To Candyce
New Years 2011
— John + Sheres

Of You
My Heart
Has Spoken

"Of you my heart speaks; you my glance seeks;

your presence, O Lord, I seek."

Psalm 27:8

Of You *My* Heart *Has Spoken*

Selected columns by
Bishop J. Peter Sartain

Diocese of Little Rock
2000-2005

ARKANSAS CATHOLIC
LITTLE ROCK

■

Fourth Printing July 2006
Third Printing May 2006
Second Printing June 2005
First Printing March 2005

Printed in the United States of America
Edited by Malea Hargett
Designed by Emily Burgin Roberts
Published by Arkansas Catholic
Diocese of Little Rock
P.O. Box 7417
Little Rock AR 72217
(501) 664-0125
www.arkansas-catholic.org

All material previously published in
Arkansas Catholic

INTRODUCTION

Dear Friends,

For the past five years, I have had the pleasure of writing a weekly column for *Arkansas Catholic*. I have always enjoyed writing, but the challenge of a weekly column was new to me when I became bishop of Little Rock.

As with preaching, I quickly discovered that putting some thoughts down in writing every week was of immense help to me. In a very pragmatic way, doing so helped me organize and clarify my understanding of many issues. But in a more personal and fruitful way, it helped me remember what I am to be about; for you see, a preacher always preaches first to himself. Thus, my columns are first and foremost about lessons I hope to put into practice myself.

We decided to title this selection of columns "Of You My Heart Has Spoken." You might recognize that as my episcopal motto, taken from Psalm 27:8. Each week, what I endeavor to say comes from prayer and reflection on our Catholic faith in the context of ministry among you. You have given me much food for thought, and I have tried to lay everything on the altar, asking God's thoughts and response. As I mentioned the day of my episcopal ordination, the "You" in my motto is God, but it is also you, the people of the Diocese of Little Rock, whom God has called me to shepherd.

I hope you find these words helpful on your way to the Lord. Thank you for your inspiration, your support, and your prayers.

Sincerely in Christ,

Bishop J. Peter Sartain
March 6, 2005

J. Peter Sartain
Sixth Bishop of Little Rock

2500 N. Tyler St.
P.O. Box 7239
Little Rock AR 72217

Born: June 6, 1952
Memphis, Tennessee

Ordained a priest: July 15, 1978
Memphis, Tennessee

Ordained a bishop: March 6, 2000
Little Rock, Arkansas

OF YOU MY HEART HAS SPOKEN

TABLE OF CONTENTS

March 6, 2000

We were made for God

Seeking the face of God in prayer

Living the life of Christ

A people on pilgrimage

Seasons of the Church: Advent-Christmas

Seasons of the Church: Lent-Easter

Loving from the cross

Family, friends, mentors and models:
A cloud of witnesses

To life!

MARCH 6, 2000

Hidden behind the moments is God's grace

The room shook. That's what many people have told me, in those exact words or similar words, about their experience of my episcopal ordination on March 6.

Some of those making the comment had been physically present in Robinson Auditorium, others had watched the liturgy on television; but their reaction was the same.

The room shook.

They did not mean that there was physical shaking of the building, of course, but that they experienced God's presence and transforming grace in a way we do not experience every day. I felt it, too, needless to say. God was at work on March 6.

Was it the beautiful music? Yes, that was part of it. Was it the presence of 45 bishops? Yes, their presence contributed to the liturgy in a powerful way. Was it the fact that the auditorium was packed with 2,500 faith-filled Catholics? No doubt everyone's presence made a difference. Was it the love of my family and friends? Many people have commented that they will always remember my mother and sisters walking up on the stage to greet me after I had been installed as bishop of Little Rock.

Yes, it was all these things, and more. Everyone who participated could point to the particular moment or aspect of the liturgy that moved them.

But most of all, without a doubt, what made the room

"shake" was the grace of God poured forth upon the Church in the sacrament of holy orders. God was being God — loving and merciful, saving and transforming, awesome and mysterious; and we were being the Church — attentive and receptive, obedient and humble, full of praise and thanks. We experienced the power of the sacraments, we felt what it means to be at the heart of the Church.

I have often remarked since that day that I am still "taking it all in." The reality of my vocation sinks in a little more each time I celebrate confirmation, or hear someone call me "Bishop" (after all, less than 30 days ago I was very accustomed to people calling me "Father Pete"!), or whenever I'm engaged in a discussion about the future of our diocese. But I am most profoundly aware of the effects of March 6 when I am sitting alone in my chapel, or driving down the interstate, or asking God's blessing on someone who has just asked for prayers. It's at those times that "the room shakes" with silence.

What a blessing it is whenever we can talk about our experience of God in liturgy or prayer in a way that describes how we felt and what happened to us.

What a blessing it is whenever we can talk about our experience of God in liturgy or prayer in a way that describes how we felt and what happened to us. God was at work, and we knew it — we felt it! Those are experiences to treasure and remember as benchmarks along our path of faith.

But there are other times — perhaps most of the time? — when God works quietly, in a hidden and gentle way, in Christ's body, the Church. No less powerfully, no less lovingly, but more simply, and way down deep within us. The room shakes then, too; God is being God, and we are being the Church then, too. But those times require of us the willingness to go deeper than feelings and trust that, even though we do not feel the room shake, God is there. Perhaps we need to watch more closely or listen more attentively in prayer.

In a letter to her sister, Celine, St. Thérèse of Lisieux once put it this way:

"Jesus is a hidden treasure, a good beyond price that few souls find, for it is hidden... To find a thing hidden, we must ourselves be hidden."

This week, find some hidden time to give to God alone. The room will shake with the presence of God. You may not feel it, but no matter. Sometimes God shakes things up very quietly.

April 8, 2000

WE WERE MADE
FOR GOD

Movies might be about nothing, but life isn't

S ometimes I cry at movies. I used to be embarrassed by the tears, fearful that even in a dark theater someone would notice that my emotions had gotten the best of me. But now I see my tears as a gift, even a sign of maturity. I'm glad I cry at movies.

Recently I started thinking about this for two reasons. The first is that it happened again the other night. When the day's work was finished, I leaned back in my recliner, turned on the television, and started watching a movie with an emotional ending. The main character resolved a life-long search for his father when he met an elderly woman who had witnessed his father's last breath. Momentarily my eyes welled up with tears.

The other reason is a column by Father Ronald Rolheiser, which appeared in the March 25 issue of the *Arkansas Catholic* ("Post-modern nihilism helps kill hope"). Father Rolheiser's point was that today nihilism (a philosophy that holds in part that nothing can really be known or communicated because nothing really exists) often wears a humorous face; he gave as one example the "Seinfeld" television show which consciously professed to be about "nothing." Such humor, he suggests, can seduce us into an attitude of indifference; after all, if the point is to "be about nothing," then nothing really has value, and everything loses meaning. Father Rolheiser writes that this attitude is the antithesis of hope.

I couldn't agree more. I cut out the column and will reflect on it again.

So what's the connection between my tears and Father Rolheiser's ideas about modern nihilism?

Many sitcoms these days aim at being "about nothing," and their characters dwell on the surface of their day-to-day lives. Were we to examine these shows more closely, we would have to admit that it is not the issues the characters deal with (relationships, employment, sexuality, parenting, aging, etc.) that are shallow, but the way the characters deal with them. They make us laugh, but to tell the truth, no one who goes through life acting as if it is "about nothing" can find happiness.

They make us laugh, but to tell the truth, no one who goes through life acting as if it is "about nothing" can find happiness.

We know that life is about something. We've all dealt with the same issues as the Seinfeld cast, and we know that often they are no laughing matter.

In many ways, gratuitous violence on the screen plays into the same dynamic: it's possible to see so much of it that the very existence of violence seems unreal, especially to children. But violence is real, as we have sadly witnessed several times recently in our state. A movie or TV show can resolve its story in an hour or so, but the real kind of violence inflicts wounds that can last a lifetime.

I wonder if "post-modern nihilism" is also at the root of what Pope John Paul has called the "culture of death." If life is "about nothing," if we fall into the trap of living only on the surface of things, then human life in the womb, or human life afflicted with disease, or human life in its last years, has no meaning; with such indifference we can dismiss the life-struggles we see on the news as easily as changing the channel on our TV set.

The tragedy of it all is not just that we won't try to help where we're needed. Eventually we won't even notice the need.

One of the humbling privileges of being a pastor is that

people let me into their lives — their ache to be good, their struggle to deal with illness and anger, their search for God, their sorrow for sin, their need for guidance. In letting me into their lives, they are really letting God in. They know that life is about something — they deal with those "somethings" every day, and they're not always funny.

They come to God for good reason: they know that God gives hope. They know instinctively that "He who did not spare His own Son but handed him over for the sake of us all will grant us all things." (Romans 8) Following the Lord Jesus gives us strength to bear whatever comes, because only He reveals the full and true meaning of human life.

I like comedies as much as the next guy. I even laugh at shows that are "about nothing." But I'm glad I sometimes cry at movies, because my tears flow from the fact that I know life is really about "something." Certain scenes can suddenly seize my emotions and remind me of the lives that have touched mine.

In the end, of course, life is about "Someone." And that Someone holds out His hand in compassion to all, giving us hope through His abiding love and compassion.

Do you know what is the most powerful antidote to nihilism in all its forms? Love.

And God is Love.

April 15, 2000

God inspires us to love anonymously

Thank God for hidden favors. When I am able to attend Catholic High football games at War Memorial Stadium, I enjoy standing on the sidelines. Last week, as I watched several of the players practice passing the football, I noticed that the heavy metal gate leading to the stands had swung wide open where one of them would run to catch the ball. Instinctively, I walked over to shut it.

It's a habit I developed as a pastor. Keeping watch on the parish grounds, I would look for rakes on the soccer field, broken playground equipment, cluttered boiler rooms, wet floors. Parents and grandparents do exactly the same when they child-proof their homes. It's a matter of safety and prevention. We understand the dangers and temptations posed by certain hazards, so we remove them before an accident happens. Does anyone know we prevented a potential mishap? Do they thank us? Probably not. But we keep up the practice, because we love our kids, our grandkids, our friends and our parishioners.

In Chapter IV of her autobiography, St. Thérèse of Lisieux writes that without God she could have "fallen as low as St. Mary Magdalene." This was not a matter of pride but of gratitude for God's loving mercy. In fact, she writes, "Jesus has forgiven me more than St. Mary Magdalene since He forgave me in advance by preventing me from falling. Ah! I wish I could explain what I feel." She then gives an example:

"Suppose a clever physician's child meets with a stone in his path which causes him to fall and break a limb. His father comes to him immediately, picks him up lovingly, takes care of this hurt, using all the resources of his profession for this. His child, completely cured, shows his gratitude. This child is no doubt right in loving his father!

"But I am going to make another comparison. The father, knowing there is a stone in his child's way, hastens ahead of him and removes it but without anyone's seeing him do it. Certainly, this child, the object of his father's tender foresight, but UNAWARE of the misfortune from which he was delivered by him, will not thank him and will love him less than if he had been cured by him. But if he should come to learn the danger from which he escaped, will he not love his father more?"

Thérèse realized that she was just as indebted to God as Mary Magdalene, and that God wanted her to know he had loved her "with a love of unspeakable foresight in order that now I may love Him unto folly!" In other words, though her life was brief and innocent, she nonetheless had a profound experience of the mercy of God, who had prevented her from falling into serious sin.

God's mercy is to be found not only when he forgives our sins, but also when, as a loving Father, he quietly removes hazards from our path.

Whether we identify with the Magdalene or the Little Flower, the lesson is the same. God's mercy is to be found not only when he forgives our sins, but also when, as a loving Father, he quietly removes hazards from our path. Are we aware that he has done so? Do we thank him? Probably not. But our lack of awareness or gratitude does not prevent God from protecting us still.

Adults eventually come to appreciate the protective love of our parents. Where we might have once tried to worm our way out of their embrace to touch some fascinating temptation, or escape what we considered prison-like house rules, we are now grateful that they wisely shielded us from untold disasters. We probably don't know the half of it even now.

Last week, I wrote that remembering and giving thanks for

God's blessings builds trust and teaches us to imitate his goodness. It is equally important to thank God for hidden favors — the times he quietly showers his mercy on us without our even knowing it, the times he removes obstacles from our path before they trip or tempt us. We may never learn precisely how he has done this, but we can be quite certain that he has.

Cultivating gratitude for God's quiet mercy has many benefits. I would like to point out two:

First, we become less judgmental. Like Thérèse, we have no room to judge others who have fallen far from God. There, but for the grace of God, go we. We praise God when any sinner finds mercy and pray for those who refuse it. Whether or not we have ever strayed far, we are all equally indebted to him.

Second, we begin loving others in ways they may never know. Recognizing ourselves as beneficiaries of God's quiet mercy, we look for anonymous opportunities to love — prayer, hidden favors of all kinds, sacrificial almsgiving, unsolicited kindness to strangers. "When you give alms, do not let your left hand know what your right hand is doing, so that your almsgiving may be secret. And your Father who sees in secret will repay you." (Luke 6:3-4)

It's like this: As a father, God forgives us when we have strayed and protects us from hazards we never notice. He has no need of our thanks, because he simply delights in loving us. But giving thanks enriches us. How else will we know who we truly are, if we do not look for ways to better know this "love of unspeakable foresight," by whom and for whom alone we were made? And how else will we learn to fully imitate that love, unless we recognize that he often works in secret?

October 26, 2002

Words should build people up, not destroy

When I jog or walk along the Arkansas River, I often meet other joggers, walkers and skaters. As time goes by, I recognize more and more of the regulars, and we exchange quick greetings. Bikers are another story, because they typically breeze by at breakneck speed. If there are several bikers together, sharing a conversation, it's hard not to listen because they have to speak loudly above the noisy wind.

Down by the river not long ago, I heard a young couple approaching me from behind on bicycles. I have no idea what their conversation was about, but I couldn't help but notice the profanity — not just an occasional curse word, but profanity peppered throughout every sentence. As they passed, I noticed their state-of-the-art bikes and stylish clothes and helmets. When they approached me again from the opposite direction, I wondered whether their conversation had also changed course, but it had not. There was rarely a sentence spoken, by him or her, that did not include a curse word.

My first thought was about how offensive and pointless their speech was, how inconsistent with the care they had given to dressing for the ride. Why did they feel the need to speak that way, and what good did it do? The profanity got in the way of real communication.

All of us have used words carelessly. We have criticized, gossiped, cursed, ridiculed and lied. Perhaps we have purposely used words to offend someone who had harmed us, or lashed out in anger at a frustrating situation. We have manipulatingly used harsh words to get our way and have unintentionally offended others with ill-timed humor. We have added our two cents to discussions when it would have been more profitable to remain silent.

Words are cheap, and we are bombarded with so many words in the media that they have begun to lose effectiveness and meaning. One word, one opinion, is as good as another. We have gone from, "My word is my bond" to "They're only words."

Sometimes the use of words is especially appalling — as when the name of God is taken in vain. The second commandment makes clear that we are to respect and honor God's holy name. As the catechism states, "Among all the words of Revelation, there is one which is unique: the revealed name of God. God confides his name to those who believe in him." (no. 2143) The Jewish people so cherish the holiness of the revealed name of God — YHWH (Yahweh) — that they do not pronounce it. When reading the Bible, they replace YHWH with a divine title, "Adonai" (Lord).

God's name is to be used only to bless, praise or glorify him. Oaths taken in the name of God are given validity precisely because they appeal to God's fidelity and truth, and to be unfaithful to such oaths is to be disrespectful of God. Blasphemy involves abuse of the names of God, Jesus, the Virgin Mary and the saints.

According to the Gospel of John, Jesus is the divine Word of God, the complete utterance of God: "In the beginning was the Word, and the Word was with God, and the Word was God … the Word became flesh and made his dwelling among us." At the incarnation, the Son of God received the name "Jesus," the name that says everything about God and his saving plan for humanity. In other words, because of the incarnation, we can now call out the divine name, "Jesus" — that is, "YHWH saves." Early Christians professed their belief that Jesus is divine by using the title "Adonai"; they acclaimed, "Jesus is

LORD" — "the name above every other name." (cf. Philippians 2:6-11) So holy is the name of Jesus that a good gauge of whether a word or action is worthy of Christian faith is to ask, "Can I say or do this in the name of Jesus?"

Sacred Scripture is the speech of God as it is put down in writing under the breath of the Holy Spirit. If God makes use of human communication in his speech, then all human communication has in a sense been blessed. But how do I use my God-given ability to communicate through speech? The same faculty that offers prayer and praise to God should not be used for purposes contrary to his. That would truly be talking out of both sides of one's mouth.

If God makes use of human communication in his speech, then all human communication has in a sense been blessed.

Paul wrote to the Ephesians, "Let no evil talk come out of your mouths, but only what is useful for building up, as there is need, so that your words may give grace to those who hear. And do not grieve the Holy Spirit of God, with which you were marked with a seal for the day of redemption. Put away from you all bitterness and wrath and anger and wrangling and slander, together with all malice, and be kind to one another, tenderhearted, forgiving one another, as God in Christ has forgiven you." (Ephesians 4:29-32)

By extension, then, the second commandment refers to our general use of the faculty of speech. In these days of cheap words flung in every direction and in every conceivable form — from e-mails to disinformation to threats of terror — we would do well to mark our speech and restore the dignity of human communication. Every word we speak bears the awesome potential of reflecting and participating in the Word of God.

November 30, 2002

Fishing with the Lord
is catch of the day

I have no doubt that St. Peter's skills as a fisherman were much greater than mine, even though I bear his name. But last week, whether by sheer luck, weather or water temperature, I had several successful days of fishing on a small lake in Mississippi. I'm one of those who declare that fishing is fun even when you don't catch anything; my fishing buddies claim I have to say that to justify being on the water. I'll admit that my skills rarely compensate for uncooperative fish, but it is true that I simply enjoy being outside and fishing, whether or not I catch a big one.

Several months ago, I celebrated Mass at All Saints Church in Mount Ida, near Lake Ouachita, a beautiful recreational spot in central Arkansas. In my homily I spoke of a long-ago fishing expedition with a group of friends, all of whom were accustomed to being "in charge" in daily life. Since we were fishing for salmon, we needed guides. "It's hard for guys who are used to being in charge to surrender control to a guide," I said. "When you're fishing with a group like that," I asked rhetorically, "who's in charge?" "The fish!" answered a woman in the congregation. We all had a good laugh. Of course, she was absolutely right. The fish are always in charge.

In his encyclical "Novo Millennio Ineunte," Pope John Paul II invites us to "put out into the deep." He is referring to St. Luke's account of an unsuccessful night of fishing by Peter and his companions, after which Jesus invites them to cast their nets one more time: "Put out into deep water and lower your nets for a catch." (Luke 5:4 ff) "Master, we have worked hard all night and have caught nothing," whines Peter. "But at your command, I will lower the nets." They hauled in a catch so huge that their nets were at the breaking point. Peter and his friends had been relying on their wit and experience; faced with failure, they had given up. Everything changed, however, when they surrendered to the command of the Lord — "Put out into deep water."

The Holy Father's image is a beautiful and practical one. Discipleship is a continuous act of trust in the Lord Jesus, a progressive handing over of our decisions, skills, attitudes and expectations to his Word, his command. God's sights are always set on a much bigger catch than ours are.

God's sights are always set on a much bigger catch than ours are.

On a large scale, the Church is called to cast its net unceasingly in every place and time, even against all odds, in the deepest and murkiest of waters, trusting that the proclamation of the Word will "catch" those who hunger for salvation.

There is a close similarity here to Jesus' parable of the farmer who sows seed by flinging it with reckless abandon on rocks, footpaths, sand and rich soil. Nets are cast far and wide, whether or not fish are evident; seed is sown indiscriminately, whether the ground is fertile or barren. The point is, God is at work. As disciples and ministers, we cede control to God — otherwise, we risk abandoning the unyielding water, retreating in fear, rationing his gifts or falsely attributing his success to ourselves.

On a personal scale, we are to allow ourselves to be guided in all things by the Word of the Lord. The Christian life is not a relay race, in which God is merely our partner — in other words, we do not hand him the baton when we tire, only to take it up again when refreshed. Christian life is the way of surrender to the One who carries us on wings of eagles, on shoulders of shepherds, in arms of doting mothers, in cara-vans of camels. It is surrender to the One who invites us to trust in his power to do the unexpected and impossible. Put out into the deep, even if all seems lost, says the Lord. God uses our talents, to be sure, but only by surrender do we dis-cover his love and power. Only by surrender do we become his disciples and instruments.

When we approach God in prayer, particularly when we perceive ourselves to be deep in waters of distress, do we "point out" to him our need for help but retain tight control? Or do we hand over our worries to him, relinquishing control to his loving providence? That can be a frightening prospect, but it is the only way to discover the power of grace.

I have been mixing metaphors in this column — fishing, farming and running. But isn't that exactly what the Bible does? God uses whatever it takes to catch our fancy, to make an impression, to draw us into his embrace. In a sense, isn't the goal of the Incarnation to lure us, through Christ, into intima-cy with our heavenly Father?

Fishing, farming or running, the whole point is to be "caught" by God. He delights in fishing in both the deep and the shallows, farming in all kinds of terrain, carrying us in the race all the way to the finish line. Whatever it takes, he longs for us to surrender to the lure of his friendship. I hope I'm as cooperative with the Lord as the fish were with me last week.

July 20, 2002

Jesus longs to bring sheep back into fold

M ost of us know what it's like to ache for someone who is "lost." A daughter or friend has cut herself off from the family; a son or neighbor has turned his back on the Church; someone we love has set out on a path of self-destruction. We encourage, instruct, prod, and pray, to no apparent avail. Our heart aches.

Lent is the perfect time to surrender these loved ones to God, as we reflect on our own repentance and conversion; for just as God is drawing us to himself, so is he waiting patiently for them, never giving up on them, for in his eyes everyone is of inestimable value.

This past Sunday we heard the parable of the Prodigal Son, which in Luke 15 is the climax of three parables about "lost" things. Looking at the context in which Jesus tells them helps us understand where he is heading — and gives us hope for our own lost ones.

Luke 15 begins with the high-minded grumbling of the scribes and Pharisees, who have observed Jesus spending time with tax collectors and sinners. "This man welcomes sinners and eats with them," they gossip; that is proof enough of his unrighteousness. Jesus responds with parables to explain what he is doing and why.

A single sheep is lost while 99 others stay put, but the shepherd goes after the lost one. A woman has 10 silver pieces and loses just one, but she turns the house upside down until she finds it. In both cases, the result is sheer delight at finding what was lost; friends and neighbors are called in to share the joy.

It almost seems that the rejoicing is out of proportion to the finding. Was it really worth risking the safety of the 99 sheep to go on a wild goose chase for one straggler? And if nine of 10 coins are still securely in the cookie jar, is it worth losing a good night's sleep to recover only 10 percent? Why not cut your losses and move on?

The first two parables are about lost possessions, an animal and a coin. Luke uses them to introduce Jesus' main parable, about a lost soul. A young man absconds with his inheritance while his father is still alive, spends it all in short order, then finds himself homeless, reduced to caring for pigs. Things get so bad, and he is so hungry, that he would eat pig feed; but no one in this far away land lifts a finger to give him anything. That's how much they notice his plight, how little they care.

But the father has not forgotten his runaway son. His heart aches so much for him, to whom he had literally given the shirt off his back (and would again, gladly), that from his front porch he strains his eyes scanning the hills to see if there is any sign of the lost one. Any sign at all.

When finally he catches sight of the runaway, he takes to his heels, rushing to embrace and escort him home. As in the other two parables, the rejoicing is extravagant, for the lost has been found. The father throws an out-of-proportion party for a delinquent son. It makes no sense to some, but to the father it makes perfect sense. His son hadn't just run away — he had died, and now he is alive again. They "must" celebrate and rejoice.

Jesus "must" eat with tax collectors and sinners! Unsavory, unseemly, unrighteous characters, they were like sheep without a shepherd. Had he not been sent by the Father to find them? How could he not be happy that they finally faced up to their wounds and disfigurements, that they regretted the dark roads they had taken, even if their motives for repentance were not yet pure? How could he not rejoice and invite others to join the celebration? He had been sent to bring them home.

We live in the household of a Father who never cuts his losses and moves on with what's left, because each of us is of incomparable value to him, each of us irreplaceable in his eyes. He never ceases looking for those who are lost. Any parent knows how he must feel.

We live in the household of a Father who never cuts his losses and moves on with what's left, because each of us is of incomparable value to him, each of us irreplaceable in his eyes.

That's why we can always have hope for our own lost ones, for whom our hearts ache. Our prayers for them are never fruitless, nor is our love, for as we join our longing to that of the Father, they are never out of sight, never out of range of his mercy. Never.

God is always on the watch, surveying the hills to see if we and our lost ones show any sign of looking his direction, hoping we'll slow down long enough to heed his invitation to an extravagant banquet. We'll bring our blemishes and blights, our fractures and scars. He'll clothe us in glory. It will be pretty embarrassing.

He beckons us all — the repentant sinner, to be sure; but he'll even squander his mercy on those of us who for some foolish reason think we have no need to repent.

God bless your lost ones. Take courage that the Lord Jesus is on a mission to find them. They are in my prayers, and in the Father's heart.

March 31, 2001

Learning to take a break, enjoy a sabbath

A friend once told me, quoting a famous writer, "Writing is the art of rewriting what one has already rewritten." Typically when writing this column, it would be my habit to call the friend and ask for the exact quote and its source, or failing that to search the Internet for the answer. Not this week.

The quotation comes to mind for several reasons. First, because it's true. But it also comes to mind because this week I'm going to discipline myself not to follow its counsel. I'm not going to check my sources and spend a lot of time editing what's to follow below. I'm on vacation.

For someone who likes to write, as I do, the quote is good advice; but it can also fuel any tendency to perfectionism. This week I'm slowing down to let God restore what I squander whenever I work as if everything depends on me.

A story also comes to mind, this time from the Desert Fathers. I won't get it exactly right. I don't have any books handy to check its accuracy, and I'm not going to call Abbot Jerome for help. It goes something like this: A monk once came upon some other monks enjoying a day of relaxation, and he castigated their Abba for allowing such ease. The Abba replied, "Father, if a hunter always keeps the bowstring pulled back and ready to strike, he risks snapping the string. It is much the same with us. From time to time it is good to relax our efforts."

It is good for all of us to relax our efforts from time to time. Teachers need a summer break. Business people need time away from beepers and cell phones. Priests need time away from the parish for vacation and retreat. Caregivers need time away from the one in their care. It is not selfish or irresponsible to take one's rest, because a break rejuvenates us for the work we're called to do.

That such leisure can seem so foreign is probably due to the fact that we don't take adequate time during the workweek to lessen the tension on the bowstring. Moreover, every now and then it occurs to me that my working too much is actually a sign of pride — and not the good kind!

For people of faith, there is another reason rest is important. It is about Sabbath.

> *Moreover, every now and then it occurs to me that my working too much is actually a sign of pride — and not the good kind!*

Rabbi Abraham Heschel once wrote that Jewish people observe the Sabbath by a series of abstentions; they abstain from the work, noise, and business of the week in order to create an atmosphere in which they glorify God's saving presence. Just as God himself rested after six days to marvel lovingly at the wonder of his creation, so we rest from our work to recognize the wonder of God all around us — and to drink from the source of all that is. My work, after all, is but a participation in God's work.

The Sabbath was also a celebration of God's covenant with Israel and his never-ending care. Since abstention from work was fundamental to Sabbath observance, during the Israelites' sojourn in the wilderness God miraculously provided a double portion of manna on Friday so that they would not be forced to gather food on the Sabbath. On their day of holiness and rest, God still supplied their needs.

If we never lessen the tension on the bowstring, if in pursuit of perfection we keep rewriting what we have already rewritten, we forget that whoever we are and whatever our work, God alone is our strength and inspiration. Several Sundays ago the Gospel story of Martha and Mary taught a similar lesson. Jesus was not arguing with Martha about the importance of her tasks of hospitality; he was pointing out to her that by allowing herself to be distracted and troubled by such things she was failing to sit at his feet to receive the nourishment he had come to bring.

The purpose of Sabbath is not that we single out a day to honor God while allowing the rest of the week to proceed as usual. Its ultimate purpose is to let Sabbath rest — which is really "rest in God," or "sitting at the Lord's feet" — spill over into the entire week. To be mindful always of God's presence, to go to him alone for strength, to let him teach me the meaning of each task I undertake, to allow him to guide my every decision — that is what I hope and pray for.

I am blessed in being able to take a vacation, and I recognize that for a variety of reasons not everyone can do so. But there are such things as walks around the block, moments with the Bible, visits to the Blessed Sacrament, time with the kids, phone calls to long-neglected friends, curling up in an easy chair with a good book and Sundays free of work by design and discipline. They're all part of the rhythm and flow God intends for his creation.

Mind you, all that I've written above represents a lesson I'm trying to learn. Back on the job next week, I'll likely pull the bowstring taut once again. But I'm hoping that the Sabbath of this week will flood the work of next week and beyond with the loving presence of God.

August 11, 2001

Conscience has to be formed and guided

As an infant develops into a toddler, his or her newly acquired mobility presents a challenge to parents. Crawling limbs can now go where they should not go. Tiny hands can grab things they should not grab. Growing but fragile bodies can bump into sharp surfaces and tumble down stairs. Houses have to be baby-proofed; hazardous materials placed out of reach. Moms and dads get plenty of exercise following the kids around the house.

Physical growth is a natural, beautiful part of every life — it demonstrates the potential we have in countless areas and the wisdom of God's creative hand. But human development must be guided, taught and formed. No responsible parents would ever leave a little one to fend for herself, assuming she could pick up skills and lessons to be learned on her own. They teach her to walk, carefully show her the difference between "hot" and "cold," deny her certain foods that would be bad for her, protect her from hidden dangers, keep her clean, hug and praise her constantly, and love her unconditionally. They would not think of doing otherwise.

Our lives of faith must be similarly guided, taught and formed. No Christian parents would ever think of letting their son fend for himself in learning about God, since they know faith is God's gift to be cherished and passed on. They teach him about God and how to pray. They take him to church and help with his prayers each night. They give good example and show him what faith in action means. They instill in him reverence for God and a proper sense of religious obligation. They know that faith in God is essential to every human life.

There is another area of life I would like to address this week and next: the development of conscience. Here, too, we must be guided, taught and formed. No wise parents would ever think of telling little children, "Do whatever you want," for disaster would not be far away. They teach them the difference between right and wrong, good and evil. They explain the meaning of sin. They demonstrate proper behavior and respect for others. They set down rules and expect them to be followed. They lay out principles by which their children can make good decisions. They find the proper time to instruct them in sexual morality and give good example in family life. They teach them how to say both "I'm sorry" and "I forgive you." They encourage and support them when they fail.

No wise parents would ever think of telling little children, "Do whatever you want," for disaster would not be far away.

It is especially important that parents teach children the intimate connection between one's relationship with God and the formation of conscience, because growth in both is lifelong — and destined for eternity.

True morality has its source and goal in God. The moral law is God's gift to us, through which we are guided, taught, formed and led to union with him. God has given us freedom, and he never coerces us to love him or denies us the use of freedom, even in the most delicate and complicated matters. However, he also offers us the wisdom to use our freedom properly by doing good and avoiding evil. We were made for God — we were made for good — and God knows we will never be happy when doing evil. Evil is beneath our dignity, for we were made in God's image and likeness.

The fathers of the Second Vatican Council gave a beautiful definition of "conscience" in the "Pastoral Constitution on the

Church in the Modern World:"

"Deep within his conscience man discovers a law which he has not laid upon himself but which he must obey. Its voice, ever calling him to love and to do what is good and to avoid evil, sounds in his heart at the right moment … For man has in his heart a law inscribed by God … His conscience is man's most secret core and his sanctuary ... There he is alone with God whose voice echoes in his depths (16)."

Commenting on this passage, Pope John Paul II wrote:

"Conscience is the most secret core and sanctuary of a person, where we are alone with God. In the depths of our conscience, we detect a moral law, which does not impose itself on us, but which holds us to a higher obedience. This law is not an external human law, but the voice of God, calling us to free ourselves from the grip of evil desires and sin, and stimulating us to seek what is good and true in life."

If freedom is to be full and authentic, it must be educated by the formation of a right conscience; otherwise, we risk misusing our freedom and falling into evil, intentionally or unintentionally. God, our loving and protective Father, would never think of leaving us to fend for ourselves in living good, moral, and holy lives. He guides, teaches, and forms us as his children, giving us everything we need to grow in faith and goodness.

Next week I will address the formation of conscience and how conscience comes into play in many aspects of life.

July 24, 2004

Take time to form your conscience

When the communist governments of the Soviet Union and Eastern Europe fell in the late 80s and early 90s, the citizens of those countries faced immediate and critical challenges. Liberation from the tyranny and oppression they had known for so long was a great blessing. But freedom is more than release from tyranny. How would they put freedom to work for the common good?

With economies in shambles, new systems of free enterprise had to be created. Since there was little effective government infrastructure, democratic processes had to be put in place. Since civil order and public safety had been in the hands of an often terrorist military, provision had to be made for adequate and humane police protection. And since the majority of government budgets had been given to military spending, it was necessary to reorganize priorities with primary concern for people, not military might.

But there was also a subtle and ultimately more important challenge facing the people: how to use their personal freedom in a changed society. Vast new opportunities, choices and influences were open to them (particularly the young) for the first time. It was in part for all these reasons that Pope John Paul II wrote his encyclical "The Splendor of Truth" in 1993.

We Americans have much to learn from the growing pains of former communist countries. Ironically, there are many in our society who regard moral norms as a form of tyranny and oppression — they think one should be able to do as he or she pleases, "free" of all moral guidelines. According to their frame of reference, what one chooses to do is "right" and "good" precisely because he or she chooses it — not because the choice was made according to a set of moral norms.

There are others who assume (perhaps unwittingly) that if a Gallup poll demonstrates that the majority of Americans holds a particular opinion about a moral issue, that opinion must be morally correct. If we lived totally according to that approach, a majority vote would determine morality, and morality would change as the numbers change. Isn't that backwards?

Such approaches are not examples of "freedom" at all, and we should regard them with great suspicion. They would create a society which crumbles because it has no lasting foundation. Just because "I choose" something does not make it right — after all, I am capable of choosing evil. The fact that 75 percent holds this or that opinion regarding a moral issue does not make their opinion morally correct — sadly, they might be ignorant of the truth.

The fact that 75 percent holds this or that opinion regarding a moral issue does not make their opinion morally correct — sadly, they might be ignorant of the truth.

What is right, good and true has one source, and that is God. It is only in searching for his truth and obeying it that we find freedom. The path to real freedom, then, is the formation of a good conscience.

Conscience enables us to recognize the morality of something we are about to do, are in the process of doing, or have already done. It helps us take responsibility for our actions, prompts us to ask forgiveness when we fail, and produces peaceful hearts. A well-formed conscience is a messenger of God, who teaches us how to do good and avoid evil.

The formation of a good conscience is a lifelong process, and as I wrote last week, it begins with the loving guidance of parents. As we grow older and find ourselves free of parental control, we must take responsibility for the education of our consciences. That entails serious interior reflection, something not always valued in our era of quick fixes and instant gratification. Forming a good conscience requires that we slow down, reflect, pray and learn.

How do we properly educate and form our consciences? By studying the Word of God, praying for God's wisdom, relying on the gifts of the Holy Spirit, following good example, seeking sound advice from others and allowing ourselves to be guided by the teaching of the Church.

The formation of a good conscience requires humility. I must admit that there is such a thing as moral truth which, though it may not be easy and may go against popular trends, is given to us by God for our good and must be obeyed. Moreover, since this moral truth comes from God, it is meant for all humanity, not just for believers.

The formation of conscience is actually about conversion and discipleship. Am I willing to hand over every aspect of my life, every decision, and every moral judgment, to God's wisdom? Or do keep some things for myself, as if God knows best in some areas but not others? Perhaps it is easier to follow trends and opinion polls, but they will inevitably change — as will governments and presidents — and I will be left in the lurch. Only a well-formed conscience keeps me on solid moral ground. I owe it to my country to form my conscience well.

Pope John Paul II wrote:

"Let us remember: it is only by listening to the voice of God in our most intimate being, and by acting in accordance with its directions, that we will reach the freedom we yearn for. As Jesus said, only the truth can make us free. And the truth is not the fruit of each individual's imagination. God gave us intelligence to know the truth and the will to achieve what is morally good. He has given us the light of conscience to guide our moral decisions — and, above all, to love good and avoid evil."

July 31, 2004

Freedom is found through following God

I will never forget the sheer terror I felt the first time I was dragged onto the dance floor by a girl in my freshman class. Barely 14 years old, my buddies and I had gone to the Friday night dance, not planning that we would actually dance. Much to my surprise, as we sat at a table off to the side drinking Cokes, she approached. My shoes seemed to be filled with concrete, and my friends punched each other on the arm. The next thing I knew I was dancing.

I don't suppose you could truly call what I did that night "dancing." I heard the music with its 60s pulsing rumble, but I watched my feet trip on the gym floor in absolutely no relationship to the music. My partner tried to help. "Loosen up, Peter," she told me. I tried my best, but that night I had two left feet.

I never became a good dancer, but I got to the point that I enjoyed Friday nights at my high school, not embarrassed in the least to take to the floor. My clumsiness had come from the fact that I approached the rhythm and beat of the music as "rules" to which I had to apply myself. The music often went in one direction and I in another, a pretty comical sight, especially that first night.

I noticed that the good dancers were those who danced without effort, who flowed with the music. They did not seem to be following "rules" at all; they simply danced.

If you have ever been to the ballet, you've seen ballerinas leap effortlessly into the air and across the stage, perfectly in sync with the music. What appears effortless, of course, is the fruit of endless hours of physical training, the fruit of studying the music their dance accompanies. Ballet is beautiful because dancers and music are one — they are part of it, expressions of it, embodiments of it. If a ballerina's performance had no relation to her music, if her steps were totally out of sync with the orchestra, we would laugh!

Good dancers say they do not feel bound by their music, even though its rules are clear and its purpose intentional. Instead, they feel free. Interesting.

The same must be true for jazz musicians. Jazz has its musical rules, but it is also characterized by improvisation, the variety of which is endless. An improvised sax or piano piece is beautiful because it goes in many directions while maintaining its clear connection to the basic musical intent. Good jazz improvisers don't feel bound by the rules of their art. They are set free by them.

Perhaps the analogy of dance and jazz helps us understand in part the freedom that comes to those who follow God's law. Created in God's image and likeness, we were created to be fulfilled and set free by following his ways. Freedom is a gift won for us by Jesus' death and resurrection; we live out that freedom and experience its full power by living as he did. As Paul told the Galatians, "For freedom Christ has set us free." (5:1) Only sin binds us and holds us back.

Jesus recognized that what he asked would not be easy. To forgive enemies, pray for persecutors, confess sins, care for the poor and vulnerable, work for peace, endure persecution, trust in his Father, let go of hatred and prejudice, carry our crosses, profess him as Savior: these ways of God demand much of us, and we may feel out of sync with them, especially when we first take them seriously. We may hear Jesus' words leading in one direction but feel our habits or knee-jerk reactions going another.

Some of Jesus' disciples found his teaching unbearable.

When he proclaimed himself the Bread of Life, for example, they were troubled.

"Then many of his disciples who were listening said, 'This saying is hard; who can accept it?'... As a result of this, many returned to their former way of life and no longer accompanied him. Jesus then said to the Twelve, "Do you also want to leave?" Simon Peter answered him, "Master, to whom shall we go? You have the words of eternal life." (John 6:60, 66-68)

Many left, but those who believed that Jesus had the words of eternal life remained. And giving themselves to his teaching, putting it into practice, and persevering through failure and misunderstanding, they found freedom. Freedom came because like all men and women, they were created for the kingdom of God. They accepted Jesus and his teaching even though others rejected and ridiculed him. Abiding by the ways of the kingdom — its rhythm and beat, if you will — they gained freedom in Christ.

> *And giving themselves to his teaching, putting it into practice, and persevering through failure and misunderstanding, they found freedom.*

True freedom is found and experienced by following the ways of God, living according to his Commandments and the Beatitudes of the Lord Jesus. We may follow them clumsily, especially at first, but with the help of the Holy Spirit we discover that God's ways are the only perfect fit for humanity. Disciples of the Lord begin to consider his teaching not as a set of rules but as the Truth, the Way of Love, the only Path to Freedom. We were meant to tread that path and none other. We were made for God and his ways alone.

August 7, 2004

SEEKING THE FACE
OF GOD IN PRAYER

Your good health is reflected in the soul

When I bought a pair of Asics running shoes a few years ago, I noticed a familiar Latin saying printed on the box: "Anima sana in corpore sano" —"a sound mind in a sound body." It is a variation on "Mens sana in corpore sano" (translated similarly). I thought it was interesting to see Latin on a box of running shoes, but I did not give it a second thought. Whatever it takes to sell shoes, I figured.

Juvenalis, a Roman poet and satirist (55-127 A.D.), is credited with the saying, though I do not know which version is more authentic. His point was a good one. People of every generation have championed the value of a healthy body, even if the notion of health has varied greatly through the centuries. The body/mind connection is a reminder that we are whole persons, that one aspect of living directly affects the others. Intellectual, psychological and physical health go hand-in-hand. I notice that I live more serenely, think more clearly and work more energetically when I exercise regularly.

I found out the other day that the brand name Asics is in point of fact an acronym for Anima Sana In Corpore Sano. It is interesting that Asics chose "anima" over "mens," because while "mens" usually referred to the mind in its intellectual aspects, "anima" referred to the more encompassing "vital principal" of life, the "breath of life," and one's overall sense of well-being. In fact, "anima" is the Latin word used for "soul" in Church writings and the liturgy.

Juvenalis was not a Christian, but his famous adage

certainly lends itself to Christian application. With apologies to him and to Asics, I would like to suggest another variation: "A sound soul in a sound body." As summer approaches and our attention is turned toward healthy physical appearance (if not necessarily healthy living), we would do well to remember there is something deep within — but all-encompassing and literally life-giving — that begs for attention, discipline and nourishment: the soul.

Writing to the Christians at Corinth, St. Paul noted that Christian freedom is not freedom "from" restraint but freedom "for" positive striving for fullness in Christ, a natural outgrowth of faith and one's desire to share the crown of victory with him. Drawing on the Corinthians' fascination with healthy bodies and the popularity of their Isthmian athletic games, he wrote:

Physical strength is not the same as moral strength. Obsessing over one's bodily appearance is ultimately like striking at the air.

"Do you not know that the runners in the stadium all run in the race, but only one wins the prize? Run so as to win. Every athlete exercises discipline in every way. They do it to win a perishable crown, but we an imperishable one. Thus I do not run aimlessly; I do not fight as if I were shadowboxing. No, I drive my body and train it, for fear that, after having preached to others, I myself should be disqualified." (1 Cor 9: 24-27)

Paul knew that of all the things a Christian could do with the freedom he or she has found in Christ, striving for spiritual health was the most significant of all. A crown of laurel leaves may be fresh and fragrant for a few hours, and a gold medal may look good on the mantel, but both are merely man-made, momentary prizes. The life already given us in Christ is eternal, and it is worth cultivating. Why not live so as to be "sound" and "healthy" in soul? After all, it is the soul that makes the body human.

A beautiful tan, while noticeable to us and everyone who

sees us, is not an indicator of health. Hours spent in the gym or on the running track do not guarantee a life of peace. Physical strength is not the same as moral strength. Obsessing over one's bodily appearance is ultimately like striking at the air.

Attention to the soul makes attention to the body and mind complete. We are in good health only when we pay deliberate attention to our spiritual lives, when we understand, as Paul did, that for us "life is Christ." (Philippians 1:21) There is a clear and undeniable connection between a healthy mind and a healthy body, but to limit ourselves to a well-toned physique, interesting leisure reading, and the insight of self-help tools is to cheat ourselves of the fullness of life.

Benedictine Archabbot Lambert Reilly of St. Meinrad Archabbey, in "Latin Sayings for Spiritual Growth," comments on Juvenalis' famous adage: "There is a connection between what I do on my knees and how I experience the events of the day. If one is neglected, the other suffers ... The body is an expression of the soul and ultimately what we do with the soul truly determines whether we really care about our bodies."

A sound soul in a sound body. Giving attention to our spiritual lives is the path to full health, soundness, saneness and well-being. Our culture's obsession with healthy physical appearance is a constant invitation to train with and for Christ. It works both ways. Do we truly care about our body and mind? If so, we will care first for our soul.

May 24, 2003

Sign of cross strengthens us for journey

When flying, it is my habit to make the sign of the cross and ask God's blessing and protection on the flight and my fellow passengers. A few weeks ago, flying from Dallas to Little Rock, I had the good fortune to sit next to a little boy, about age 5. When he first took his seat between me and another passenger, he was in a very talkative mood, telling us what he had been doing, what he liked and disliked, and what happens when one flies in an airplane. As we sped down the runway, I shut my eyes, made the sign of the cross and said a prayer. He was watching.

"Why did you shut your eyes?" he asked.

"I was saying a prayer," I responded.

"Were you praying that the plane won't crash?" he continued.

How should I answer this, I thought to myself. "I was asking God to bless everybody on the plane so we will be safe and have a good time," I said.

That satisfied him, and within a few minutes, he was fast asleep.

I have noticed that the song, "Lift High the Cross," is very popular in Arkansas parishes. My favorite verse is this one: "Each newborn follower of the Crucified bears on the brow the seal of him who died."

What is the "seal of him who died?" The cross.

One of the most ancient, exclusively Christian, gestures is to "sign" or "seal" oneself with the cross. About 211 A.D. Tertullian wrote, "At every step of the way, when going in and going out, when putting on our clothes and shoes, while washing, eating, lighting lamps, going to sleep, while sitting down, and in whatever action we are carrying out, we imprint on our forehead the little sign [of the cross]."

This is only one of many references in early Christian writing to the practice — and importance — of signing oneself on the forehead with the cross. By the third century, it was such a mainstay of Christian devotion that theologians simply assumed it as a longstanding practice, going back to the apostles.

The prophet Ezekiel had written that the faithful would have "the mark" (an "X," or "taw," in the Hebrew alphabet) on their foreheads and would be saved from the destruction to be inflicted upon Jerusalem (chapter 9). Early Christians saw in Ezekiel's words a prefiguration of the sign of the cross, because taw was written in Hebrew as a cross. This was probably the inspiration and meaning of John's vision in the Book of Revelation that the servants of God would be sealed on their foreheads (Revelation 7).

Signing oneself with the cross literally marks one as a "Christian" — saved by Christ alone, through his death on the cross. He was victorious over every evil power, and we enter his victory through baptism. Even today, in the baptismal liturgy for children, the priest or deacon says to the one to be baptized, "The Christian community welcomes you with great joy. In its name I claim you for Christ our savior by the sign of his cross. I now trace the cross on your forehead and invite your parents to do the same." In the rites of the R.C.I.A., adult catechumens are marked several times with the cross as they prepare for baptism.

Each time we sign ourselves, then, we remember baptism, through which we were claimed by Christ. Several early

Christian writers also state that when we make the sign of the cross with faith and devotion, we demonstrate to the devil that we belong to Christ.

Although in the earliest centuries Christians typically signed only their foreheads with the cross, gradually the gesture was expanded to the one we know today, through which we place our entire body — our entire life — under the cross of Christ. We live in the shadow of his cross, shielded and protected by his unconquerable love.

We live in the shadow of his cross, shielded and protected by his unconquerable love.

Making the sign of the cross, we bring together two great tenets of our faith: salvation through Christ's death and resurrection and the holy Trinity. The catechism teaches, "The baptized person dedicates the day to the glory of God and calls on the Savior's grace which lets him act in the Spirit as a child of the Father. The sign of the cross strengthens us in temptations and difficulties." (2157)

The sign of the cross is not just a "Catholic trademark," and though it is used most importantly in prayer, that is not the only time it can be used. Any good activity can begin with it and thus be dedicated to Christ. In time of temptation, it is a way to proclaim that we belong to Christ, and not to the evil one.

The sign of the cross is not a good luck charm. Far to the contrary, it is a witness to the price paid for our redemption and the power of Jesus' trust in his heavenly Father. Luck had nothing to do with that! In fact, the cross exposes our selfishness by revealing the depth of Jesus' love.

The sign of the cross is the way to place ourselves, our homes, our children and fellow pilgrims under the loving, sheltering, victorious arms of the Savior.

June 28, 2003

External gestures reflect internal reality

A barber once told me about his first visit to a Catholic church, on the occasion of a friend's wedding. "You people sure do move around a lot during services," he said. We had a good laugh, and I explained the reasons for what he observed.

Among the characteristics of Catholic worship which a first-time visitor will notice are the many gestures we make: the sign of the cross, genuflection, kneeling, sitting, standing, praying with outstretched arms, processions, bowing and kissing the altar, to name the most common. The fact that such gestures become routine to us is both good and bad. On the one hand, we participate in the liturgy easily and without confusion; on the other hand, if we do not pay attention to what we are doing, we risk missing the rich meaning of the gestures.

When I wrote about the soul/mind/body connection last week, I reflected on the all-encompassing soundness of living that comes to those who give primary attention to their souls. Another way of approaching this essential connection is to recognize how and why we use our bodies in worship. In making liturgical gestures or using certain postures, we are sending a message both to God and to ourselves.

Using our bodies in worship is first and foremost a way of saying that every aspect of human life can and should be directed toward the worship of God. Human life is not separated into component parts, some of which are the concern of God, others of which are not his concern. The Son of God took on flesh and blood that we might be saved "body and soul."

Salvation in and through Christ has many ramifications for the Christian, needless to say. From the standpoint of the moral life, it is easy to understand that what we do with our bodies is of immense importance. In fact, all of Christian moral teaching derives from the very truth that our bodies and souls have been saved by Christ, are destined for eternity with him, and are meant for his praise and glory in this life. It makes perfect sense, then, that we would pray with bodily gestures.

Reflecting on the posture of standing during prayer common in his day, Origen (3rd century A.D.) wrote: "Nor may anyone doubt that of the countless postures of the body, the posture with hands outstretched and eyes uplifted is to be preferred to all the others, because one then carries in the body too, as it were, the image of that special condition which befits the soul during prayer."

There is an important reciprocity between one's internal disposition in prayer and one's external posture or gesture.

His point was a simple but profound one: the body itself prays and "gives image to" the prayer of the soul. However, this is not a mere visible expression of something that could otherwise remain private and invisible. There is an important reciprocity between one's internal disposition in prayer and one's external posture or gesture. Origen writes that through posture, the soul produces a "suitable icon" of itself in the body, and the habit of using posture in prayer enhances and strengthens the soul's inner disposition. In fact, he writes, if we neglect the posture, we risk harming the inner disposition. It works both ways.

Writing about the same time as Origen, St. Clement of Alexandria also reflected on the meaning of gestures in prayer, using a particularly interesting example: "That is why we also raise our head toward the height and stretch out our hands to heaven and, while reciting the concluding words of the prayer together, stand on tip-toe, in that way seeking to follow the yearning of the mind upward into the spiritual world." While we no longer stand on tip-toe at the conclusion of common prayers, we can certainly understand Clement's teaching.

Christian theology does not see the body standing on its own, beside the soul. Rather, the two form a perfect unity, for it is the soul that makes the body human. Thus, the whole person prays, body and soul. Catholics embrace that truth so completely that it would be uncomfortable for us to remain sitting during an entire liturgy.

We would do well to pay deliberate attention to those gestures and postures which have become second nature to us, to remember their meaning, and to renew interiorly the message we are sending to God and ourselves by making them. They can truly deepen our prayer and express our longing for God.

The best way to begin? By slowing down.

One last comment about the prayer of body and soul. We should never underestimate the power of quiet reverence and proper dress in church. Both speak volumes about the quality of attention we are giving to our presence and participation in the liturgy, and about our respect for God and fellow parishioners. Just as there is reciprocity between interior disposition and exterior posture, so is there reciprocity among the members of Christ's Body. We can be an enhancement — or a distraction — to the worship of the Body of Christ.

"I urge you therefore, brothers, by the mercies of God, to offer your bodies as a living sacrifice, holy and pleasing to God, your spiritual worship." (Romans 12:1)

May 31, 2003

God calls us to childlike love, simplicity

I carry in my wallet a ragged piece of lined paper torn from a tablet, on which is written a series of numbers in no particular order. In ink with a child's scrawl, some of the numbers are large, and some are small; some are backwards, and some are upside down. The little piece of paper was a gift from Joseph, age 4.

Crossing the street from the rectory to the church one afternoon a few years ago, I saw Joseph's family car leaving the parking lot. When his mom saw me, she pulled to the curb, rolled down the window, and announced proudly, "Joseph has a gift for you." Smiling broadly but not saying a word, Joseph handed the slip of paper to me. His older sister and brother watched approvingly from the back seat.

I looked at the paper and noticed all the numbers. Not really understanding what I had just received, I said, "Thanks, Joseph! This is really good."

His mom explained, "You know what that's for, don't you, Father? You use it when you go out to eat. When the restaurant hostess asks about the size of your group, you check the table Joseph made for you and tell the hostess, 'Party of 5' or 'Party of 6.' This helps you know how to give her the right number."

"Oh, I understand now," I replied. "Joseph, you're a smart man for thinking of something like this. I'm going to put it my wallet and use it the next time I go out to eat." His broad smile broadened.

That small slip of paper is a child's perception of the world of adults. It is precious to me because it is a gift from Joseph and because it puts the cash, credit cards and driver's license I carry alongside it in their proper place. In the scheme of things, they are fleeting, insignificant and valueless. Joseph's table represents the childlike love and simplicity I am to have in my relationship with God, and thus it has great value.

Joseph was trying to be truly helpful to me. He was helpful, of course, but not in the way he had planned. I can count without his table, but I need to be reminded not to let the sophisticated trappings of the adult world lure me into a sense of self-sufficiency. All of us are children in the eyes of God, and our insight into the mystery of God is hazy and simplistic at best. It is for us to recognize that we are his children and give him what we can with a loving heart.

It matters not to God that I do not understand everything — what matters is that he understands me, and that I love and give myself to him.

It matters not to God that I do not understand everything — what matters is that he understands me, and that I love and give myself to him. When I preach a sermon or write this column, I am aware that my reflections are like scattered words and numbers scribbled by a child compared to the magnitude of the mystery I try to explore. God laughs at my cash, my credit cards and my Northwest Airlines WorldPerks number. I think he smiles with loving approval at my naïve attempts to proclaim his glory.

I need constant guides to simplicity, frequent lessons in reliance on God. I need to grow in spiritual childhood, to surrender any false sense of sophistication, which is merely a mask for pride. The only place to have these needs met is prayer.

Psalm 131 is one of the shortest psalms, yet it is packed with wisdom:

O Lord, my heart is not proud,
nor are my eyes haughty;
I busy not myself with great things,
nor with things too sublime for me.
Nay rather, I have stilled and quieted
my soul like a weaned child.
Like a weaned child on its mother's lap,
so is my soul within me.
O Israel, hope in the Lord,
both now and forever.

Whether parent, scholar, nun, attorney, physician, or bishop, we are children to God. Even if charged with the most complicated or exalted tasks, we are called to uncomplicated and humble trust in him. Even if we fancy ourselves experts in some field, we have only scratched the surface of the fullness of truth found in God. Prayer is our rest in God's lap, our grounding in his love, where he shares his understanding of us with us.

It is said that on December 6, 1273, the great theologian St. Thomas Aquinas was given profound spiritual insight while celebrating Mass and he stopped writing from that day forward. He told a friend, "Such things have been revealed to me that all I have written seems to me as so much straw." The priest who attended him at his deathbed 15 months later said that hearing Thomas' final confession was like listening to the first confession of a child of five.

March 13, 2004

Call upon the Lord always
with all your heart

One of my nieces was once rushed to a hospital by ambulance with a diagnosis of meningitis. Thanks to prayers and good medical care, she recovered quickly and was well enough to be released within a few days. I drove her and my sister back home one night, and during the long drive my sister cradled the little 3-year-old in her arms. "Hold me, Mommy," she kept saying, even though her mom was holding her tight. "Hold me, Mommy, hold me."

Listening silently at the wheel, I realized that when we call out to God, our prayers are part supplication ("Comfort me, guide me, Lord") and part proclamation ("You comfort me, guide me, Lord"). Aren't our cries to God also professions of faith in him? Isn't the very fact that we call out to him an indication that we place our lives in his hands?

At about the same time as my niece's illness, a longtime friend died of leukemia in his mid-40s. He was a man of deep faith and devoted love for his wife and daughters. One day toward the end of his life, when he could no longer speak, I entered his hospital room to bring holy Communion; he raised his hands high in the air and applauded — the only way he could outwardly welcome the Lord.

After his death, his wife suggested I read the last of his many journals. Its pages chronicled a man's journey of faith, prayer and surrender. One entry stated, "The simple childlike repetition of the name of Jesus can work real miracles for us." At the top of a page near the end of the journal, he wrote: "October,

1991. Chip's Novena Prayer to Jesus; composed one sleepless night. Praise God." Below were 75 three-word prayers, written one underneath the other, his personal litany. They included the following:

"Forgive me, Jesus. Fill me, Jesus. Shepherd me, Jesus. Warm me, Jesus. Cool me, Jesus. Heal me, Jesus. Use me, Jesus. Push me, Jesus. Pull me, Jesus. Send me, Jesus. Cradle me, Jesus. Take me, Jesus. Urge me, Jesus. Remember me, Jesus. Mold me, Jesus. Teach me, Jesus. Humble me, Jesus. Purify me, Jesus. Hear me, Jesus. See me, Jesus. Help me, Jesus. Pardon me, Jesus." The last prayer on the page was, "Possess me for eternity."

When Pope John Paul II preached his first homily in St. Peter's Square in 1978, he said, "Do not be afraid!" In 1993, when he published "Crossing the Threshold of Hope," he repeated those words. Having survived an attempt on his life and serious illness, having watched the downfall of communism and escalating persecution of the Church in other parts of the world, and having seen increasing threats to human life and dignity, he began and ended his book with reflections on the same words, "Do not be afraid."

This is sacred biblical counsel. An angel told Mary at the annunciation, and the shepherds at the birth of Jesus, "Do not be afraid!" Joseph was told, "Do not be afraid to take Mary your wife into your home." An angel told the women at the tomb, "Do not be afraid!" Jesus said to his disciples, "Do not fear, little flock," "Do not let your hearts be troubled."

At a critical and troubled time in his ministry, Paul received a vision of the Lord, who said to him, "Do not be afraid. Go on speaking, and do not be silent, for I am with you." As John began the Book of Revelation he recounted how he saw Christ in glory, who said, "Do not be afraid. I am the first and the last, the one who lives. Once I was dead, but now I am alive forever and ever."

The holy witnesses of the Bible clung to God's promises and

grew in faith. Their cries were acts of faith, proclamations of God's loving kindness. And even as they spoke their cries, they knew they were safely in God's arms. The one upon whom they called was near, and there was no reason to be afraid.

And even as they spoke their cries, they knew they were safely in God's arms. The one upon whom they called was near, and there was no reason to be afraid.

A 19th-century Russian spiritual classic titled "The Way of a Pilgrim" relates the journey of an anonymous Christian who yearns to understand Paul's admonition to "pray without ceasing." Early in his travels he comes upon an elder who says, "The ceaseless Jesus Prayer is a continuous, uninterrupted call on the holy name of Jesus Christ with the lips, mind and heart; and in the awareness of his abiding presence it is a plea for his blessing in all undertakings, in all places, at all times."

The beautiful book recounts the pilgrim's discovery of this "prayer of the heart," an ancient tradition going back to the monks of the Egyptian desert. As he travels about Russia, he discovers the fruit of prayer, the revelation of God's abiding presence in one's heart. In fact, he learns, prayer becomes unceasing when it descends from the lips into the heart.

In the course of a day, we have unceasing opportunities to call upon our Lord. Teach me, Jesus. Guide me, Jesus. Give me strength, Jesus. I love you, Jesus. Forgive me, Jesus. Calling upon him, we proclaim our faith in his saving love; and the duties of the day — as hectic or lonely or challenging as they might be — are transformed by the revelation of his presence. Gradually we begin to realize that the very reason we were led to call out his name in the first place was that he was there all along.

Pray always, and do not be afraid.

June 30, 2001

Sometimes we 'pray for the sake of praying'

"Ars gratia artis," "Art for the sake of art," is a phrase known originally as "the motto of the true artist." It refers to art executed for no other purpose than the beauty it renders visible, for no other recompense than the joy of expressing what lies deep within the artist.

We have seen this phrase whenever we have watched the opening credits of a Metro-Goldwyn-Mayer movie. A lion roars through the MGM seal, and above its head is written, "Ars gratia artis."

Some years ago I saw a movie by comedian Mel Brooks, and as the first frames were projected on the screen with the familiar MGM seal, it was Brooks, not a lion, who roared. A Latin phrase appeared above his head which read, "Ars est pecunia" — "art is money."

Brooks was spoofing the classic motto and the commercialization of art. Billions of dollars are made from movies, and even obscure paintings bring in big bucks. Mass-produced sketches and sculptures may be beautiful, but production is geared toward profit. Are there still artists out there who execute their craft for its own sake? Sure there are. Brooks was taking a jab at himself.

Perhaps the motto of the true artist is a good way to further our understanding of the nature of Christian prayer. Let's call it prayer for its own sake.

It is easy for us to understand how profit cheapens art.

Likewise, we understand that kindness to others for the purpose of obtaining a favor from them is not pure love. Genuine, gratuitous deeds of love arise out of love; husbands and wives sacrifice for one another because of their love. They delight in seeing the joy their love gives to one another. Love for the sake of love.

Several times in this column I have written about intercessory prayer. I consider it one of my central responsibilities as a priest and bishop, a responsibility I cherish. Last week I commented that Jesus eternally intercedes for us before the Father. Our participation in the communion of saints means in part that we benefit from the intercession of all believers, living and dead.

When I wrote about the risen Christ as the "contemplative Christ," I had in mind something even more extensive than his eternal intercession for us before the Father. Contemplative prayer is prayer for its own sake — prayer for no other purpose than to be one with God in love. Contemplation is about love.

Contemplation involves giving ourselves to God in prayer without expecting anything — an answer, a favor, or even a feeling of God's presence — in return. That can be very difficult, because we tend to heap on our prayer the same expectations we have of our efforts in other areas of life, particularly the expectation that there must be some measurable sign of success.

The most common criteria we use to evaluate the "success" of prayer are "answers" and "feelings." No doubt about it, God hears and answers our prayers. When we pray for a particular intention, we ask God to guide us patiently in discerning his answer; we also add, with Jesus, "thy will be done."

The issue of "feelings" in prayer is a tricky one. Certainly God does at times grace us with feelings or emotions which assure us of his presence and love. But to tell the truth, God works at a level much deeper than feelings, a level so intimate that feelings do not have the capacity to adequately communicate his grace. Thus we never assume because we did not feel something at prayer that God was not at work in us. Whenever we give ourselves to him in prayer, he is there.

The beginning of contemplative prayer takes us beyond our need for "answers" and "feelings." It is prayer for the sake of prayer; it complements and completes intercessory prayer and helps dispose us to God's work within us. It involves making time simply to be in God's presence, with no claim on receiving an "answer," no expectation of "success," no hope for profit or a certain "feeling" — in other words, for no other reason than that we love God. This kind of prayer mirrors God's generosity, for he gives himself without holding back, no strings attached, and continues to give even when we are ungrateful or indifferent.

It involves making time simply to be in God's presence, with no claim on receiving an "answer," no expectation of "success," no hope for profit or a certain "feeling" — in other words, for no other reason than that we love God.

I will give only one brief "instruction" in this regard; anything else might muddy the message. Take five minutes every day, whether on your knees, in your favorite chair, or before the Blessed Sacrament, and quietly give yourself to God. If you would like to use words, make them simple, something like, "I love you, I am yours." That's it.

Frequently when we begin to give ourselves to this kind of prayer, we fear we are not doing it properly because it requires no particular strategy or "work" on our part. We wonder, because it is not difficult, whether we will accomplish anything.

There is a valuable lesson here. This kind of prayer is one way we surrender to God and rely entirely on his grace. We let go of expectations of him and of ourselves — and admit that perhaps all too often we would like to "take credit" for prayer.

This is prayer for the sake of prayer, love for the sake of love, prayer for the sake of love. It is how we communicate with God on his own terms.

May 12, 2001

Directions aren't always about distance

One of our priests, an alumnus of St. John Home Mission Seminary in Little Rock, recalls that the public speaking instructor at St. John's had an annual assignment for new students: give a speech about how to get from Point A to Point B. He was a wise teacher, for the one who can give clear directions is a communicator indeed.

When I have needed directions to parishes around the state, my secretary has painstakingly taken down instructions dictated over the telephone by pastors, deacons, nuns and parish secretaries. I quickly discovered that giving directions is an expression of one's perspective. It is therefore an art, not a science.

Asked about distance, some people respond with time. How far is Fort Smith from Little Rock? To some, it is "two-and-a-half hours." To others, it is "157 miles."

Some people will direct, "turn left at Arkansas 22." Others, "go west on Arkansas 22."

Do not inquire of some people the names of streets, for street names are of no consequence to them. Ask instead about landmarks. "Do I go past Harvest Foods?" "Is it the road before or after the power station?" "Do I turn left or right at the funeral home?"

Distance is entirely a matter of perception. The first time I visited one parish, I was told that the left turn would be "about 3 miles from the gate." It was 8 miles. Visiting another parish, I was told the bend would appear several miles down the road. It was less than a mile.

One would think that left is left and right is right, but apparently that is not the case. "Turn right at the courthouse" can mean several things, I have learned, and often it does not mean what one would think. Courthouses are usually at the center of town squares, and it is understandably difficult for folks who are accustomed to approaching a courthouse from one corner to explain what one would do when approaching it from another.

"Look for the sawmill sign" is equally confounding. Expecting a big sign (especially since it was included in the directions), I find a small sign, and preoccupied with the sawmill, I miss the church.

"It's where K-Mart used to be," some people will confidently announce. If only I had lived here 10 years ago, I say to myself, like those who used to shop at K-Mart where it used to be, I wouldn't be lost now.

For Father Bill Thomas, pastor of St. John the Baptist in Hot Springs, directions are not essentially a matter of time or distance. They are a matter of prayer. "It's three rosaries from Hot Springs to Little Rock," he explains. And he means it.

The Bible sometimes uses time to express distance. Fleeing the enraged Jezebel, Elijah left his servant at Beer-sheba and "went a day's journey into the desert." (1 Kings 19:4) The reluctant Jonah was sent by God to preach repentance at Nineveh, a city so enormous that "it took three days to go through it." (Jonah 3:3) A "day's journey" was a distance of 10 to 30 miles, depending on circumstances.

A "Sabbath day's journey" was much shorter, about .60 mile, because of rabbinical restrictions on Sabbath travel. Luke reports that after Jesus ascended into heaven, the apostles "returned to Jerusalem from the mount called Olivet, which is near Jerusalem, a Sabbath day's journey away." (Acts 1:12) It was very close.

As for God giving directions, he has his ways, and "hearing" and "following" them requires a special point of view.

Take Abraham, for example, to whom God gave startlingly direct — but bewilderingly hazy — instructions: "Go forth from the land of your kinsfolk and from your father's house to a land that I will show you." (Genesis 12:1) It was not the "where" that was important, but the "going forth" — a sign of trust that God would show the way, even if his directions would be given on a need-to-know basis. Hundreds of years later, the author of Hebrews commented, "By faith Abraham obeyed when he was called to go out to a place that he was to receive as an inheritance; he went out, not knowing where he was to go." (Hebrews 11:8-9)

It was not the "where" that was important, but the "going forth" — a sign of trust that God would show the way, even if his directions would be given on a need-to-know basis.

Jesus told the apostles he was going to prepare a place for them and would return to take them with him. "Where I am going you know the way." Thomas protested, "Master, we do not know where you are going; how can we know the way?" "I am the way and the truth and the life. No one comes to the father except through me" (John 14:1-6), said Jesus. God does deal with us on a need-to-know basis. All we need to know is Jesus.

Everyone seeks help navigating the personal and spiritual roads of life. When we lose our bearings and fret about where to turn next, it is time for prayer, a time for trust that God will show the way.

With God, it's not so much "where" I am to go but "toward whom." It's not so much "how" I will get there but "with whom." Jesus' promise that he would be with us was not an empty one, and there is deep freedom to be found in knowing that our sure-footed Savior will lead us along unknown paths.

I think Father Bill has it right. The best measure of distance between two points is prayer.

August 9, 2003

Need a Hail Mary Pass?

S everal weeks ago, I confirmed six inmates at the Federal
Correctional Institution at Forrest City. I was accompanied
by Sister Maxine Vogan, Father Ed Graves and several lay
Catholic volunteers from Forrest City and Wynne who regularly visit the unit. From the moment we arrived, it was obvious
that the Catholic volunteer group was a favorite of the
Protestant staff chaplain. As she escorted us through the security procedure, there was lots of laughter.

"Do these people give you a hard time?" I asked. "No," she
said, "This is a fun group."

A large number of inmates were present for confirmation.
They were attentive and smiling, happy to be present for Mass
and happy to see the volunteers they have come to love.
Among the Catholic inmates there are several key leaders who
have organized Bible study, instructions in the Catholic faith,
liturgical music and common praying of the Liturgy of the
Hours. They take our faith seriously, and confirmation was a
celebration for all.

At the end of the evening, we went through the departure
procedure, once again escorted by the chaplain. As we were
about to say our good-byes for the evening, she said to me,
"Bishop, can I ask you a question?" "Sure," I replied.

"Will you explain to me what a 'Hail Mary pass' is?"

"A desperation pass," someone in the group called out.

I filled in the blanks, explaining the origin of the Hail Mary
prayer (the Ave Maria) from Scripture and what the phrase

means in football. (At the end of a half, and especially at the end of a game, when the team on offense is losing and has just enough time for one play, the quarterback throws the ball almost blindly toward the end zone, hoping one of the receivers can catch it for a score).

Although we Catholics usually think first of the prayer when we hear the words "Hail Mary," they have also come to refer to any desperate measure or final effort in a project.

The chaplain's question was one I had never been asked, and it made me smile. I began to wonder: would the Blessed Mother mind having a popular phrase refer to her as some kind of desperation move?

I don't think she would mind at all.

As a child, along with the Hail Mary I learned the traditional prayer known as the "Memorare."

> Remember, O most gracious Virgin Mary,
> that never was it known
> that anyone who fled to thy protection,
> implored thy help, or sought thy intercession,
> was left unaided.
> Inspired by this confidence, I fly unto thee,
> O Virgin of virgins, my mother.
> To thee I come, before thee I stand
> sinful and sorrowful.
> O Mother of the Word Incarnate,
> despise not my petitions, but in thy mercy
> hear and answer me. Amen.

The Memorare has been attributed to St. Bernard of Clairvaux (1090-1153), probably because it contains themes common to his writing, but it is doubtful that St. Bernard was the author. Its popularity and the theory of its authorship were promoted 500 years after his death by a French priest, Father Claude Bernard (1588-1641). Interestingly, Father Claude was known as the "Poor Priest" and was dedicated to ministry among prisoners and those condemned to death for their crimes.

In his apostolate of evangelization, Father Claude frequently encouraged prisoners to seek the intercession of the Blessed Mother, and to great effect; many were reconciled to God because of his counsel. He once printed more than 200,000 leaflets with the Memorare in various languages and distributed them wherever he thought they would give consolation and encouragement.

I suppose one could say that the Hail Mary and the Memorare are prayers of desperation, but only if at the same time one sees them as prayers of hope and confidence.

I suppose one could say that the Hail Mary and the Memorare are prayers of desperation, but only if at the same time one sees them as prayers of hope and confidence.

When Mary and Joseph brought Jesus to the temple, holy Simeon told her, "You yourself a sword will pierce." (Luke 2:35) We "fly" to Mary because the Scriptures testify to her unfailing hope in God, even in the midst of her own suffering. She is happy when we ask her intercession, no matter the circumstances, because that gives her another opportunity to take us to her Son. She knows that no situation is desperate when handed over to him.

There are thousands of people incarcerated in the federal and state facilities of Arkansas. Pray for them and their families, that they might find hope in God, as Mary did. I have first-hand knowledge that many of them are praying for us.

August 28, 2004

Give us the confidence you had in the Father

Have you ever had a sleepless night? We can toss and turn in bed for all sorts of reasons.

Perhaps we've been working too hard, and instead of counting sheep we count budget numbers or work plans. We're ill, and the illness or the medication that cures it keeps us on edge. Maybe knowing that we have to get up extra early for some special reason, our mind stays alert through the night lest we oversleep.

Maybe we're waiting for the phone call about a sick relative or friend, or listening for the sound of the front door, signaling that the son or daughter is home from a date. Perhaps there's a spectacularly frightening storm brewing outside, or a frightening storm brewing inside, in our hearts and minds, and we're full of anxiety and worry.

A brief but beautiful passage in the Gospel has always appealed to me in this regard, and when it appeared in the cycle of daily Mass readings several weeks ago I decided to reflect on it with you in one of my weekly columns.

Read Matthew 8:23-27. Mark and Luke also report this incident. While Jesus was in a boat with some of his disciples, a violent storm suddenly came up on the sea, so violent that the boat was filling with water. Jesus was fast asleep. The story continues, but I like to linger at this scene.

I've pictured it in my mind many times — surrounded by thunder, lightening, wind, waves and a frightened band of disciples, Jesus is fast asleep. I don't know about you, but when I'm in the middle of a storm — the kind produced by nature or the kind that can brew inside me — I don't find it easy to sleep. But Jesus did.

It wasn't that Jesus was free of troubles (we are told that at times he was "troubled in spirit"), or that his sleeping indicated a lack of concern (though that might have been what some of his disciples first thought).

Instead, I picture his sleep as a sign of trust in his Father. Jesus was so united with his Father in love and prayer that he knew that the Father would take care of him, no matter what was brewing around him.

He knew that nothing on earth has the power to hinder God's love from extending a protecting hand. He knew that storms would pass, but his Father's love would not.

He knew that nothing on earth has the power to hinder God's love from extending a protecting hand. He knew that storms would pass, but his Father's love would not. And so he slept peacefully during this storm.

I think that's why, when the disciples woke him crying "Lord, save us! We are perishing!" he replied, "Why are you terrified, O you of little faith?" He knew that placing one's faith in the Father stills any storm. He rebuked the wind and sea, and there was great calm.

Amazed at what they had seen, the men said, "What sort of man is this, whom even the winds and the sea obey?"

Without a doubt this was only one of many storms Jesus' disciples would experience as the years went by, but their experience with him that day must have stayed with them, just as he intended. He had power to calm storms! But before they witnessed that power, the disciples saw Jesus sleeping trustingly in the Father's love. No storm could shake that peaceful sleep.

One of the mid-day prayers in the breviary contains a phrase that always comes to mind whenever I picture the Lord

Jesus asleep: "Give us the confidence you had in the Father..."

Give us the confidence you had in the Father, and we will sleep in peace.

Give us the confidence you had in the Father, and we can weather any storm.

Give us the confidence you had in the Father, and we will calm others.

Give us the confidence you had in the Father, and that will be enough for us.

Amen.

July 22, 2000

Changed forever through the Eucharist

When I visited a lifelong friend at the time of his wife's sudden death two years ago, he took me to their bedroom and showed me a spot with two comfortable chairs, a table and lamp between them. "That's where we used to sit in the evenings, Pete. We really didn't say much or carry on long conversations. We would read or she would do some sewing. After 31 years of marriage, it was just wonderful to be in one another's presence."

They had many conversations about kids and grandkids, about laying new floors and how to spend retirement, about their own parents' health and their future together. But they also had precious times when nothing was said, because simple presence said it all.

St. John Vianney noticed an elderly man visiting church every morning before work and again every evening after work. One day out of curiosity he asked, "Mr. Chaffangeon, what do you say to our Lord during your visits?" The old man responded, "I say nothing to him, Father. I look at him and he looks at me."

It is logical and correct for us to think of prayer as conversation with God. We pour out our hearts in words of praise and intercession, words of confusion and hope. He responds with his Word, his consolation, his peace-filled silence. But another, vitally important way of praying is simply to be in God's presence. Not that there's nothing on our minds or nothing we feel like saying to him. There are times when simple presence says it all. We look at him, and he looks at us.

As with most things in life, we assume that prayer must accomplish something, that it must end in a thought or a resolution or a feeling. Certainly sometimes that happens, but quiet presence before God — nothing accomplished, nothing in particular said — solidifies and deepens our relationship with him, spilling over to every aspect of our lives.

There is no doubt that my friend's quiet hours in his wife's presence were both the result of many conversations and the reason why some things did not need to be said. It was enough every evening just to be together.

I think of prayer, and especially prayer before the Tabernacle, in that way. The Lord Jesus is present in the reserved Blessed Sacrament, because he emptied himself so completely on the cross (and therefore at Mass, during which his one sacrifice is made present to us) that his presence remains in the consecrated bread after Mass as real, true and personal. We reserve the Blessed Sacrament in order to take Communion to the sick and so that we might prolong our being present to the Lord in loving adoration, as he is lovingly present to us.

As for myself, I have many conversations with him before the Tabernacle. I talk too much, but he listens patiently, touching my heart with a word or a thought, a decision or a reminder of some kind. But I also try to spend time simply looking at him as he looks at me. Nothing accomplished, nothing said. His Eucharistic presence is ample evidence that he wants to be with me, ample evidence that he desires my presence, too.

During the Year of the Eucharist, each deanery of our diocese is spending time in Eucharistic adoration as a way of deepening our mutual presence with our Lord. I hope that the holy hours being conducted around the state will enliven our desire to be in his presence. I hope most especially that they will enliven our participation at Mass by awakening in us a desire to offer ourselves completely along with the bread and wine. We are changed when we participate in the Eucharist, because the gifts we make of ourselves are taken by the Lord and offered with his gift — himself — to the Father. Fed with his Body and Blood, we are sent to live as he lived, to empty ourselves for others. When we pray in his Eucharistic presence, he takes us beyond words, and our relationship with him — our desire to give ourselves to him — is deepened. Every aspect of that dynamic is important.

We are changed when we participate in the Eucharist, because the gifts we make of ourselves are taken by the Lord and offered with his gift — himself — to the Father.

It is for that reason that Eucharistic adoration flows from the Mass and leads us back to Mass. Jesus' abiding presence in the Blessed Sacrament is his way of drawing us continually into his presence. "Father, they are your gift to me. I wish that where I am they also may be with me, that they may see my glory that you gave me, because you loved me before the foundation of the world." (John 17:24-25) He longs for us to be with him eternally in heaven, and he gives us a true taste of his heavenly presence when we pray, especially before the Blessed Sacrament.

Many years ago my friend started attending daily Mass and making a weekly hour of adoration. I think his time of prayer spilled over to his marriage, and his marriage spilled over to his prayer. His closeness to the Eucharist gave him strength, particularly when his grief was overwhelming.

He and his wife had given themselves completely to one another and, together, to God. God took their gift and made it holy. My friend still regularly just looks at God, and God looks back. Nothing accomplished, nothing said. Their profound love is expressed just by being together.

January 22, 2005

LIVING THE LIFE
OF CHRIST

Three priests and three preachers meet on a road …

For a number of years, it was an after-Christmas tradition that several priest friends and I would spend a few days hiking, eating and relaxing in the Smoky Mountains. We always hoped it would snow while we were there, and once or twice the weather obliged.

One such year, as we were driving down the mountain on a highway punctuated by treacherous patches of ice, we came upon three men standing befuddled next to their SUV, which had slid into a shallow ditch. Apparently they had been trying for some time without success to get back on the road. We stopped to help.

Six sets of hands and a couple of jacks did the trick. Within 30 minutes they were ready to be on their way. As they were expressing gratitude for our help, one of them asked, "What do you guys do for a living?" "We're Catholic priests," one of us responded.

The three of them broke into friendly laughter, and one said, "You're not going to believe this. We're Baptist preachers."

I have a feeling that six sermons were preached the following Sunday about Good Samaritans, about slipping off the road of life, about religious differences or about letting go of prejudice. It was the kind of serendipitous experience for which a homilist is always on the prowl, the kind that lends itself to a variety of interpretations. I would have liked to have been in the pew for the other five sermons.

Had we ministers begun our acquaintance elsewhere with a discussion of theological differences, things might not have turned out the same. I have a feeling that had that day been the beginning of a lasting friendship, differences would have always given way to mutual love and respect — because of the way we met. Impelled by the Holy Spirit (for the Spirit works in such uncomplicated ways), six strangers met on a slippery mountain to work together as God intends. There was no doubt that faith was the inspiration for our stopping to help and their willing acceptance of our offer.

Had we ministers begun our acquaintance elsewhere with a discussion of theological differences, things might not have turned out the same.

The Lord Jesus had promised to send the Holy Spirit, the advocate and consoler, to remind us of all he had taught and keep us in faithful discipleship. But the promise was not just a matter of helping us keep things straight in our heads. The Spirit would be given to ensure the proper functioning of the body of Christ, the Church.

As St. Paul would explain, the Spirit and his gifts are given for the common good. "To each individual the manifestation of the Spirit is given for some benefit. To one is given… wisdom; to another… knowledge; to another… gifts of healing; to another, mighty deeds; to another, prophesy; to another, discernment of spirits… But one and the same Spirit produces all of these, distributing them individually to each person as he wishes." (see 1 Cor 12)

St. Cyril of Jerusalem offered the analogy of water. "Water comes down from heaven as rain, and although it is always the same in itself, it produces many different effects, one in the palm tree, another in the vine, and so on throughout the whole of creation. It does not come down, now as one thing, now as another, but while remaining essentially the same, it adapts itself to the needs of every creature that receives it." So it is with the Holy Spirit, taught Cyril.

St. Basil the Great compared the Spirit to the radiance of the sun. "Like the sunshine, which permeates all the atmosphere, spreading over land and sea and yet is enjoyed by each person as though it were for him alone, so the Spirit pours forth his grace in full measure, sufficient for all, and yet is present as though exclusively to everyone who can receive him."

Joined to the body of Christ through baptism, confirmation and Eucharist, we are given the one Spirit; and we receive his gifts so that we might undertake our particular role in the body as God intends. St. Paul taught that by following the Spirit's lead, we work with him in building up the Church. It is my experience that the most humble paths, and the most simple faithfulness to love and responsibility, make parishes and dioceses strong. Nothing flashy, nothing extraordinary. Just faithfulness to the Lord, day in and day out. Just "following the Spirit's lead" in the most commonplace of opportunities. Without the humble, the great never has a chance.

Of the lessons gleaned from that chance encounter in the Smokies a few years back, one has always stuck with me. Some regular disciples of the Lord took a few days away from their assigned tasks and happened to meet along the road. Watered and warmed by the same Spirit, they worked together toward a common good, and off they went to the next opportunity. Unspectacular as it sounds, in many ways it was the microcosm of everything you and I are called to be. Our common goal is God. Our common path is love.

June 14, 2003

We can bear all things with Christ's help

One evening several years ago, I received word that an elderly friend, who lived at a nursing home and was dying of cancer, wanted to see me.

Later that night we enjoyed a spirited half-hour visit in her darkened room. She was 88 years old and just a wisp of her former self, but she was full of life, wisdom and love for God. We had a rather loud conversation, all of it within earshot of her roommate, who insisted that we were not bothering her, and who kept saying we should turn on the light to see one another better. Before leaving, I stopped by the bed of my friend's roommate to say good night.

She took my arm, stroked it several times, and said softly, "You're so young and happy and good. Stay that way. Don't ever let 'em cheat it out of you." I was expecting to say good night, to tell her I would say a prayer for her, too. But she caught me totally off guard by offering some stunning advice.

I knew exactly what she meant when she said, "Don't let 'em cheat it out of you." She wasn't referring to any person, but to the hardships of life and the temptations that accompany them. In other words, don't let hard times cheat you out of happiness by making you bitter. Don't let anger get hold of you and make you dwell on the negative. Don't let anything like that cheat you out of happiness and goodness.

I think her advice was similar to that offered by St. Paul to the Ephesians: "Do not grieve the Holy Spirit of God, with

which you were sealed against the day of redemption."
(Ephesians 4:30) Don't let anything cheat you out of the peace
of the Spirit — not bitterness, passion or anger, not harsh
words, not slander or malice of any kind. These are temptations for all of us when pushed against the wall. We were given
a precious gift of the Spirit at baptism, and it would be tragic
to allow anything in life to "cheat it out of us" by giving into
bitterness. I think we know instinctively what Paul meant.

Jesus knew well the difficulties that come with living out his
Father's will in this world. He confronted rejection and misunderstanding. People were out to get him. On the cross he cried
out in abandonment. He never gave in to bitterness over his
predicament, however, but forged the path of pure love and
forgiveness. He did not let his trials and passion cheat him out
of his love for the Father or his love for us. With all his might,
he clung to his Father.

While St. Thomas More was imprisoned in the Tower of
London, he composed numerous prayers and meditations.
One in particular has always appealed to me, and I keep a copy
in my breviary. More's "A Godly Meditation," written in 1534,
begins: "Give me thy grace, good Lord, to set the world at
nought, to set my mind fast upon thee." He prays for the grace
to keep his mind fixed on God as he suffers imprisonment and
separation from family, to grow in faith and love while in the
Tower. He asks God to help him "To think my most enemies
my best friends, for the brethren of Joseph could never have
done him so much good with their love and favour as they did
him with their malice and hatred."

He was referring to Joseph, son of Jacob and Rachel, who
was sold by his envious brothers to slave traders, who took him
to Egypt. After a series of painful trials, Joseph became a high
officer to the Pharaoh and eventually helped his father and
brothers during a terrible famine (see Genesis, chapters 37-50).
It is a beautiful story, which comes to a climax in Genesis 45,
when Joseph reveals his identity to his brothers and declares
how God's hand was at work in his saga. More referred to this

biblical account, because Joseph had recognized how God used the painful events he endured, and the misdeeds of his brothers, for good purpose. In other words, Joseph did not let what had happened to him cheat him of faith in God or love for his family. More would not let himself be cheated, either.

Neither should we ever allow ourselves to be cheated out of the peace God gives. When life's challenges, certain people, painful events or our own sinfulness threaten to cheat us, Paul reminds us to be like the Lord Jesus: in the face of everything, be kind, compassionate and mutually forgiving (Ephesians 4:32). In fact, that is the best way to stand our ground, to cling to God, to affirm with confidence and hope, "Nothing is going to cheat me out of the happiness that God intends for me." It is also a way of sharing in the victory Jesus won over sin and death.

In fact, that is the best way to stand our ground, to cling to God, to affirm with confidence and hope, "Nothing is going to cheat me out of the happiness that God intends for me."

As Paul affirmed in Romans 8, nothing will be able to separate us from the love of God in Christ Jesus our Lord. Nothing can cheat us out of God's love. Holding on to that profound truth gives us strength to bear all things.

July 27, 2002

Parishes should be 'No Gossip Zones'

E very parish to which I have been assigned has had its share of conflicts — between priest and parishioner, parishioner and parishioner, teacher and parent, child and child. Conflicts are inevitable whenever two or three of us come together, no matter who we are; but I have always been saddened by conflicts in parishes.

Parish conflicts are often accompanied by gossip, which can be harmless (there was once a rumor circulating through the parish that I was one of triplets!) or devastating (untruths or truths about someone's personal failings or private family struggles). Why do we have a need to perpetuate such things, to make them our business? I suppose the reasons are as varied as our personalities.

Several years ago I contemplated making the parish I served a "No Gossip Zone." It would have been an all-out campaign, with signs at the driveway entrances and on the sports fields, pledge cards taped to refrigerators, stickers on telephones, Sunday homilies and lessons for the school children. I had seen reputations damaged and spirits crushed by gossip, little kids shedding crocodile tears because of stories spread about them, gossip used as fuel for arguments and as rationales for decisions. I wondered, why couldn't we see the insidious nature of rumors, why couldn't we understand that parish conflicts injure the Body of Christ?

Like families, parishes are schools for love, where we learn to put the lessons of Christ into practice, where we focus on his summons to put aside the habits of the marketplace and take up a new way of living. I would like to suggest seven steps toward peaceful parish life.

1. Remember the Eighth Commandment. According to the catechism, calumny is "a false statement which harms the reputation of others and gives occasion for false judgments concerning them." It is a sin.

2. Direct is best. When we walk into a conversation that is nothing more than gossip, we can say, calmly and simply, "I don't think we should be talking about this." No further explanation is necessary.

3. Judging is best left to God. It is said that many centuries ago a Christian monk in the Egyptian desert committed a fault known to all. A council was called to which the holy man, Abba Moses, was invited; but he refused to attend. When finally a messenger was sent to him because everyone was waiting, he relented and set out for the meeting. He filled a leaky jug with water and carried it on the journey. The others said, "What is this, Father?" The old man said to them, "My sins run out behind me like water, and I do not see them, and today I am coming to judge the errors of another." Hearing this, the others said no more to the offending brother and forgave him.

4. Speak only in the name of Jesus. Every one of us has a multitude of opinions, but tossing our opinion into the ring of conflict might only kindle the flames. Before we speak, we ask ourselves, "Can I say this in the name of Jesus?"

5. Recognize the subtle seduction of evil and step aside. Satan would like nothing more than to cause division in the Church. By refusing to jump needlessly into petty parish conflicts, we rob evil of its power. "If you resist and fight every time there is trouble in the Church, you give evil its power. Merely move aside as would a martial arts master, and evil will collapse of its own weight on the floor beside you." (William C. Martin, "The Art of Pastoring: Contemplative Reflections")

6. Pray for those who are the subject of gossip. Most of the

time, we have no legitimate need to know all the facts when the parish is rife with rumor. But the smoke tells us that someone is hurting and needs our prayers. If we know him or her well enough, we might offer personal support and counsel as well. Prayer and love bring Christ's healing, put out fires, and strengthen the community.

Most of the time, we have no legitimate need to know all the facts when the parish is rife with rumor. But the smoke tells us that someone is hurting and needs our prayers.

7. Write the letter but don't mail it right away. When angry about a certain issue, some people find it helpful to write a letter to vent their frustrations, much like a whistling kettle vents steam. If that's the case with us, after writing the letter, wait a few days. If we judge that it meets the test of criteria 1-6 above, and if it offers constructive help, we might consider mailing it. If it does not meet the necessary criteria, or if we are not willing to sign our name to it, it belongs in the trash.

Perhaps you're wondering if lately I have been hearing about conflicts in parishes around the state. It would be nothing new. But not wanting to spread gossip, true or false, I'd rather not talk about it. I have enough of my own sinfulness to say grace over, on most issues my opinion is not worth more than anyone else's, and I've discovered that being aware of the conflict but not reacting too quickly, I will soon hear that it has dissipated. As for letters, I've learned that revising the revision of the original keeps me out of trouble and my wastebasket full.

Prayer brings me back where I need to be. It's the life-blood of the Body of Christ, the sustenance of my relationship with God, and the deepest expression of my love for fellow parishioners, especially those who are hurting.

February 24, 2001

The Lord knows the sadness of our losses

As I think back over the funerals at which I have presided through the years, I am struck by the variety of family circumstances and causes of death. The funerals of the well-known were attended by great crowds. Others were quite small, often because the deceased had outlived most of their friends and relatives. Some loved ones had known that they were going to die; we had the chance to say "good-bye," to reminisce and celebrate as death approached. Others were suddenly wrenched from us; there were no good-byes, because no one knew death was near.

At some funerals, there was evidence of strong and tender family bonds; at others, subtle hints of strained and fragile relationships. In every case, in funerals large or small, of the young or the old, by death expected or unexpected, with loving warmth or painful coolness, families were left to grieve.

Many know the story of St. Augustine and his mother, St. Monica, who lived in the fourth century. Although he had been raised by a devout Christian mother, Augustine's early life was marked by sin and selfishness. With the help of his mother's prayers and tears, he eventually accepted the grace of conversion. He tells the story in his "Confessions," and in Book IX he movingly gives an account of his mother's death.

"On the ninth day of her illness, when she was aged 56, and I was 33, this religious and devout soul was released from the body ... I closed her eyes and an overwhelming grief welled into my heart and was about to flow forth in floods of tears.

But at the same time under a powerful act of mental control my eyes held back the flood and dried it up. The inward struggle put me into great agony ... Why ... did I suffer sharp pains of inward grief? It must have been the fresh wound caused by ... a precious bond suddenly torn apart ..."

Augustine explains that when they did not see him cry, his friends wondered if he lacked all feeling. Inwardly he was being torn apart because he missed his mother terribly, but he thought it a sign of weakness to cry aloud. Even at her burial, he was profoundly sad but could not bring himself to cry.

"... throughout the day I was inwardly oppressed with sadness and with a troubled mind, and I asked you [God], to the utmost of my strength, to heal my pain. You did not do so."

Without success, he tried everything to get his mind off the pain. But little by little, he recalled his mother's kindness and gentleness, "of which I had suddenly been deprived," and he began to weep.

"I was glad to weep before you and about her and for her, about myself and for myself. Now I let flow the tears which I had held back so that they ran as freely as they wished. My heart rested upon them, and it reclined upon them because it was your ears that were there, not those of some human critic who would put a proud interpretation on my weeping."

He had been dead, and now he tearfully mourned the loss of his mother, who had in a sense prayed him back to life.

"Let anyone who wishes read and interpret as he pleases. If he finds fault that I wept for my mother for a fraction of an hour, the mother who had died before my eyes, who had wept for me that I might live before your eyes, let him not mock me but rather, if a person of much charity, let him weep himself before you for my sins ..."

His mother had cried tears of mourning when he was dead in sin and had prayed that he might come to life again in the eyes of God. He had been dead, and now he tearfully mourned the loss of his mother, who had in a sense prayed him back to life.

He also prayed for her. "I now petition you for my mother's sins ... I know that she acted mercifully and from her heart forgave the debts of her debtors. Now please forgive her debts if she contracted any during the many years that passed after she received the water of salvation."

Monica had not asked that her body be sumptuously wrapped and perfumed, or that her grave be marked by a special monument. "She desired only that she might be remembered at your altar which she had attended every day without fail, where she knew that what is distributed is the holy victim who 'abolished the account of debts which was reckoned against us.'"

He concludes Book IX: "So as a result of these confessions of mine may my mother's request receive a richer response through the prayers which many offer and not only those which come from me."

Every November, we pray for the repose of the souls of the dead. Many of you lost loved ones during the past year, and the Lord knows the sadness you feel at losing them. May your hearts rest and recline in your tears, for the Lord himself hears them. May the prayers of the whole Church give strength to you and your beloved dead. And may they receive eternal peace in the heart of God.

November 9, 2002

Death doesn't separate us from loved ones

Twenty years ago Marie and Mike were on my list of First Friday Communion calls. They lived near the parish, so I usually scheduled a stop at their house toward the end of my route. A visit with Marie and Mike was filled with sweetness and faith, the kind that put a smile on my face and made the whole day worthwhile. They never had children, and their lives were marked by single-hearted devotion to one another, and together, to God. After Marie took sick, Mike did the shopping, cleaned the house, and saw to it that she had everything he thought she deserved.

Entering their home was taking a step back in time. The house seemed quiet, even silent, to me, but sunlight flooding through the open curtains made the silence warm and peaceful. Figurines collected over many years were displayed lovingly on shelves and mantels; photographs of parents from another country covered the walls. The place was immaculately clean, and lace doilies protected chair backs and tabletops. These were simple, working class people, typical of so many in that parish; they worked hard for what they had, and when several plants that employed thousands in the area closed, they grieved their neighbors' misfortune.

They dressed in their Sunday best for my monthly visits, welcoming the presence of the Lord with a reverence I have never forgotten. Invariably, after they received holy Communion we would look at photographs. Mike was a musician, and he was particularly proud of the pictures of his

Catholic high school band. There he was, sitting in a line-up of early 20th century teenagers in suits and feathered alpine hats, proudly holding his french horn. I don't remember the details, but Mike once told me about playing french horn for the Army during World War I. Marie, who had heard his stories so many times, listened proudly.

When Marie died, Mike was lost and heartbroken. He continued to keep the house as tidy as ever, but without Marie he spent more time away from home — at church, with friends, shopping. He tried heroically to fill the void opened by her death, and parishioners went out of their way to speak to him with kindness.

When I was transferred to another parish, I lost track of him for several years. But one day after a funeral, I decided to spend a few extra moments at the cemetery visiting my father's grave, and I caught sight of Mike standing in prayer next to Marie's grave. We enjoyed a pleasant conversation, catching up on the latest news.

We decided that from then on, whenever either of us was at the cemetery, we would visit each other's family grave sites; he would say a prayer at my father's grave, and I would do the same at Marie's. I have tried to be faithful to that promise, and I have no doubt he was. When Mike himself died a few years later, a visit to their graves would make me smile all over again, as I recalled our monthly Communion calls and their faith-filled love. In fact, I started asking them to pray for me.

Every All Saints and All Souls Days I think of Mike and Marie, because they remind me of the intimate connection we have with Christ and one another through the communion of saints. In his "Credo of the People of God," Pope Paul VI wrote:

"We believe in the communion of all the faithful of Christ, those who are pilgrims on earth, the dead who are being purified, and the blessed in heaven, all together forming one Church; and we believe that in this communion, the merciful love of God and his saints is always attentive to our prayers."

There is one Church, and all members share in the spiritual riches of Christ — and share them with one another. The Church is a communion of love, and all members should have only one desire for one another — deep union with Christ. Thus, just as we pray for the living, so do we pray for the dead, and the dead pray for us. Our prayer is an expression both of our union with Christ and our longing for that union to be brought to perfection for everyone.

Our prayer is an expression both of our union with Christ and our longing for that union to be brought to perfection for everyone.

St. Thérése of Lisieux is often quoted as saying, "I want to spend my heaven doing good on earth." As he lay dying, St. Dominic said to his brothers, "Do not weep, for I shall be more useful to you after my death and I shall help you then more effectively than during my life." Death does not place any barrier among the members of the Church that cannot easily be bridged by prayer.

Thus we also remember souls undergoing God's cleansing mercy in purgatory. Christians have prayed for their dead from the earliest days, precisely because we long to be united with one another forever in Christ. Our longing is the result of our love! Prayer gives voice to our longing. We should not forget that the souls in purgatory pray for us, too.

The gifts I received from Mike and Marie did not cease when they died. I still benefit from them — not just in memory, not just by example, but in a very real way in Christ. Since what they shared with me during our monthly visits came from Christ, I have every reason to believe that we still "exchange" those gifts today.

May their souls, and all the souls of the faithful departed, rest in peace.

November 4, 2000

When it comes to faith, taste shouldn't matter

"De gustibus non disputandum est." There's no accounting for taste.

In my opinion, there is no better lunch than three Krystal or White Castle cheeseburgers, a bowl of Krystal chili, and a diet coke (Unfortunately, in my first three months in Arkansas, I have not found any Krystal or White Castle restaurants).

Many years ago one of my sisters liked to wear a certain perfume that I'm told was very expensive. She liked to wear a lot of it. But to me it smelled like insecticide. Please don't tell her I told you this.

There's no accounting for taste.

We all have our preferences in food, in entertainment, in cars, in clothes. For the most part, we can follow our tastes; doing so is just part of life. But sometimes we let our tastes take us too far, even into the realm of our relationship with God. These days, it is not unusual for folks to choose a church as a matter of taste: "I like his preaching." "I like their music." "They have Mothers' Day Out." "I like the freedom they give me to believe what I want." "I like this teaching of the Church, but I don't like that one." "They have activities for the whole family." "They don't have all those rules."

Americans, particularly Southern Americans, live in a very competitive church environment. Which church has the best preacher, the best-equipped school, the best worship, the best activities for children, the most Bible study groups? Folks make their decisions about which church to join, or where to attend Mass today, based on such questions. This is not just a Catholic phenomenon (several Protestant church leaders recently told me they notice it in their congregations as well), but it is certainly operative among some Catholics.

This "search for my taste" religious quest is dangerous to our Catholic faith, because its starting point is misplaced. Where we start makes all the difference when it comes to faith.

Here's the question that resides at the starting point: Who is faith all about — me or God?

Here's the question that resides at the starting point: Who is faith all about — me or God? In one sense the answer is "both." But unless we understand that God is the starting point of our faith (specifically, God's revelation of himself to us), our religious expectations will be misplaced, and we will never know the deep joy that faith has to offer.

Several years ago an article in a national newspaper addressed the consumerist attitude about church membership. It is characterized by the question, "What's in it for me?"

I can tell you from a pastor's perspective that the consumerist attitude is a temptation for us as well. The pressure is intense to invent programming of all kinds, to stock our schools and parish facilities with the latest gadgetry, to wonder why folks are going to church there and not here, to do more and more and more. I have fallen into that trap myself, until I spent a few moments alone with God in prayer.

We are not consumers. We are disciples. Consumers buy, use, throw away, and move on to the next product. Disciples respond to a call they sense from God and give their entire being to the "pearl of great price" they discover in him; after they have given all they have, they say, "We are useless servants.

We have done no more than our duty." (Luke 17:10)

Faith begins with what God has revealed to us about himself; it is the God-given grace to believe in him and to respond to him. By surrendering to faith, by allowing ourselves to be totally immersed in the way of Jesus Christ, we are led far beyond where our tastes could possibly take us. Tastes are very limiting, for they are all about "me." Faith is limitless, because through faith we allow God to embrace us into his very life. Tragically, we often expect much less of God than he wants to give us.

The world, our workplaces, and our families don't need us to be merely satisfied by our church membership, as I might be satisfied by the service I get from my plumber; they need us to be holy. Jesus taught that we become holy by giving ourselves (letting faith take us where we might never go), not by looking to see what we will get.

Is good preaching important? Absolutely.

Should we have the best possible children's activities and Bible study groups? No doubt about it.

Should we have beautiful music at Mass? Definitely.

Should our schools be the best we can make them? Without question.

Each of those components of church life can make faith grow, and part of the glory we owe God is to give him the best. But if we let our church attendance rest on our taste in how each of those components is carried out, we have put a bushel basket over our faith.

So let's do a check-up on our starting point:

After Mass, consumers ask, "Did I like that, or not?" "What did I get out of it?"

Disciples ask, after Mass, "What did I bring, and what did I offer?" "Did I surrender myself today to what God has revealed about himself, knowing that he will lead me where I need to be, far beyond where my tastes would ever carry me?"

Taste can take us only so far. Only surrender to God in faith can take us all the way to eternal life.

June 10, 2000

Showing more reverence for the Eucharist

A t the end of the closing Mass of our diocesan Encuentro Hispano this past Saturday, there was a Eucharistic procession through the large meeting tent and around its perimeter. Led by Juan Guido, incense bearer, I carried the monstrance containing the Blessed Sacrament as choir and congregation sang Spanish Eucharistic hymns. Since 2,000 people were present for the Mass, the procession lasted several minutes. Passing through the crowd, I was struck by the reverence and attention of young and old alike.

At one point along the way, I noticed that people began touching my vestments as I passed by. Their gesture momentarily caught me off guard, but then I began to think of the instances in the ministry of Jesus when people sought to touch him.

"She said to herself, 'If only I can touch his cloak, I shall be cured.'" (Matthew 9:21; Mark 5:28)

"He had cured many and, as a result, those who had diseases were pressing upon him to touch him." (Mark 3:10)

"Whatever villages or towns or countryside he entered, they laid the sick in the marketplaces and begged him that they might touch only the tassel on his cloak; and as many as touched it were healed." (Mark 6:56; Matthew 14:35-36)

"Everyone in the crowd sought to touch him because power came forth from him and healed them all." (Luke 6:19)

"People were bringing even infants to him that he might touch them, and when the disciples saw this, they rebuked them. Jesus, however, called the children to himself and said, 'Let the children come to me and do not prevent them; for the kingdom of God belongs to such as these. Amen, I say to you, whoever does not accept the kingdom of God like a child will not enter it.'" (Luke 18:15)

Processing through the crowd last Saturday, holding the monstrance high, I felt tangibly the reverence of those present for the Blessed Sacrament. Recalling these Scripture passages, I realized how desperately all of us long to touch the Lord Jesus, to be in his presence, to be nourished by his grace. Those who beat their breasts, or made the sign of the cross, or touched my vestments expressed their belief in the Real Presence and their acknowledgement that the Lord was with us. Their actions spoke louder than words.

In many ways, modern culture has lost its sense of reverence, and we would do well to consciously recover it in daily life. There are many reasons we have neglected to cultivate gestures of reverence in recent years, among them an unconscious disparagement of "old-time" practices and a tendency to focus more on ourselves than on the Lord when we go to church.

However, we do ourselves — and God — a great disservice when we neglect to show reverence. Signs of reverence (for example, respectful silence, bows, genuflections, signs of the Cross, appropriate dress, attention, arriving early and remaining for the entire Mass, receiving holy Communion worthily) increase our awareness of God's presence and help us to be more attentive to what he wishes to do for us. They transfer focus from us to him. Reverence is the very least we owe God, and we do owe it to him.

If we act the same in church as we do in a business meeting, in the classroom, in the family den or on the sports field, we have failed to recognize that God is there. Calling to mind those in the Gospel who traveled miles merely to see the Lord, who stretched their hands through the boisterous crowd hoping to touch just the tassel of his cloak, we should be embarrassed to think that, though present in church, we have paid him no mind. We should act differently in church, but we also need to act differently in church. We need to physically, tangibly, re-direct our focus from ourselves to God.

We need to physically, tangibly, re-direct our focus from ourselves to God.

When Jesus told his disciples they should not prevent the children from coming to touch him, he taught a great lesson. Luke places this passage strategically to contrast the behavior of children with that of some of the Pharisees and the wealthy. The childlike demonstrate naturally their total dependence on God.

Gestures of reverence bring us closer to the Lord. They are a means of paying attention to him, disposing ourselves to listen for his word, and showing our love for him. Our churches should be oases of quiet prayer, where the clamorous crowds — needy and sick and self-righteous and childlike and distracted and spiritually poor and too busy with too many things — come to show God reverence … and be renewed even by touching the tassel of his cloak.

October 2, 2004

Informal education
a lifelong pursuit

This time of year reminds me of my first day of school. Kindergarten was still optional in those days, so first grade was my first experience of formal education. With four older sisters, several of whom liked to "play school" at home (that meant they were the teachers, I was one of the students), I probably had the equivalent of kindergarten in our backyard. In fact, one of the moms in our neighborhood said she liked her kids to play at the Sartain's house "because it is so educational." Even with all the practice at home, I was still terror-stricken that first morning at St. Paul School and even escaped the classroom momentarily to follow my mom back to the car; but it wasn't long before I settled into a very familiar routine.

At some point during my grade school career (and after I had developed a distaste for "play school"), Mom decided that we kids needed to read during the summer, so we made regular trips to the public library. The expectation was that we would read one hour every day after lunch. That hour was sheer agony for me. I usually took the timer from the stove in the kitchen, put it next to me as I lay on the bed "reading," and listened as the timer slowly ticked away the hour. My sisters joke that I always read the same book: "Grant Marsh, Steamboat Captain."

Every September for 21 years straight, it was "back to school" again; and through the years school became such a part of me that it was rather strange after ordination not to be going "back to school" come September.

In a sense, "back to school" always implies growth and progress, no matter how old we are. We "advance" to the next grade, signifying that we have reached a certain level and are ready to move forward. There is always more to learn, always room to grow, always progress to be made. As much as I looked forward to the various "graduations" I celebrated with the passing of years, and as happy as I was to be out of school when seminary was finished, I still felt a certain void that first September without a "back to school."

It didn't take long before I realized how much I still needed to learn, how I had only skimmed the surface in school. The task of learning was left up to me, and now I had to be responsible for my own education, growth and progress. No doubt a big part of the void was that I missed my school friends. But I've come to understand that even more important was the fact that no matter how old we are, we need to learn. There is something about continually expanding our knowledge that keeps us alert and alive. Learning keeps us on our toes and assures that we have a perpetually fresh outlook on life.

There's another reason, an ultimate reason, for people of faith to keep learning — seeking the truth brings us closer to God.

There's another reason, an ultimate reason, for people of faith to keep learning — seeking the truth brings us closer to God.

Last week one of our seminarians who is a civil engineer told me that there is something "beautiful" about mathematics. Not being a mathematician, I have never experienced that beauty. But I understood perfectly well what he was saying. His education and personal interests have given him insight into the world of numbers such that he gets a glimpse of God's wisdom in the midst of it all. Philosophers, writers, physicists, astronomers, anthropologists and theologians could say the same thing.

But so could farmers, who know intimately the change of seasons and the scents of fertile soil, because they have to keep their senses alert and tuned to the subtleties of nature. And so could teachers, who hone their skills in the summer because they treasure the opportunity to see their students' eyes light up when they understand a new concept. And so could lots of folks with no formal education, who possess an earthy wisdom for the deepest truths of life because they work hard and care lovingly for their families and friends.

My point is simply that for people of faith, God's creation is ripe with his wisdom ready for harvest. No diploma or degree is necessary for this education, only a desire to see more clearly and grow in the knowledge and love of God.

No doubt, there are scientists and scholars who don't believe in God, who might even claim that their education led them to disavow their faith. But knowledge is incomplete without faith. An authentic quest for knowledge is at the same time a quest for God. The love of learning is actually a desire for God —unwittingly perhaps for those who don't believe in him, and wondrously rewarding for those who do.

So it's "back to school" once again. As we watch our kids and grandkids start up that familiar fall routine, let's not excuse ourselves from school this time around. Pick up a good book. Read a poem. Write a poem. Study a language. Open the Bible. Watch the seasons change. Ask the kids what they're studying. Ask an elderly person about his or her experience of the old days. Most important of all, while doing these things or others more to your taste, consciously offer your effort to God in prayer. Ask him to help you get underneath it all and uncover his wisdom and beauty.

He who created all things and knows all things and teaches all things will draw you close to him, and so make you hunger for more.

August 19, 2000

Summers shouldn't be spent by computer

When I think of summers growing up at our house, I think of opera and baseball, chili and floor wax, and fun with friends and neighbors.

My father loved both opera and baseball. We were often awakened on Saturday mornings by his favorite operas — almost always Italian, sometimes French, never German. Later in the day, the living room radio featured the Texaco Metropolitan Opera broadcast from New York. There was competition on television, however, in the form of baseball; which entertainment won out each week depended on the selection of sopranos and teams.

In the early 1900s, my grandfather had been known for "Sartain's Chili," a special concoction served at the soda fountain of his drug store in South Pittsburg, Tenn. The story goes that he had been given the recipe by a man from Mexico who once worked for him, and my father later reconstructed the recipe to the best of his recollection. Pots full of chili were brewed at our house on Saturday mornings, then frozen in plastic containers for later consumption. You couldn't help but notice it was chili day when you walked through the door.

Although I don't know the recipe myself, I can tell you that it called for a special kind of red bean (specially ordered from either Iowa or Idaho, according to my mother), powdered cumin, and bottles of Mexene red chili powder (also specially ordered). Most clearly in my mind, however, is that the recipe began with cutting up slabs of white suet to be rendered on the stove; the resulting liquid grease was an essential ingredient of the chili. We would eat some of the "cracklins" left in the skillet, and occasionally mom would bake them in cornbread. Today nutritionists would probably ask, "What were you thinking?"

There were hardwood floors in our house, and we five kids, the dog and our skates did them no favors. Saturday afternoon was the time to clean the floors, and the heavy, oily smell of Johnson's wax would linger for hours.

Summers were hot, but we had air conditioning. I was in and out of the house all day long, playing with the Broyles, Beards, Pates, Callicotts and Sterns. If we held the outside door open too long, my father would yell, "You're letting out the BTUs!" — a reference to the air conditioning.

Bicycles gave us a certain freedom, but it was confined to our neighborhood — a school park around the corner, the shopping center a mile away, the woods that dotted our area before new houses were built and church, where I took my turn serving early Mass, weddings and funerals. I wore out several bikes growing up, exploring new places and visiting school friends out for the summer.

After supper there was softball or badminton with the neighbors in our backyard until dark, or maybe a game of horseshoes across the street, improvised with broad, heavy washers and open cans buried in the neighbors' front yard. Across the street we also had a special kind of baseball, just for the guys, which called for a regular bat and red rubber ball; rules were as usual, except that to tag someone "out" you simply threw the ball at him as he ran to the next base.

Southerners know about chiggers, and summer nights our legs itched like crazy until they were soothed with cool rubbing alcohol or a hot bath before bed. I slept well every night.

I'll admit that sometimes I got bored during the summer, watched too much TV and whined to my parents for something to do. I didn't always like their suggestions, such as cutting the grass or reading a book. But there were always things to do, good things, and rules which for the most part kept me out of trouble.

With the end of the school year, kids all over Arkansas will be free for a few months. The older ones might have jobs, but all of them will have free time. It's fascinating to me that some of the most popular forms of entertainment these days, especially those involving computers, are solo entertainments that do not engage a young person in honest-to-goodness human interaction. Even if computer entertainments develop skills and can be educational, there are hazards in such solitary play. Growing up should be "growing up with" friends and family, interacting in ways that strengthen character and teach the fundamentals of relationships.

Growing up should be "growing up with" friends and family, interacting in ways that strengthen character and teach the fundamentals of relationships.

I've been thinking about my childhood summers these past few weeks, and about the kids of Arkansas. Lord God, keep them safe, give them joy and laughter, and help them grow up in the company of loved ones and pets and friends. In fact, Lord, teach them how to be friends! May their young days be filled with sights, sounds and scents that stimulate their imaginations, strengthen their bodies, and touch their souls. May they be under the watchful eyes of grownups who playfully interact with them and nudge them down the right path.

It was fun growing up in our neighborhood, because we did it together.

June 9, 2001

A PEOPLE
ON PILGRIMAGE

Ultreya! Onward!
Follow the path of the Lord

I'm the kind of person who likes to be inspired. I can be inspired by an engaging biography, spiritual reading, a touching movie, a stirring sermon or simply by being in the presence of an inspirational person. Such inspirations serve as a kind of encouragement for me along the journey.

Since the Middle Ages, the most famous pilgrimage site in Spain has been Santiago de Compostela, in honor of St. James the Apostle. At one time this shrine rivaled Rome and Jerusalem in popular significance. The Spanish call the Milky Way "El Camino de Santiago," because it resembles the endless columns of candle-carrying pilgrims streaming to Compostela. Even today Catholics from across Europe make the journey by car, bicycle and on foot. In the old days, as pilgrims passed through villages on their way to Compostela, locals would shout, "Ultreya!" — "Onward!" — as a cheer of inspiration and encouragement. They knew that the graces awaiting at the destination were worth the hardship of the journey.

There has always been the added sense for Christians, however, that such journeys themselves bestow blessings. By God's grace we already hold within us the rewards of our destination, which is not so much a place as it is a state of eternal union with God. We are always beginning the pilgrimage, always on pilgrimage, and always arriving at deeper union with God. That's why I'm inspired by people, readings, movies and sermons that remind me of what God wants to give me right now, as a foretaste of what's in store in eternity.

On March 6 I will celebrate my first anniversary as bishop of Little Rock. It would be an understatement to say that it has been a year of grace and challenge. I am filled with gratitude for your kindness and openness, and for the evident signs of God's presence in our midst. Traveling around the state, I have begun my acquaintance with many of you, but I soon came to the realization that my goal to visit every parish and mission in the first year was unrealistic. I look forward to finishing the inaugural pilgrimage this year.

I considered approaching this first-anniversary column with a variety of formats, but in the end I decided to write some simple words of encouragement. I would like this column to be a kind of "Ultreya!" for you.

Stay the course set by faith. The path of life is not identical for everyone and has surprising twists and turns.

Stay the course set by faith. The path of life is not identical for everyone and has surprising twists and turns. Its hazards are sometimes unpredictable, and its trials can be baffling. But along everyone's path, no matter where it leads or how it winds, faith sets a clear course. Trust in God to give light and guidance. We cannot see beyond the bend just ahead of us, but God can. In prayer and reflection on God's Word, we listen to him show us the way and calm our frayed nerves. Even in the most frightening and incomprehensible circumstances life sets before you, stay the course set by faith.

Follow the Lord Jesus Christ as the only Way, Truth and Life. The New Testament is absolutely clear about this core of our Christian faith: Jesus Christ is the one mediator between God and humanity, the only savior of the world, the only way to the Father. Strive to know him by pouring out your heart to him in prayer, by following his ways and imitating his example of sacrificial love. This is the way of love for which you and I were made by God, and God has revealed it to us completely in Jesus. Cling to him. As his mother said, "Do whatever he tells you."

Stay close to the sacraments of the Church. We Catholics are doubly blessed because we are a people of both word and sacrament. In the seven sacraments the Lord Jesus himself comes to us and continues his saving ministry in the Church. To stay away from the sacraments is to deprive ourselves of the food we need most. To stay away from the sacraments is to miss precious face-to-face encounters with Christ.

Have hope. Hope is not the same as wishing, nor is it the same as praying that the odds will be in favor of what we "hope" will happen. Instead, hope is confidence in the truth God has revealed to us about himself and his promises. The truths that are the foundation of hope are not mere theories, good ideas or goals awaiting us at some point in our future. They are added lights along the path of life and sound criteria to be used in making concrete decisions. They are truths about which God has given repeated, unmistakable evidence throughout history: You were made for God. God loves you. God forgives you. God is extending a hand in friendship to you. God has a plan for you. God is patient with you. God will never abandon you. God wants you to be with him forever. In God's eyes, revealed to us in Jesus, it is always too soon to give up, it is never too late to start again. Hope in God.

I would like to thank everyone, especially my brother priests, for your kindness and prayers during my first year as your bishop. You are an extraordinary blessing at this stage of my pilgrimage to God. May we accompany one another to even greater union with him.

Ultreya!

March 3, 2001

Celebrate freedom,
celebrate our ancestors

Last summer I was treated with a visit by a family from Pistoia in north-central Italy. The Benesperis have been to the States so many times that their son, Massimo, has learned to navigate the American interstate system with the ease of a native. At home in Pistoia, Massimo and his father, Rolando, have a business repairing motorized scooters. His mother, Grazia, teaches religion in their parish. Every year they vacation with their aunt, Fedora, who was once my parishioner.

Fedora came to America about 50 years ago to marry a widowed Italian businessman with a young daughter. She outlived him by many years and eventually married another local Italian, Nick. She tells her life story as one would a fairy tale, and looking in her eyes one gets the sense that she has savored every moment, though the tale is not one of luxury and ease. As the years went by after Nick's death, Fedora kept more and more to herself; she went to work every day as a seamstress, did her shopping and went to church. Because she still speaks only broken English, there aren't many neighbors or friends in whom she can confide.

Rolando, Grazia and Massimo come to check on Fedora, help tend her garden, repair the garage door, tune the car — and make sure she gets out of the house, at least to go to church.

I once celebrated the funeral of another elderly parishioner, whom I had met only casually after Sunday Mass. Her accent gave her away as French. When she died unexpectedly, I asked her few surviving relatives about her background and learned the story of a courageous young woman trapped in the insanity of Nazism.

Tia was once detained for interrogation by the Nazis and separated from her terror-stricken little boy; her husband was killed. Once released, she searched frantically and against all odds to find her son. She reasoned that he had been herded on a refugee train with hundreds of displaced families and plotted out the routes they might have taken him. Running through train stations, scanning the long processions of crowded, open-windowed cars, she repeatedly called out his nickname. After searching relentlessly for weeks, one day she heard a small, familiar voice respond to her calls. He was fine, and they were together again.

Have you ever heard the stories of the Italian immigrants of Sunny Side Plantation in southeast Arkansas, or Tontitown in the northwest? Or the Germans of Logan County, Altus, the St. Joseph Colony, Little Rock, and the Swiss-Germans and Austrians of northeast Arkansas? Or the Africans brought forcibly to Arkansas as slaves? Or the Irish of Rocky Comfort and Fort Smith? Or the Slovaks of Prairie County? Or the Poles of Marche? Or the Laotians and Vietnamese of Little Rock and Fort Smith? Or the Mexicans of De Queen and Danville?

They are stories of determination, heartbreak and heroism, and they share a common theme, the thirst for freedom —religious freedom, economic freedom, political freedom, personal freedom, freedom from persecution and freedom to raise their families in peace. Once in Arkansas, the newcomers built railroads, farmed the land, and worked their trades, creating the infrastructure we take for granted today.

Just as significant for us, however, is that they also built the Church. In many ways, the history of immigration into Arkansas is the history of Catholicism in Arkansas. Many of our churches, schools and hospitals are the products of their hard-earned money, their ingenuity and their physical labor; for as they established themselves in this new homeland, they put their faith into practice and made sure it would be passed on to the next generation. It is not an exaggeration to say we stand on their shoulders.

Now this heritage is renewing itself, and we Catholics are uniquely poised to set the tone in Arkansas for welcoming newcomers, no matter their language or country of origin. In fact, to look upon immigrants and refugees as "foreign" to us is to be ungrateful and forgetful of our past. Seeing them, we see ourselves. As the Book of Leviticus reminded the Israelites, "You shall treat the stranger who resides with you no differently than the natives born among you; have the same love for him as for yourself, for you too were once strangers in the land of Egypt." (19:33-34)

Now this heritage is renewing itself, and we Catholics are uniquely poised to set the tone in Arkansas for welcoming newcomers, no matter their language or country of origin.

An interesting passage from the Fourth Lateran Council (1215 A.D.) reveals how the Church has always expressed pastoral concern for immigrants and refugees: "We find in most countries, cities and dioceses people of diverse languages who, though bound by one faith, have varied rites and customs. Therefore we strictly enjoin that the bishops ... provide the proper men, who will celebrate the liturgical functions according to their rites and languages." That obligation is no less important today.

This Independence Day, let's remember not only the sacrifices made by our forebears to secure and preserve our nation's freedom; let's also remember with pride the immigrant inheritance of our diocese. When you see the young Mexican mother on the street, beautiful children in tow, think of your great-grandmother tightly holding the little hand of your grandfather in a strange, new, Arkansas town. When you see the elderly Vietnamese man, who once traveled here by crowded boat from half a world away, remember the cost of freedom, so easy to forget.

Faith gives us the eyes and heart to understand that these newcomers reveal more features of the face of the Church, the face of Christ. Welcoming them, we welcome him.

July 7, 2001

Pilgrims must share graces from their pilgrimage

Much of what we know about the liturgy of the late fourth century comes from Egeria, a Spanish nun who chronicled her journey through Asia Minor, Palestine and Egypt in "Diary of a Pilgrimage." Egeria's writings are important not only because of the factual information they provide, but also because they are the fruit of a spiritual pilgrimage. Encountering the faith and prayer of fellow Christians in a part of the world previously unfamiliar to her, she grew in faith and enriched the Church with her diary.

Like our Jewish ancestors, Christians have taken to the world's highways from the very beginning, hoping to deepen their faith. Jerusalem, Bethlehem, Nazareth, Capernaum, Antioch, Rome and other towns attracted believers who wanted to walk in the footsteps of Jesus and the apostles. With the passing of centuries and the expansion of Christianity, the number of holy places grew because God's grace was in evidence everywhere. Today, thousands of Christian shrines around the world attract millions of pilgrims seeking God.

It is not the pilgrims' physical presence at these sites that makes the difference — one need not leave home to find God, and a casual tourist can visit holy places without any effect. It is faith that impels pilgrims, and the desire of their hearts that transforms a journey into a pilgrimage. A pilgrimage away from home is also a pilgrimage within, because it is a symbol of our yearning to draw closer to God. The saints are often our guides.

Such was the case March 8-15, when 47 pilgrims from Arkansas (including a few from Texas, Tennessee and Kentucky) traveled to Mexico to visit some of the holy places of America. Each of us carried the names of those for whom we had promised to pray and our own desire for certain graces. Along the way, we met Our Lady of Guadalupe, Our Lady of the Remedies, St. Juan Diego, Blessed Sebastian of Aparicio, St. Philip of Jesus, and other saints beloved to the Mexican people.

Mexico is a country rich in history. The earliest inhabitants may have arrived there as early as 20,000 years before Columbus reached America, and their descendants created a succession of highly developed cultures — the Mayan, Aztec, Zapotec and Toltec among them. As we visited the ruins of those ancient civilizations (the Pyramids of the Sun and Moon at Teotihuacán, for example) I was struck by the spiritual search that inspired such extraordinary architectural and engineering accomplishments. These ancient peoples were stretching their arms toward God, though they did not know him.

Every human person naturally and spontaneously seeks God. As St. Augustine wrote, "You have made us for yourself, O God, and our hearts are restless until they rest in you." When St. Paul visited Athens in the mid-first century, he noticed many idols in the city and knew that the Athenians were unwittingly searching for the true God. He went to the Areopagus and spoke.

"You Athenians, I see that in every respect you are very religious. For as I walked around looking carefully at your shrines, I even discovered an altar inscribed, 'To an Unknown God.' What therefore you unknowingly worship, I proclaim to you. The God who made the world and all that is in it, the Lord of heaven and earth, does not dwell in sanctuaries made by human hands, nor is he served by human hands because he needs anything.

"Rather it is he who gives to everyone life and breath and

everything. He made from one the whole human race to dwell on the entire surface of the earth, and he fixed the ordered seasons and the boundaries of their regions, so that people might seek God, even perhaps grope for him and find him, though indeed he is not far from any one of us. For 'In him we live and move and have our being,' as even some of your poets have said, 'For we too are his offspring.'" (see Acts 17)

Ever the master evangelizer, Paul brought many to the one true God. Spanish missionaries first introduced the Christian faith to the Mexican people in the early 16th century, facing many obstacles as they did so. Things changed dramatically when Our Lady appeared to Juan Diego in 1531, because it was God's plan that her apparitions would open the hearts of the Mexican peoples to him. Through her they were led to the God they had been seeking for millennia. The first disciple of Jesus, the mother of all, she is the best of evangelizers.

The first disciple of Jesus, the mother of all, she is the best of evangelizers.

Our Lady of Guadalupe, named patroness of America by Pope John Paul II, remains the most powerful spiritual influence for the Mexican people. They call themselves "Guadalupanos" because it was she who led them to her son. We were privileged to spend most of a day at the Basilica of Our Lady of Guadalupe in Mexico City.

Pilgrims bear responsibility to bring home what they receive at the holy places. I noticed throughout the week that several in our group took notes of what they heard and saw. I have no doubt that, like Egeria many centuries ago, our Arkansas pilgrims will share with family and friends how God touched them in Mexico. In the next several columns, I plan to share with you how God's grace was extended to us, quietly and powerfully.

March 20, 2004

Different ages, personalities, but one faith

This is the second in a series on the diocese's pilgrimage to Mexico March 8-15, 2004.

At 84, Margaret Driscoll is no novice at life, but family members questioned whether she should be making a pilgrimage to Mexico. All kinds of things could happen. With typical determination, Margaret apparently responded to all objections by announcing, "I am going to Mexico."

When I boarded the tour bus in Mexico City, I introduced myself, and she did the same, telling me in a pronounced New England drawl that her name is "Mah-gret." For the rest of the trip she was Mah-gret to me. She never missed a beat and contributed plain-spoken faith, candor and humor to the pilgrimage.

Our last night in Mexico City, many of us attended a performance of the famous Folkloric Ballet, a selection of Mexican dances. Margaret announced she was wearing a dress from Pakistan. What was she doing in Pakistan? Volunteering in the Peace Corps in the late 1990s, of course. "I taught English as a second language," she explained. "Adjectives are my specialty."

We sat together at the ballet on the far side of the theater. Several people offered to change seats so I could be closer to the center, but I declined. Margaret leaned toward me and suggested wryly, "I have often said that ballet is best seen from the side."

Deacon Chuck and Anita Marino make quite a pair. Educators by profession, they have taught and traveled around the world. Work eventually brought them to Chuck's home town of Camden, Ark., and from there they moved to Fayetteville, where Chuck was principal of St. Joseph School. He and Anita now minister at St. Raphael Parish, where they bring joy, laughter and consolation.

Chuck was a cheerleader at the University of Arkansas, and it shows. He stirs up enthusiasm and life wherever he goes, at times much to the embarrassment of Anita. Their good humor is more than that, however; it is their way of drawing people together to form community. In a group of almost 50, Chuck and Anita were a glue that united us.

No one will forget Chuck's rendition of the "Dance of the Deer Hunt" from the ballet, particularly his imitation of the dying deer's quivering hind legs. He responds willingly to requests, so don't be afraid to ask for a performance.

Maria Martinez and her husband Eduardo are the parents of seven and own a restaurant in Little Rock. Maria is a native of Santa Maria Del Rio, San Luis Potosí; Eduardo is from Nuevo Valle, Guanajuato. While on the bus our last day in Mexico, I asked Sister Mickey Espinoza, several priests and Maria to comment on the week. Taking the microphone, Maria explained that the pilgrimage had been an important time for her to deepen her Catholic faith, her love for the Virgin of Guadalupe, and her appreciation of Mexican culture. She recognizes how important it is to pass on her culture to her children, now that they make the United States their home.

Ezequiel Oseguera and his wife Rosa are the parents of four and own a restaurant in Hot Springs. Ezequiel was born in Blythe, Calif., but his family is from Santa Inez, Michoacán; Rosa is from Uruapan. Ezequiel travels frequently to Mexico for business and family visits. He was a gentle, faith-filled presence in our group, as he quietly tended to the needs of other pilgrims. He spoke of his powerful experience at Cursillo a few years ago, and how it prepared him for the tragic death of his father, which came just a few weeks later.

Forty-seven personalities, 47 lives of faith united for a week in a desire to draw closer to the Lord. Perhaps one of the most important things we learned was that we were not the only pilgrims in Mexico March 8-15.

Sunday morning, we celebrated Mass at Nuestra Señora de los Remedios, a hill-top shrine just outside Mexico City. Many local folks joined us, mixing easily in the pews with our group and participating in the bilingual liturgy. Several women and men, quite elderly and feeble, were carrying flowers. A woman on our pilgrimage told me that when she turned to offer the sign of peace to one of the elderly men, she was moved to tears, so evident was his faith.

In a deeply biblical tradition, they bring all they have to God — their beautiful flowers, their colorful dress, their cultural dance, their poverty, their prayers, their faith.

For the Mexican people, pilgrimage is part and parcel of the daily spirituality of Catholicism. In a deeply biblical tradition, they bring all they have to God — their beautiful flowers, their colorful dress, their cultural dance, their poverty, their prayers, their faith. They confidently ask Our Lady to intercede for their needs. And they return to give thanks, because the awareness of their dependence on God is both simple and profound.

In ancient times, many Jewish people made an annual pilgrimage to Jerusalem. "Pilgrim Songs" (psalms) were composed to accompany these journeys. The author of the Letter to the Hebrews suggests that the Christian life is a pilgrimage to the Heavenly Jerusalem. We should not lose heart when the going gets tough, because even now we are surrounded by an encouraging "cloud of witnesses" (see Hebrews 12).

How lovely is your dwelling place,

O Lord of hosts!
My soul yearns and pines for the courts of the Lord …
Happy they who dwell in your house!
Continually they praise you.
Happy those whose strength you are!
Their hearts are set upon the pilgrimage. (Psalm 84)

March 27, 2004

Being a 'foreigner' is a state of mind

This is the last column in a series on the diocese's pilgrimage to Mexico March 8-15, 2004.

Pilgrims find themselves in a unique situation. On the one hand, they are drawn to holy shrines which "belong" to them as part of their religious heritage. On the other hand, the citizens of the country where the shrines are located likely speak a language other than theirs. They might think to themselves, "These people speak a foreign language," when in fact it is the pilgrims who speak the language foreign to the country they are visiting.

We joke about attempts to express ourselves in another language: we speak in a loud voice; we add "o" to the end of every word; we speak our native tongue but with the accent of the country we are visiting. None of these attempts is successful, of course, but they are expressions of our frustrating inability to speak for ourselves. We are grateful when someone comes along who can give voice to what we are trying desperately to say.

We had many funny stories to tell when our Arkansas group visited Mexico a few weeks ago. Asking directions, bargaining for reduced prices, ordering lunch, reading church signs, and understanding answers to questions were a challenge to us. In a sense, many of our pilgrims discovered what it is like to feel "voiceless" and "foreign." That can be a very helpful experience.

Popular wisdom holds — correctly or incorrectly — that citizens of certain countries are decidedly unhelpful when it comes to accommodating foreign visitors who do not speak their language. Nothing could be further from the truth for the Mexican people. They went beyond the call of duty to communicate with us and make us feel at home. We may have felt voiceless and foreign at times, but there were plenty of folks around to help us get our bearings.

Experiencing travel in another country gives us reason to ask whether we are equally accommodating to visitors and immigrants, the voiceless among us, here at home. Do we go out of our way to help them, to make them feel welcome, to put words to their needs?

There is a subtle form of prejudice to which we can fall prey without realizing it. When we are unable to communicate with someone because of a language barrier, we can unwittingly treat him or her as invisible. We may unwittingly begin to consider those who speak a language other than ours as somehow "foreign" in a personal way — as if in the deepest sense they are unlike us, separated from us, and unrelated to us, or as if they are not even there. As Christians, we can never say that about any other human person.

When we are unable to communicate with someone because of a language barrier, we can unwittingly treat him or her as invisible.

During our pilgrimage in Mexico, many of us began to realize that this was to be not only a journey to holy places, but also an encounter with holy people. The Mexican people, deeply Christian and devotional by nature, awakened in us a longing to restore a simpler, more direct approach to the spiritual life — for God is as close as a sacrament celebrated, a prayer whispered, a blessing imparted, a beloved child. Our encounters with Mexican men, women and children were dramatic reminders that they are our sisters and brothers in the Catholic faith. We gained insight into what it means to be the Church.

In every country around the world, Catholics take seriously

their responsibility to be a voice for the voiceless. The Holy Father constantly speaks on behalf of the poor, victims of war, the sick, refugees, immigrants, and the abandoned — he gives voice to the needs of those who cannot speak for themselves (or to whom no one will listen). He gives the example so that we will recognize that the reason we do this is not out of "charity," as if lending our voice to the poor is an act of benevolence. He gives the example because he knows who his brothers and sisters are. No one is invisible to Christ, nor should they be to us.

Being part of the Church teaches us what God has always intended for the world: one people, splendid in their diversity, on a common pilgrimage to eternal life. God intends the Church to be the vehicle through which the world is restored to its original destiny, renewed for us in Christ.

Msgr. Scott Friend reminded us during the pilgrimage that God is sending such a large number of immigrants to Arkansas because he trusts us. He is sending his beloved children — our sisters and brothers — because he knows we will welcome them as family, help them build a good life, and share in the gifts they bring. After all, we share an eternal destiny with all people.

Not long ago a young Mexican man in Arkansas planning to be a priest wrote that he has noticed a significant change in himself. As he put it, "I have begun to see myself as a disciple of Jesus and not just as a person from another country."

May we in the Diocese of Little Rock create such an environment, and give such a welcome, that everyone feels at home here, no matter which language they speak. There should be a marquis inscribed on our hearts and in our parishes: "No foreigners here. Just sisters and brothers in the Lord."

April 3, 2004

If our world is small, we make God small

I keep a certain photograph on a bookshelf in my home as a reminder that God's creation and his loving concern extend far beyond what I see on any given day.

It's a simple photograph of eight dark-skinned kids, one of them holding a soccer ball. I took the picture in 1990, when I visited Yemen to give retreats to the Missionaries of Charity.

Each day as I walked from the apartment where I was staying to the sisters' convent, I passed a group of children playing soccer on a dusty, gravelly vacant lot. Little girls and boys, some in native dress, played together and took little notice of me. After several weeks of watching them, I decided to take their picture on my last day. Much to my surprise, as soon as they spotted my camera all the boys gathered in a group and, with big smiles, posed enthusiastically. One put his hand up and waved. I snapped the picture.

My first morning in Yemen, I had prepared to celebrate Mass for the sisters by taking a look at the day's Scripture readings. In the Gospel passage from Luke, Jesus decried the fact that the crowds failed to understand the significance of the word he was preaching. It was so clear, he said, that anyone — even non-believers — would repent at hearing what he had to say. In frustration he said to the crowds:

"The queen of the south will rise at the judgment along with the men of this generation, and she will condemn them. She came from the farthest corner of the world to listen to the wisdom of Solomon, but you have a greater than Solomon here." (Luke 11:31)

The queen of the south to whom Jesus referred was the Queen of Sheba, who had once traveled many miles just to speak to Solomon, whose profound wisdom was legendary.

A footnote in my Bible indicated that Sheba was modern-day Yemen. I was in Sheba, whose queen had once traveled to a far-away land to praise the God of Israel for a king named Solomon and shower him with rare, priceless gifts!

Because of strict laws, I was not allowed to wear my Roman collar there, and I had to restrict the number of books and religious materials I brought with me.

We all face the temptation to be so caught up in our personal concerns that we neglect the rest of "the world."

But in a small way, for just a few weeks, I was called to bring the wisdom greater than Solomon to the land of the queen who had sought him out several millennia ago.

The world would be very small if we were left to our own resources to define its boundaries. And if our world is small, we make God small. And if we make God small, we miss the overwhelming universality of the word of God and the gift of salvation in Christ Jesus. My world could very easily shrink into preoccupation with the 75 counties of Arkansas. We all face the temptation to be so caught up in our personal concerns that we neglect the rest of "the world." The Gospel does no such thing, and our Christian faith does no such thing. If we keep our eyes on Christ, he expands our understanding of the universality of his love.

St. Gregory of Nyssa once said, "As no darkness can be seen by anyone surrounded by light, so no trivialities can capture the attention of anyone who has his eyes on Christ. The man who keeps his eyes upon the head and origin of the whole universe has them on virtue in all its perfection; he has them on truth, on justice, on immortality and on everything else that is good, for Christ is goodness itself."

I would add that such a person also has his or her eyes on the whole world and prays that peace will reign for all God's children. Listening to the word of God expands our world, for we begin to see just how great is God's love, just how wide is his mercy. We begin to see that our love and prayers should extend far beyond the space we inhabit every day.

When I watch the news and learn of conflicts in Israel, Afghanistan, Iraq and Yemen, I remember that the people of those lands are my sisters and brothers, deserving of my prayers and love. They may seem to be a world away, but they inhabit the same world as I, the world my Savior came to save.

So now in my home I have a photograph of a pickup soccer game in a dusty Yemeni neighborhood. I look at it from time to time, especially when my world has become too small, and recall that for three weeks in 1990 I was called to proclaim the wisdom of Christ in a country where no Christian churches are permitted, where I was not allowed to identify myself as a priest, where Catholic sisters serve the poorest of the poor only by special invitation and permission of the government.

In Yemen I gained a deeper love, respect, and awe for the saving Word who makes me who I am. May all creation know the peace of Christ, and may we be its ambassadors, wherever life takes us.

June 1, 2002

'Shepherd-brothers' guiding one Church

As I write this column, I have just returned from the Jubilee of Bishops in Rome. About 1,500 bishops attended the three-day event, the largest such gathering since the Second Vatican Council. As a new bishop, I found the experience extraordinary in a number of ways.

First, there were the celebrations themselves. On Friday afternoon, October 6, we assembled at the Basilica of St. John Lateran for a penitential liturgy. Archbishop Giovanni Battista Re, prefect of the Congregation of Bishops, presided and preached. His words were both comforting and challenging, reassuring and thought-provoking. He reminded us to be shepherds of the Word of God, of prayer, and of love.

He said, "We must take care never to be reduced to 'managers' of our pastoral concerns. The 'good shepherd' and the 'manager' are two quite different things! ...To be a father means to know how to encounter people, giving attention to everyone ... Everyone we meet should feel accepted, esteemed and loved."

On Saturday morning there was a "missionary celebration" in the Basilica of St. Paul Outside the Walls; at noon an audience with Pope John Paul II; and at 5 p.m. the recitation of the rosary in St. Peter's Square before the Statue of Our Lady of Fatima.

Each decade of the Glorious Mysteries was introduced by a cardinal and a bishop, and the prayers were led by families from Oceania, Asia, America, Africa and Europe. The final decade was led in Portuguese by Sister Lucia, the sole surviving witness of the apparitions at Fatima.

It was heartwarming to watch the young families, small children in tow, step up to the microphone before tens of thousands of onlookers. Not only was the rosary a beautiful devotion to the Blessed Mother; it was also a poignant reminder of the universality of the Christian message. The whole world was joined in prayer.

Sunday morning the bishops concelebrated Mass with the Holy Father in St. Peter's Square before a crowd of several hundred thousand. At the end of Mass, we joined him in entrusting the Third Millennium to Mary. The touching prayer was a request that all inhabitants of the earth, whatever their situation, experience God's providential care and protection. There was a tangible feeling of unity in that vast crowd as we visited in the square after Mass.

My eyes were opened by several encounters with brother bishops.

A highpoint of the jubilee for me was the opportunity to meet brother bishops from around the world. In his homily Friday afternoon, Archbishop Re reminded us that we are to be not only "shepherd-fathers" to our dioceses, but also "shepherd-brothers" to one another. My eyes were opened by several encounters with brother bishops.

At the penitential liturgy I sat next to a bishop from Sudan, and I told him I had recently met a Sudanese family in Helena. He said, "Since the war, my people are scattered everywhere." I thought to myself, I will take care of my brother's people now scattered in Arkansas.

After Sunday Mass I met Archbishop Josip Bozanić from Croatia. I think we spied each other because we were among the youngest there! We decided to get together for lunch before returning home, and it was then I discovered that he is archbishop of Zagreb, ministering in another war-torn part of the world. I asked him about the most daunting part of his ministry, and he responded that it is helping his people understand the meaning of freedom. Croatia declared its independence from the Socialist Federal Republic of Yugoslavia in 1991, and the transition from communism to democracy has posed many difficult challenges.

One of Archbishop Bozanić's predecessors in Zagreb was Cardinal Alojzije Stepìnac, recently beatified by Pope John Paul, and remembered for his courageous stands against the Nazi's and Communists who once occupied his country. During World War II, Blessed Stepìnac spoke out for the political rights of all people — not only his fellow Croatians, but also Jews, Serbs, Slovenes and Gypsies; he was instrumental in saving the lives of several hundred Jews. In 1946 Stepìnac was found guilty of Nazi collaboration at a mock trial and sentenced to 16 years hard labor; he died in prison in 1960.

Upon my return home I read the U.S. State Department's 1999 Annual Report on International Religious Freedom in Croatia and learned that since his installation as archbishop of Zagreb, Bozanić has promoted reconciliation and the return of refugees, spoken out forcefully against corruption, and promoted the need for dialogue and respect among ethnic groups. In May of last year he made a particularly strong public challenge to the government in a homily at a Statehood Day Mass attended by President Franjo Trudjman.

It was during lunch that I realized the deeper meaning of the Jubilee of Bishops to which the pope had invited us. As Archbishop Bozanić and I enjoyed some pasta at a small restaurant on the Borgo Pio, I couldn't help but marvel at his awesome responsibilities and his courageous leadership in a fragile corner of the globe. But he was just as interested in Arkansas as I was in Croatia! We invited each other to visit our respective dioceses, and I look forward to welcoming him one day to Arkansas.

That afternoon, two "shepherd-brothers" from widely divergent backgrounds made the needs of one another's Churches our own. I think that's what the Holy Father intended.

October 21, 2000

(Update: Archbishop Bozanić was named a cardinal by Pope John Paul II on October 21, 2003 — three years to the day after this column appeared in *Arkansas Catholic*.)

Like Peter, we all have to suffer for Christ

The Appian Way, the oldest and most famous Roman road, was opened in 312 B.C. by the consul Appius Claudius, from whom it takes its name. Known as "Regina Viarum" ("Queen of Roads"), it was once lined with luxurious villas, temples and burial monuments. Just outside the Gate of St. Sebastian on the Appian Way stands a small church known as "Domine Quo Vadis."

According to an ancient legend, the Christians of Rome urged St. Peter to flee during Nero's persecution. A fourth century account by Pseudus Linus describes the scene:

"Thus Peter, on hearing these pleas and being of a sensitive nature — he was never able to witness the tears of the suffering without weeping himself — was won over by these laments ... The following night, following the liturgical prayer, he said goodbye to his friends, entrusting them to God with his blessing, and he left alone.

"He was about to walk through the city gates when he saw Christ coming toward him. He paid reverence to him and said, 'Lord, where are you going?' ('Domine, quo vadis?'). Christ replied, 'I am going to Rome to be crucified again.' Peter said to him, 'You will be crucified again, Lord?' And the Lord said to him, 'Yes, I will be crucified again.'

"Peter replied, 'Lord, I am going back to follow you.' Then the Lord rose up toward the heavens. Peter watched him go and wept with joy. When he came to himself, he understood that the words referred to his own martyrdom, namely, how the Lord would suffer in him, as he suffers in all those who are chosen. Peter returned to the city joyously, glorifying God."

In the Gospel of John, Jesus refers to Peter's death: "'I say to you, when you were younger, you used to dress yourself and go where you wanted; but when you grow old, you will stretch out your hands, and someone else will dress you and lead you where you do not want to go.' He said this signifying by what kind of death he would glorify God. And when he had said this, he said to him, 'Follow me.'" (John 21:18-19)

Peter was crucified June 29, 67 A.D., on the Vatican Hill (upside down, according to tradition, because he did not consider himself worthy to be crucified like the Lord). Pseudus Linus writes that he offered these words of consolation to those who witnessed his martyrdom:

"Great and profound is the mystery of the cross! God draws all things to himself through the cross. The cross is the sign of life, for which the empire of death was destroyed. You showed this to me, O Lord. Open the eyes of all these too so that they may contemplate the consolation of eternal life."

The story of Quo Vadis illustrates that Peter's martyrdom was a decisive moment for the early Church. At a time of fierce persecution, Christians began to understand both the importance and the risks of their own witness to Christ, and they were encouraged to persevere as had Peter and the Lord himself. When Pope John Paul II visited the church in 1982, he said that the legend has particular importance for all the successors of Peter, who are to give their lives for the Gospel in every circumstance.

When I visited the church of Quo Vadis the other day, I realized that Peter's encounter with the Lord on the Appian Way teaches everyone a very personal lesson. At once faith-filled, impetuous, stubborn, courageous and fragile, Peter had to learn the wisdom of the cross step-by-step. Invited by Jesus to walk toward him on the water, he stepped out of the boat but soon began to sink, distracted by the wind and waves. When Jesus said he would suffer and die, Peter could not fathom that such a thing could happen. At the end, terrified and pelted by the questions of others warming themselves by the fire, he denied knowing Jesus.

Who has not set out to follow Christ, only to be distracted by storms swirling about? Who has not tried to tell the Lord there must be a better way?

Prone to discouragement and slow to understand, he was nonetheless chosen — and given courage to persevere when the going got tough. Fleeing a city perilous to Christians, Peter met the Lord once again and saw that his cross was in fact the cross of Christ, in which he had been invited to share.

Who among us has not been discouraged or disheartened by the trials of life, by our own frailty? Who has not set out to follow Christ, only to be distracted by storms swirling about? Who has not tried to tell the Lord there must be a better way? Who has not needed a challenge to persevere in the face of obstacles? Who has not been confronted with opposition to the Christian faith? Who has not reached out to the Lord for strength on the rough road?

The legend of Quo Vadis teaches a valuable lesson. Peter was weak but always ready to meet Jesus, even on the Appian Way — the Roman superhighway, his intended escape route from the cross. When burdened and tempted to give up we ask Jesus in prayer, "Lord, where are you going?" he responds, "I have been this way before you. It is my suffering you share. Where am I going? To carry your cross."

And we to him respond, "Lord, I am going back to follow you."

May 22, 2004

Our pope leading the way of discipleship

On May 18, a new book by Pope John Paul II was released by Mondadori publishers in Italian, Spanish and Polish: "Alzatevi, Andiamo!" ("Rise, Let Us Be on Our Way").

The Holy Father takes the title from Mark 14:41-42. Finding Peter, James and John asleep in the garden as he underwent his agony, Jesus said, "The hour has come. Behold, the Son of Man is to be handed over to sinners. Rise, let us be on our way."

The pope's latest book is a reflection on the unfolding of his vocation and an encouragement to all who follow Christ. Alluding to the title, he writes, "Even if these words denote a time of trial, a great struggle or a sorrowful cross, we must not let them make us fearful. They are words that also carry with them that joy and peace which are the fruit of faith…

"The love of God does not load us with weights too heavy to carry, or with demands we are unable to face. As he asks, he offers the necessary help … Echoing these words of our Lord and Savior, I repeat to each of you, 'Rise, let us be on our way.' Let us entrust ourselves to Christ. It will be he who will accompany us on our walk, all the way to the destination that he alone knows."

The book offers the pope's account of Christ's accompaniment along his personal journey. If there is anything that can be said of the Holy Father, it is that he has always willingly and courageously walked the way of the Savior. As he now confronts the effects of illness and advanced age, he still finds Jesus at his side, and he eagerly continues his walk. His body has weakened, but his heart is as vigorous as ever.

May 18 was chosen for the book's release because it was the Holy Father's 84th birthday. Fortunately for Bishop McDonald and me, it was also the day of our private audience with him.

Since this was my first visit "Ad Limina Apostolorum," I did not know what to expect. I had been told I could invite our seminarians studying in Rome for a brief introduction and photograph before the private audience began, so Jason Tyler (Morrilton) and Matthew Glover (Little Rock) joined us. I also invited Mauricio Carrasco (Springdale), who is spending five weeks in Italy with the University of Arkansas. Sporting a new tie and borrowed black suit coat, he looked just like a seminarian!

The five of us arrived early and were ushered through a series of rooms in the Papal Palace. When finally our time came, we were led into a large, bright hall, a kind of personal study. The Holy Father was seated at one end of the room; there were two chairs at his right, one for me and one for Bishop McDonald. After we greeted him, I introduced the three young men who accompanied us. A photograph was taken of the group, then Bishop McDonald and I were left alone with the pope.

What does one say to the pope? To be honest, I don't remember everything I said. We began by wishing him a happy birthday. After I gave a brief profile of our diocese, he surprised me by saying, "There are many Hispanics in Arkansas." I told him about the tremendous immigration of Spanish-speaking Catholics and what a blessing they are. He asked about family life and vocations.

His ready sense of humor shone through clearly. When I mentioned that in October 1978, I had the privilege of being in St. Peter's Square the evening he was elected, he responded with a smile, "Five o'clock." I said, "Holy Father," I will always remember that night." Smiling again, he said, "I will remember, too."

The audience was a particularly moving experience for Bishop McDonald. As bishop of Little Rock, he made at least five ad limina visits and had private audiences with two popes. As bishop emeritus, he has both a paternal relationship with us and a fraternal relationship with John Paul II. They are brothers aged in wisdom, seasoned in mission and schooled in discipleship; they are long-time companions along the way of Christ.

The Church will reflect on Pope John Paul's insights for years to come, so broad is his grasp of Christian faith.

The Church will reflect on Pope John Paul's insights for years to come, so broad is his grasp of Christian faith. He will be remembered as a profoundly influential figure of the late 20th and early 21st centuries, a spiritual guide with uncommon clarity and wisdom, and a world citizen with a truly comprehensive vision.

How would he prefer to be remembered? If his personal memoirs offer any clue, I think it would be as an apostle who believed with every fiber of his being that Jesus is Lord and Savior, who ever kept vigil with Christ, who eagerly responded to the call ("Rise, let us be on our way"), who trusted in Jesus' companionship along the journey, and who simply did what he was asked to do.

"So you also, when you have done all that is commanded of you, say, 'We are unworthy servants; we have only done what was our duty.'" (Luke 17:10)

Because he takes the call of Christ so seriously, I do not think it occurs to John Paul II to take his rest. Everything about him speaks untiringly of Christ. Drawing near the "threshold of the apostles" last week, I, too, heard Jesus say, "Alzatevi, Andiamo!" through him.

May 29, 2004

SEASONS OF THE CHURCH: ADVENT-CHRISTMAS

What we can learn from Simeon and Anna

When Jesus was first brought to the Temple by his parents, how did Simeon and Anna know he was the One for whom they had been waiting?

Joseph and Mary were devout Jews who faithfully observed the Law of Moses. St. Luke writes that they came to the Temple when Jesus was 40 days old for the ritual purification of Mary after childbirth and the consecration of their first-born to the Lord. They made the symbolic offering prescribed for the poor. It was there that they met two prayerful children of Israel, Simeon and Anna.

Simeon and Anna were part of the "anawim," God's poor, who are mentioned countless times in the Old Testament. The anawim were objects of God's tender love and care, examples of humility and generosity, who trusted not in their own resources but solely on the providence of God. Unshaken in faith despite the misfortunes that had befallen them, they were examples to others who struggled to keep their sights on the Lord.

Simeon was "righteous and devout, awaiting the consolation of Israel, and the Holy Spirit was upon him. It had been revealed to him by the holy Spirit that he should not see death before he had seen the Messiah of the Lord." (Luke 2:25-26)

Anna was 84, a widow most of her life. "She never left the temple, but worshipped night and day with fasting and prayer." (Luke 2:37)

I am certain it is fair to say that everyone knew Simeon and

Anna, because they were always in the Temple. Having rooted themselves deep in the hopes of Israel, they never left the house of God. "Why would we be anywhere else?" they must have thought. The Messiah is coming!

Both of them instantly recognized Jesus as the One for whom they had been waiting. Simeon took the baby in his arms and praised God, declaring that he could now die in peace because he had seen the salvation promised by the Lord (v. 29-32). Anna saw the baby, gave thanks to God, and began speaking about him to "all who were awaiting the redemption of Jerusalem." (v. 38)

How did they know he was the One? Because he was the focus of their waiting.

Simeon and Anna could have focused on waiting for a solution to their problems. Since they were poor, I am sure they had concerns about food, clothing and shelter. Were they lonely, and did they pray for companionship? Did others look at them suspiciously, snickering at their permanent presence in the temple? As a widow, Anna was particularly vulnerable. Who was taking care of her in her old age? Knowing that he would not die until he saw the Messiah, did Simeon worry that his creaking joints and unsteady gait would get the best of him in the meantime?

They had plenty to pray about, plenty to ask, plenty of answers to wait for. Yet they waited only for the Lord.

They had plenty to pray about, plenty to ask, plenty of answers to wait for. Yet they waited only for the Lord. It is precisely here that we find the blessedness of their situation and the reason for the clarity of their insight: they were not looking for an answer or a solution, but for the Messiah.

Advent is a time for us to take up the spirit of Simeon and Anna. It is easy to focus energy and attention exclusively on seeking answers to our prayers, but to do so can actually be another way of focusing on ourselves. Advent calls us to move our focus away from the answers we await and toward the One who answers every prayer. It can be frightening to take such a leap, but in reality it is very liberating to do so.

Simeon and Anna recognized the Savior when he was brought to the Temple because it was he for whom they looked, and only he. Their needs were great, and I doubt they were bashful in prayer. They must have poured out their hearts to God time and again. Their knees must have been calloused and achy from all the praying. But long ago they had let go of looking for answers in favor of relying, simply and hopefully, on God.

In a sense, Advent is a time to taste heaven. We will know then, beyond a shadow of a doubt, who the Messiah is. Then, there will be no more waiting, no prayers to be answered. Then, there will be only God, the One on whom we have always depended for everything, even when we franticly looked elsewhere for answers. In heaven, we will pray for our loved ones who are still in this life, and our prayer will be something like this: "Lord, may she turn to you. Lord, may he rely on you. Lord, may they recognize you."

This Advent, may the words of Psalm 62 be our dearest prayer:

> "In God alone be at rest, my soul;
> for my hope comes from him.
> He alone is my rock, my stronghold,
> My fortress: I stand firm.
> In God is my safety and glory,
> The rock of my strength.
> Take refuge in God all you people,
> Trust him at all times.
> Pour out your hearts before him.
> For God is our refuge."
> (Psalm 62:6-9)

December 6, 2003

This Advent, break out of your routine

One autumn Sunday afternoon many years ago, I drove to my mom's house for a visit. As I pulled into her driveway, I could hear my nieces and nephew playing in the back yard. Once inside, I looked out the kitchen window and saw them playing in the fallen leaves.

One of my nieces caught a glimpse of me spying through the window. She stopped in her tracks and yelled to her sisters and brother, "Drop your leaves! Peter's here!" They did drop their leaves and ran inside to greet me, as if they had not seen me in years. Needless to say, it made me feel good that they were willing to drop everything, even a fun afternoon among the leaves, just to see me.

Years passed, and they turned their attention to other, more grown-up, interests. One day I called my sister's house to speak with her. My leaf-dropping niece, by then in the eighth grade, answered the phone. The conversation went something like this:

"Hi, Katy, it's Peter. How ya doin'?"
"Good."
"What are you doing?"
"Talking to you."
"How's school?"
"It's OK."
"Is your mom there?"
"Yes."
"May I speak with her?"
"Mom, it's Peter" (almost as if to add, "… again").

I asked myself, what happened to the excitement I used to hear when I called or visited? I suppose it grew up, busied itself with homework, music and relationships, and settled nicely into a routine.

Early Christians were excited about their new faith and the return of the Lord Jesus. When his second coming was not as soon as they had expected, they settled into the routine of every-day living. Some simply returned to their former way of life, numb to the prospects that their Lord was going to come again.

As we begin Advent, we hear Jesus say that back in the days of Noah, folks went about regular business right up to the day Noah entered the ark. "They did not know until the flood came and carried them all away." (see Matthew 24) He warns us that it will be the same with his second coming. "So too, you also must be prepared, for at an hour you do not expect, the Son of Man will come."

Salvation is not something off in the distant future, so far away that it makes no demands on us in the present.

Jesus says, "You also must be prepared." Salvation is not something off in the distant future, so far away that it makes no demands on us in the present. The Lord Jesus will come again, at an hour we least expect; but he is also present now, especially in the sacraments, in his word, in the poor and in our prayer. Each moment holds out to us the promise of coming face to face with him.

It is easy to fall into a routine, forgetting that Jesus is with us and will come again. Paul sums it up this way: "Brothers and sisters: You know the time; it is the hour now for you to awake from sleep." (Romans 13:11) He continues, reminding us in so many words to awaken from our routine and rekindle our excitement for the coming of the Lord.

Jesus says that preparedness for his coming involves the kind of careful watchfulness we would have when guarding our homes from intruders. Perhaps he would also point out that we are to be on the watch for his presence as we would be for the perfect gift for our most cherished friend.

Cardinal John Henry Newman (+1890) wrote:

"Do you know the feeling ... of expecting a friend, expecting him to come and he delays? Do you know what it is to be in unpleasant company, and to wish for the time to pass away, and the hour strike when you may be at liberty? Do you know what it is to be in anxiety lest something should happen which may happen or may not, or to be in suspense about some important event, which makes your heart beat when you are reminded of it, and of which you think the first thing in the morning?

"Do you know what it is to have a friend in a distant country, to expect news of him, and to wonder from day to day what he is now doing, and whether he is well?... To watch for Christ is a feeling such as these.

"He watches for Christ, who has a sensitive, eager, apprehensive mind; who is awake, alive, quick-sighted, zealous in seeking and honoring him; who looks out for him in all that happens, and who would not be surprised, who would not be over-agitated or overwhelmed, if he found that he was coming at once."

In the coming weeks, we will hear prophets and apostles rouse us to watchfulness. Their words arise from a hunger for God so deep that it is almost beyond telling, so intense and utterly personal that it consumes them. Perhaps this Advent we will reach beneath our routine — beneath even the routine of our anxieties — and discover anew who it is for whom we truly hunger. May we be ready to drop everything when we catch him spying us through the window.

November 27, 2004

Balancing your checkbook and your life

I once went for about five years without balancing my checkbook. Apparently there was a month when I could not balance it to the penny, so I just let it go. I still kept approximate records, I recorded every check I wrote, and I always made sure the bank statement indicated I had more money than my checkbook. But for at least five years, I never tried to reconcile the two. There was nothing morally wrong with this — I never wrote a bad check, and I paid all my bills. I simply chose to let that part of my life be more or less OK, and I didn't worry about it.

Eventually I decided this was crazy and I needed to be more responsible, so I closed down that account and opened a new one. Now at the end of each month, I account for every cent. I'm embarrassed to admit that I enjoy balancing my checkbook.

Any unbalanced checkbooks at your house?

Or more to the point, are there any parts of our lives that we are neglecting because they're not screaming out for attention? Neglecting because they're OK — not good, not bad, but approximately OK? And even more to the point, might it be that our relationship with God is one of those areas?

In the Scripture readings for the first Sunday of Advent, Jesus reminded his disciples that in the days of Noah, when the flood was about to come, folks were going about business as usual; as he put it, they "were eating and drinking, marrying and being married, right up to the day Noah entered the ark. They were totally unconcerned until the flood came." Jesus knew that using this image of the destructive flood would grab his disciples' attention, but he was not trying to frighten them. He was simply reminding them that he will return at any moment, without advance notice. And wouldn't it be a shame if we were so totally self-absorbed that we were not prepared to meet him?

Wouldn't it be a shame if we let ourselves settle into complacency about our relationship with God — accepting the fact that it's not good, but not bad, but approximately OK — and therefore let it go unchecked, unbalanced and untended? That was Jesus' concern about us.

It was also St. Paul's concern about the Christians at Rome. Since we believe that the Lord will come again, he told them, we should already be living our lives in the light of his coming. It is easy to be lulled into complacency, seeing as how the Lord didn't return in Paul's lifetime, or for the past 2,000 years for that matter. We can get so wrapped up in the business of life that it's easy to let the spiritual remain "approximate."

But Jesus and Paul knew that Christianity is not just about waiting for something to happen at some future point. After all, God is not waiting until the end of the world to shower upon us the benefits and blessings of faith; he wants us to know them even now.

If we think of the Christian life solely as a process of "getting ready" for something, we begin to see salvation as something out there in the future — and therefore something that may or may not make demands on our lives today, or something whose blessings we will reap only after death.

For the Christian, "waiting" means that each moment of life offers the possibility of coming face to face with God and the grace he wants to give us to live in peace, to the full. The problem is not that the Second Coming is so far away from us in time, that we have so long to wait; the problem is that we don't pay enough notice to God's presence now. Maybe we settle for "not good, not bad, but approximately OK" in our relationship with God and with the way we put our faith into practice. But God wants to give us more than that.

The problem is not that the Second Coming is so far away from us in time, that we have so long to wait; the problem is that we don't pay enough notice to God's presence now.

Advent is the time to ask if during the past year we have relegated our relationship with God to an unexamined, unbalanced, unchecked corner of our lives — settling for the fact that we know he's there, but admitting in our heart of hearts that our response to him is not whole-hearted, but just approximately OK The tragedy of it all is that we let ourselves settle for much less than what God wants to give us.

It's Advent. The coming of the Lord teaches us to put things in their proper balance again.

December 8, 2001

'Awake, O my soul!'

The woodpecker that has taken a liking to my house gets up earlier than I do. Now I get up earlier than I used to.

My woodpecker goes to work before dawn, takes long and irregular breaks throughout the day, and is very good at what he does. The many holes in my wood siding are proof of his diligence and skill. A few months ago, we placed six large fiberglass owls at strategic points along the roofline (I'm told that woodpeckers do not like owls). This ploy seemed to work well at first, but my woodpecker caught on and has returned. Someone tells me Wal-Mart stocks fearsome bobble-head owls, but I have a feeling my woodpecker would think they were merely nodding in approval.

So I get up a little earlier now. No harm done, except to the house.

I've decided that the woodpecker has come to teach me something, and I've been wondering lately if it has to do with Advent.

This time of year, we are called to a different kind of awakening, an awakening to the nearness of the Lord. In a figurative sense, alarm clocks set at the regular time do not rouse us early enough for his coming. We need a bit of shaking, a bit of rumbling — a bit of knocking? — to stir us spiritually for Christmas.

We use the word "apocalyptic" to describe the kind of biblical writing aimed at shaking us up to understand what will happen at the end of time. Apocalyptic literature such as the book of Revelation uses highly symbolic language to capture the mystery of how things turn out in the end. Visions of earthquakes, lightning and awesome winged creatures give apocalyptic writing an aura of seriousness and urgency, as they communicate exactly what is at stake — God's final and definitive victory over the forces of evil.

Advent summons us to keep in mind the end of the world, when the Lord Jesus will return to hand over everything in creation to his Father. Jesus himself makes use of apocalyptic imagery to remind us that some day that end will come; at the same time, he cautions us not to believe those who say they know when that will be. He encourages us to be faithful, not fearful.

We speak of Jesus' "second coming" because there was a "first coming." The Incarnation, the conception and birth of the Son of God in flesh and blood, was the beginning of our salvation. The prophets foretold such a coming, the people of Israel ached to see it, and the Virgin Mary marveled that it was to happen in her. The angel's announcement caught her off guard and even troubled her. "Who am I?" she asked, wondering how such a thing could happen in one as insignificant as she. The news must have seemed, well, apocalyptic.

The Lord is near. If we expect him to conform to our schedule, to get to work once we have awakened, we will miss what he is doing and fall right back to sleep.

The Lord also comes to us in the Church, and Advent is a true wake-up call to his presence in Word, sacrament, private prayer and deeds of love. Knowing that we are about to celebrate the birth of our Savior, and aware that his birth signals the beginning of his final victory, we understand that Advent is not business-as-usual. The Lord is near. If we expect him to conform to our schedule, to get to work once we have awakened, we will miss what he is doing and fall right back to sleep.

Advent gives us the opportunity to be shaken out of our complacency by the stir of the prophets, to feel the ancient ache of the people of Israel, to wonder with Mary at the paradox of God's plan, and to recognize our need for a Savior. The message of Advent is as broad as the cosmos (God redeems creation in his Son, through whom he created everything) and as personal as my need for healing (Lord, I am not worthy to have you under my roof, but only say the word).

As John the Baptist preached a message of repentance in preparation for the Lord's coming, the crowds asked, "What then should we do?" The tax collectors asked, "Teacher, what should we do?" And soldiers asked, "And what is it that we should do?" John's answers were simple and direct: Change your lives. Be fair, be generous, be gentle. Let go of anything that is incompatible with his coming (cf. Luke 3).

No doubt, John was an irritant, dressed in clothes of camel hair, unrelenting in his prophesying, indiscriminate in his condemnations. Yet he was sent to awaken God's people. Some covered their ears and fell back to sleep, but others caught fire with the expectation of salvation.

An irritating woodpecker awakens me each morning, knocking on the outside of my bedroom wall. I've decided he's there for a purpose, to teach me to welcome the "Daybreak from on high" (Luke 1:78) for whom John prepared the way. He's a small creaturely reminder that if I do not reawaken spiritually, I will miss the unfolding of Advent. The Lord is near! What a shame it would be if I kept on with business as usual, slept through his coming, and failed to welcome him. He would come nonetheless — but I would be no different.

"Awake O my soul; awake, lyre and harp! I will wake the dawn." (Psalm 57:9)

November 29, 2003

Jesus' humility was bright star to guide way

When I think of the night Jesus was born, I like to imagine it as cold and crisp, stars glimmering brightly in a clear sky like candles in the hands of a thousand vigilant pilgrims. Goats and sheep shifted sleepily in their pens, while the occasional bark of a dog echoed off the hills — followed by the annoyed "Shush!" of its master. A breeze spread the lingering aroma of suppers cooked over smoldering hearths and campfires.

Joseph took a full, deep breath, then sighed in relief and wonder. I wonder if Mary was hungry. Their baby's full-throated cries pierced the evening's still, and the dog howled. Mary and Joseph smiled.

Hanging like a huge painting on the night sky was the moon, which somehow seemed much closer than usual, its mysterious, distant features clearly discernible.

That night it was a lamp so bright that travelers could have effortlessly found their way down the crude roads by its light. It would have been easy to forget that the moon was not a star, that it simply reflected the extraordinary light of the hidden sun.

As I picture that first Christmas, I like to think that the brightness of the moon that night did not come from the sun. Instead, it came from the Savior, whose glory illumined the heavens, shining on the moon and radiating far past it. The true light of the world had come.

In his homily for the closing of the Holy Door at the beginning of 2001, and again in his apostolic letter, "Novo Millennio

Ineunte" ("At the Beginning of the New Millennium"), Pope John Paul recalled a favorite ancient image of the Church.

"The theology of the Fathers loved to speak of the Church as 'mysterium lunae' (the mystery of the moon), in order to emphasize that, like the moon, she shines not with her own light, but reflects Christ, who is her Sun." (Homily, no. 3)

The night Jesus Christ was born, the reflected light of the sun paled in comparison to the light shining from a stable in Bethlehem. Though imperceptible to shepherds watching their flocks, it was seen by angels, who sang God's praises.

The Son of God, through whom all things came to be, had taken on flesh and blood, and the prayers of the ages were answered.

Who could have guessed that we would share in the mystery, that we would be called to reflect the glory of the Son of God and draw others to him?

Who would have thought that God could become so fragile, so small, so helpless? Who could have guessed that we would share in the mystery, that we would be called to reflect the glory of the Son of God and draw others to him?

Who could have known that humility would be the brightest light of all?

It had been a long journey just for the census, a long and worrisome day looking for lodging and a safe place to give birth.

Joseph lovingly admired his son and pondered the trip home, wondering when Mary would feel well enough to travel again.

He tried his best to stay awake with her, because he did not want to miss a thing, especially should she have any need. But crouched against the gate of the stall, his arm and warm cloak around her shoulders and his head against hers, his eyelids grew heavy, and he fell asleep.

December 22, 2001

Will you feed, shelter and welcome Jesus?

S ince no one would take the poor travelers in for the night (they probably have no money, and she looks as if she'll give birth at any moment, and it would be just too much of an inconvenience at such a busy time as census), God set his Christmas table in a trough used to feed animals. Little did anyone know that stingy night that God's was to be a lavish banquet of choice food, a feast of endless abundance.

"If only we had known," the innkeepers might have said later, "we would have provided a proper room for them, and a nourishing meal." But they did not, and still there is enough food forever, and room for all.

They asked very little, this weary pair, and finally someone agreed to their simple requests: just a spot out back away from the wind, among the animals would be just fine, we'll be no trouble — and yes it seems the baby will come very soon — don't worry, we have food in our sacks, and blankets, too, just a place to rest and wait, we'll pay for some hay and water for the donkey, thank you for your kindness. Shalom, good night to you as well.

And there he was born, the one through whom all things came to be. St. Luke hopes we take note that this happened in a town whose name means "house of bread," and that Jesus was placed in a manger where creatures come to feed. He needed next to nothing, this little one who would one day give everything for us.

A fifth century song for Christmas morning ("A solis ortus cardine") captured the contrast: "The blessed maker of the world assumed a servant's form … He deigned to have hay for a bed, and did not refuse the shelter of a manger. He does not suffer even a bird to hunger, and yet he was fed with a little milk." He provides the world its food but is content with just a little for himself.

Soon strangers from the east brought gifts to the child, sensing by God's hidden wisdom that something earth-shaking was afoot. They left their riches at his feet but left with more than they had brought. Did they know whom they were visiting? One thing is certain: by grace they were changed on their star-crossed journey to the manger. St. Matthew means more than geography when he reports that they went back to their own country "by another way."

The child grew in wisdom, age and grace. Still asking little or nothing, he gave everything to the poor and confused, the forsaken and lost, the stingy and ungrateful. They sought him out by the thousands. "I am the bread of life," he would tell them. "No one who comes to me will ever be hungry."

He would prove his love to the end, by the end he suffered on the cross. A soldier pierced him with a lance, and from his side sprang a fountain of blood and water. Having given his body and blood for us, the banquet was eternally set — the only banquet we would ever need, the Eucharist we share even today, and will forever.

He is our brother (flesh of our flesh), our food (satisfying Word and Precious Body and Blood), our Savior (God from all ages, our origin and destiny). Will we feed on him? That is the invitation of Christmas.

But there is another invitation, too: Will we feed him? Will we bring him our gifts? After all, he asks so little.

The truth is, we have the chance to recognize and welcome him, to feed him and shelter him, every day. John Paul I, who served as pope for just 33 days in 1978, once wrote that parents, by caring for their children, honor Jesus. "Husbands and wives are themselves Magi, who deposit their gifts at the foot of that cradle every day: privations, anxieties, nightlong vigils, detachment. They receive other gifts in return, new impulses to live and become holy, a joy purified by sacrifice, the renewal of their mutual affection, and a fuller communion of souls."

That is the way he intended it to be: that we would let him feed us, and filled with him we would feed the world.

That is the way he intended it to be: that we would let him feed us, and filled with him we would feed the world. Learning to love as he loved, we would find how rich is his banquet, how inexhaustible his generous love. Whether mothers or fathers, sons or daughters, priests or religious, nurses or teachers or leaders of nations, that is the way he intends it to be. We who have the privilege of knowing who he is — unlike the miserly innkeepers of the first Christmas — are to let him in. He will feed us, and we will become food ourselves.

On that night when no one was in any mood to take poor strangers in, God poured out his heart to us, giving us what was most precious to him, his only Son. We are Magi, too, and lay gifts at his feet every time we love as he loved.

May we know him in prayer, in sacrament, in love, in daily life. He asks so little and gives us everything.

Merry Christmas!

December 18, 2004

Disciples proclaim:
'See what God is doing'

In the year 325 A.D., St. Macarius, then bishop of Jerusalem, took the occasion of the Council of Nicea to inform the Emperor Constantine of the neglected condition of the holy places in his diocese. As a result, Constantine ordered the construction of churches to commemorate three major events in the life of Jesus, including one at the site of Jesus' birth at Bethlehem. A year later architects went to work on the design. The Basilica of the Nativity still stands on that site, having endured repairs and rebuilding after invasions, fires and earthquakes.

A document from the Council of Jerusalem in 836 A.D. tells an interesting story about the basilica. In 614 A.D., the Persian soldiers of Chosroes II destroyed all the sanctuaries of Palestine but spared the basilica at Bethlehem. When they saw the mosaic of the adoration of the magi, who were depicted in Persian dress, they recognized their own countrymen in the scene and decided to let the basilica stand.

They did not believe in Jesus as Savior, but they recognized themselves in an artistic representation of his birth and thus participated unwittingly in the fulfillment of a central biblical theme about the Messiah — that he would make all people one.

The Advent-Christmas-Epiphany season begins and ends with the prophets' dream that all creation will return, together, to the true God. Isaiah had written, "In days to come, the mountain of the Lord's house shall be established as the highest mountain and raised above the hills. All nations shall stream toward it; many peoples shall come and say: 'Come, let us climb the Lord's mountain, to the house of the God of Jacob, that he may instruct us in his ways, and we may walk in his paths.'" (Isaiah 2)

Baruch echoes Isaiah with these words: "Up, Jerusalem! Stand upon the heights; look to the east and see your children gathered from the east and the west at the word of the Holy One, rejoicing that they are remembered by God." (Baruch 5)

And again, Isaiah: "On that day, the root of Jesse, set up as a signal for the nations, the Gentiles shall seek out, for his dwelling shall be glorious." (Isaiah 11)

"Raise up your eyes and look about; they all gather and come to you; your sons come from afar, and your daughters in the arms of their nurses ... all from Sheba shall come bearing gold and frankincense, and proclaiming the praises of the Lord." (Isaiah 60)

Isaiah and Baruch escort us through Advent with these hopeful words, and the Gospel writers carefully situate the birth of the Messiah in deeply symbolic accounts. Matthew first gives us the genealogy of "Jesus Christ, the son of David, the son of Abraham," then tells of Joseph's dream, the visit of the Magi, the flight to Egypt, and the massacre of the innocents. Mark begins by telling of the crowds gathering at the Jordan to be baptized by John, and how Jesus was proclaimed God's Son by a voice from the heavens after being baptized himself.

Luke goes into great detail about the births of John and Jesus, the shepherds and angels, and the presentation in the temple, showing by means of characters who meet the infant that he is "a light for revelation for the Gentiles."

John awes us by opening his Gospel with the same words that open the Old Testament: "In the beginning..." He proclaims Jesus as the eternal Word of God, through whom everything was created; as the "true light, which enlightens everyone."

In the Acts of the Apostles (chapter 17) Luke reports St. Paul's visit to Athens. After having had some days to tour the city, Paul became exasperated with all the idols he saw there, noting that there was even an altar inscribed "To an Unknown God." While preaching at the Areopagus, Paul said, "What therefore you unknowingly worship, I proclaim to you. The God who made the world and everything in it... gives to everyone life and breath and everything. He made from one the whole human race to dwell on the entire surface of the earth... so that people might seek God, even perhaps grope for him and find him, though indeed he is not far from any one of us."

In sending his Son in flesh and blood, God begins to bring to a climax his eternal will that all creation be joined with him as one. John reports that Jesus had prayed to his Father "that all may be one," reiterating this central theme of the New Testament.

If we recognize what God is doing — reconciling the world to himself in Jesus — will we not want to work with him for this purpose?

From the beginning, apostles and missionaries have been sent to proclaim the good news: "See what God is doing!" Perhaps this Christmas we will listen to the Scriptures as having that perspective: "See what God is doing!" If we recognize what God is doing — reconciling the world to himself in Jesus — will we not want to work with him for this purpose?

Like St. Paul, Christian missionaries have often brought others close to God without their knowing it, because each time we love others with the love of Christ, we bring him close to them, and bring them close to him — even if they do not recognize it. When the Persian soldiers stopped in their tracks at the mosaic of the basilica in Bethlehem, without knowing it they drew close to the Savior because they identified with their countrymen in the scene. They were unwitting participants in God's work of making us one!

May this Christmas be a time of drawing close to the Savior for all of us. He is Emmanuel, God-with-us. May those who grope for him without knowing it, find him. May those who know him but ignore him, awaken. May we who know him and love him, follow him.

See what God is doing! A hope-filled Christmas to you all.

December 23, 2000

Grief can help unite us with Advent readings

The early years of the Sartain family are generously chronicled in a series of home movies, the first of which were taken before I was born. My father loved gadgets, and as home movie cameras became available, he followed us kids with great interest, recording our every move with enthusiasm. Bright light was a necessity for these pioneering cameras, and indoors he used a hand-held bank of flood lights so blinding that we squinted painfully as the film rolled — not exactly the best way to produce a natural pose.

In a metal cabinet located in my mother's bedroom closet you can still find canisters of these old movies, many of them labeled in grease pencil. Those produced before I was born feature fairly generic titles: "Kids At Zoo," "Kids At Grandma's," etc. But several canisters stand out with such titles as "Peter On Slide" and — my personal favorite — "Our Son." When I was born, the fifth child and first son, my father figured the event deserved special recognition.

About 10 years ago one of my sisters transferred some of the movies to videotape and gave them to the rest of us as Christmas gifts. I followed suit several years later with the remainder and added a sound track composed mostly of theme songs from television shows of the 50s and 60s. I took great pains to emphasize my first appearance on the screen. "Peter Learns To Walk" features Handel's "Hallelujah Chorus" and Copland's "Fanfare for the Common Man." The temptation was too hard to resist.

I think my sister and I had the same objective: to preserve part of our family history, and in a certain sense to do so in the spirit of my father, who loved this kind of project and first made it possible. The fact that the project was destined to be a Christmas gift added another layer of significance, for Christmas celebrations are part of every family history.

This time of year I am keenly aware of families who are celebrating the holidays for the first time without a loved one who has recently died. The grieving process is almost always heightened during the holidays — precisely because holidays bring back family memories — and navigating these days can require special strength and ingenuity.

Many of us heap loads of expectations on the holidays — what they should be like, how we should feel, where we should be, who should be there with us. But circumstances often change, and holidays can become heavy if we force unrealistic expectations into changed circumstances. If those expectations are not met, many people end up sorely disappointed.

When we have recently lost a loved one, holidays can be particularly hard to handle and cause us to turn inward even though surrounded by friends and family. At times like these it is helpful to give deliberate direction to our naturally inward gaze. Let me tell you what I mean.

The inward orientation of grief offers a prime opportunity to deepen one's understanding of the meaning of the holidays. Thanksgiving can be re-enlivened as a day of gratitude for blessings big and small, most especially perhaps for the blessing of the one who has died. A reflective attitude gives us the opportunity to thank God for the blessings our loved one brought us and helps us remember other blessings that may have been forgotten as in a closet for years. Giving thanks strengthens our hope and gives us courage, because it brings to mind friends and loved ones who have constantly streamed through our lives from the beginning.

Those who are grieving can experience the Christmas

mystery in a new and wonderful way. The very fact that they are grieving gives them a heightened understanding of themes that appear in the Scriptures of Advent and Christmas. Who better than they can grasp the longing of the people of Israel? Or the expectation of the world to come, when all will be reunited in Christ? Or the poverty of spirit shown by the Virgin Mary, who despite the troubling questions passing through her mind accepted God's will with an open heart, who heard Simeon predict that one day her heart would feel as though it had been pierced by a sword?

Who better than they can grasp the longing of the people of Israel? Or the expectation of the world to come, when all will be reunited in Christ?

Who better than they can comprehend the sinking fear that arises upon hearing painful news, such as Joseph and Mary felt when they suddenly discovered on their way home from Jerusalem that their son was lost? Or what St. Paul described as the inward groaning of all creation as it awaits redemption? Or the frightening void exposed by grief that can be filled only by God himself? Grieving people understand these things better than most.

Though such "first holidays" may appear to be the end of holidays as we knew them, they can occasion a deepening of our appreciation of the Christian mystery and the reason we need Jesus Christ, who came to destroy death forever.

May God bless you who have said good-bye to your loved ones in recent years, and may their passing through your hearts during the holidays be an occasion for gratitude and strengthened faith. May your longing for them be transformed into a prayer of longing for the Savior. I assure you, God listens attentively to such prayers that rise to him out of our depths.

November 25, 2000

News of Christ's birth started as a rumor that spread

A rumor does not have to be a bad thing. I am referring to the kind of excitement and speculation that erupt when potentially good news begins to spread. "Have you heard she may be coming home for Christmas?" "Did you know he's a finalist for the scholarship?" "Someone told me her cancer may be in remission!" "I saw them speaking and smiling the other day — could that mean they are reconciled?"

Word passes from one to another — a word of hope and anticipation, a word spread not because it is scandalous but because it is good. The crescendo increases as more and more folks are in on it; and though nothing yet has come to pass, just the thought builds good will, brings us together, and sets us to thinking generous thoughts.

"Could that be?" we might say. "Wouldn't that be wonderful? I hope it's true!" The word is so full of hope that we are surprised when someone discounts it or doesn't join in the excitement.

As Jesus began his public ministry, the good news of his preaching and accomplishments traveled like wildfire, and in those whose hearts were open, wondrous speculation began.

After he engaged the cynical Samaritan woman in conversation at Jacob's well, her heart was touched so deeply she could not keep the story to herself. She told the townspeople, "Come see a man who told me everything I have done. Could he possibly be the Messiah?" Many came to believe in Jesus on account of her testimony. (John 4:4-42)

One day after teaching by the Sea of Galilee, Jesus asked the apostles to cross to the other side with him. They embarked, and other boats followed. But a sudden and violent squall came up, and waves began breaking over the boats. Everyone was terrified — everyone except Jesus, who was sound asleep. They awakened him, he rebuked the wind and sea — "Quiet! Be still!" — and calm ensued immediately. Filled with awe, the disciples rumored to one another, "Who then is this whom even wind and sea obey?" (Mark 4:35-41)

Though rumors about Jesus were nothing new, their effect on others was unpredictable. In fact, it was a rumor that brought together astrologers from the east, King Herod, chief priests and scribes.

Three foreigners were in town inquiring about a star and a newborn king for the Jews. Worried, Herod consulted the experts. "What does Scripture say about where your Messiah will be born?" "Bethlehem of Judea," they answered. Then, feigning intimate confidence in the magi, he suggested they follow the star, find the new king and bring back news of his location.

Put on the right track by experts, their unwitting search for faith ended in triumph. But the experts, who believed in both Scripture and God's promise of a Messiah, were indifferent to the rumor and did not budge.

Off they went, enlightened by Scripture, ambassadors now of Herod himself. And finding Mary, Joseph and the child, they believed; but it was revealed to them in a dream to avoid the duplicitous Herod, so they traveled home by another way, guided no longer by a star but by the Light of the World.

A confusing turn of events, to say the least. Pagan astrologers, acting on rumor and inspiration, left home and family to look for a Messiah. Put on the right track by experts, their unwitting search for faith ended in triumph. But the experts, who believed in both Scripture and God's promise of a Messiah, were indifferent to the rumor and did not budge. They held the key but did not turn it.

Danish philosopher Søren Kierkegaard (1813-1855) once wrote:

"Although the scribes could explain where the Messiah should be born, they remained quite unperturbed in Jerusalem. They did not accompany the Wise Men to seek him. Similarly, we may know the whole of Christianity, yet make no movement. The power that moved heaven and earth leaves us completely unmoved.

"What a difference! The three kings had only a rumor to go by. But it moved them to make that long journey ... What a vexation it must have been for the kings, that the scribes who gave them the news they wanted remained in Jerusalem!"

Rumors about the birth of a new king were enough to stir the astrologers to the star-lit desert roads, but soon there was no longer any rumor for them. Matthew reports that they went back to their own country "by another way." Nothing would ever be the same again, now that they knew the truth.

Preaching to fourth-century catechumens, St. Cyril of Jerusalem remarked:

"The incarnation was not merely a rumor or something men imagined; it took place in very truth. The Word did not pass through the Virgin as through a channel but was really made flesh out of her body; he really ate as we ate, and drank as we drink. For if his assumption of human nature had been only a pretense, so would our salvation be only a pretense."

Not a rumor at all, it turned out, but the Eternal Truth. He is not the kind of news to treat casually: he is the star that guides, the power that moves heaven and earth, the "rumor" to take to heart, as did the Virgin Mary. For he did not pass through her but became flesh in her. In a sense it was the same for the nomadic magi, the cynical Samaritan woman and the storm-tossed apostles: the good news who is Jesus did not pass through them as rumor but took flesh and remained in them. So may it be this year for you and me.

Merry Christmas!

December 20, 2003

We should have a 'ready heart'

Like many of you, I have a list of daily prayer intentions. Included are personal needs, family members and friends, the clergy and religious of the diocese, and the many intentions you have asked me to remember in prayer. Among individuals on the list are Mayor Dailey, Gov. Huckabee, President Bush, Vice President Cheney, Secretary of State Powell, Al Qaeda mastermind Osama bin Laden, Israeli Prime Minister Ariel Sharon, Palestinian leader Yasser Arafat, North Korean President Kim Jong II and Iraqi President Saddam Hussein.

It is a diverse list, to be sure, but its makeup springs from hope in God and from what I believe is a Christian obligation to pray and work for peace.

Throughout the Advent/Christmas season, our biblical readings have mentioned the names of far-away places, mostly Middle-Eastern, and many the subjects of intense political and archeological interest even today. I am always struck by the timelessness of the names, for biblical lands and peoples are also modern lands and peoples. Age-old struggles and animosities kindle much of what still erupts on the world scene.

Thus, biblical hopes are also modern hopes. The birth of Christ still confronts all people with the challenge to hope in God alone and the need for courage to act in accordance with that hope. In other words, Christ's birth confronts us with the fact that God had made things new. Will we live according to the new order God has established in his son?

It would be easy to study world history and conclude that the Christmas message has been missed, or that because certain situations do not seem to have changed, they will never change. If we allow ourselves to think that way, we run many risks — the risk of losing hope, the risk of depending on ourselves and succumbing to vengeance as the only way out of conflict, the risk of deciding that peace is a spiritual pipedream and not a God-given reality, the risk of absolving ourselves of responsibility for the world situation and of the solemn duty to better it.

Taken seriously, Advent and Christmas mitigate all those risks by reminding us once again of the good God does, even in the deepest darkness.

On New Year's Day, I read a meditation written in 1945 by Jesuit Father Alfred Delp shortly before he was executed by the Nazis on the false charge that he had conspired in an attempt on Hitler's life. Titled "The Shaking Reality of Advent," the essay is full of hope.

"Walking up and down in my cell, three paces this way and three paces that way, with my hands in irons and ahead of me an uncertain fate, I have a new and different understanding of God's promise of redemption and release.… The horror of these times would be unendurable unless we kept being cheered and set upright again by the promises that are spoken."

The promises of God, proclaimed by prophets, angels, apostles and the Lord himself, speak to us unrelentingly of the way things are, in their deepest reality. They give us the vision of God's order of things, and of God's grace at work, when the world situation or our personal situation would otherwise obscure this truth. God's promises are not just indications of "where he is taking us" and "what he will do"; they are proclamations of where we are now, and what he is doing now. They set us upright again.

Awareness of God's promises makes us messengers, just as he sent angels to bear glad tidings to an ancient people. Delp writes, "So many need their courage strengthened, so many are in despair and in need of consolation, there is so much harshness that needs a gentle hand and an illuminating word, so much loneliness crying out for a word of release, so much loss and pain in search of inner meaning. God's messengers know of the blessing that the Lord has cast like seed into these hours of history."

God has cast his seed of blessing into our hour of history as well. My daily prayer list is one way I work with him to make his blessing known and lived. I pray that those who hold the weight of the world in their hands will think beyond themselves and desire something better for their people. God has many ways of setting us upright, and none of them works better than trusting in his promises. They give us bearings, as lighthouses on a raging sea. And because we know those promises and believe with all our hearts that they are true, we proclaim them.

> *God has many ways of setting us upright, and none of them works better than trusting in his promises.*

Delp knew that we messengers of hope are not simply to tell others of the peace the son of God has come to bring. If we believe in his promises and in his coming, we will be people of peace in every situation we confront each day. Our humble, practical love of others will vigorously protest the violence that holds so tight a grip on our time. We will be like John the Baptist, shouting out the Advent of God in a world where nothing seems to have changed for millennia.

But things have changed — forever — because of the birth of Christ, and we know it. Delp wrote that "Advent's holiest consolation is that the angel's annunciation met with a ready heart" in Mary. In 2003, may our hearts stand always ready to take God at his Word.

January 11, 2003

Christmas is almost over, but not the Light

As I was sitting in my recliner one night several weeks ago, a flash of light shone through the window and caught my peripheral vision. Startled, I turned my head in that direction and caught a brief glimpse of what looked like a meteor racing across the sky. Fireworks? No, I thought, this was something different. I would check the newspaper in the morning.

Sure enough, it was a meteor that had been visible across much of northern Arkansas. It was a fascinating sight, fleeting but brilliant, and it reminded me that there is much in creation to admire in awe and wonder. God's light shines everywhere, in more ways than I can count.

My Christmas tree will remain in place until January 11, the feast of the Baptism of the Lord and the end of the Christmas season. The lights on my tree have created a pleasant atmosphere in the house, and I have enjoyed having them around for the past few weeks. I will miss them when the tree comes down.

It is no accident that we use light to celebrate Christ's birth, because the liturgy does the same. At Christmas midnight Mass, we heard the beautiful passage from Isaiah (9:1-6) announcing that "The people who walked in darkness have seen a great light; upon those who dwelt in the land of gloom a light has shone." At morning Mass, the Evangelist John (1:1-18) proclaimed, "This life was the light of the human race; the light shines in the darkness, and the darkness has not overcome it." And on Epiphany, Isaiah (60:1-6) again announced, "Rise up in splendor, Jerusalem! Your light has come, the glory of the Lord shines upon you" — and, of course, we heard the captivating account of Magi guided by an eastern star.

Light is everywhere during Christmas, and our candles and electric lights can remind us of the birth of the Light of the World. He is not like a meteor, however, which flashes briefly across the sky but then evaporates. He is the light that illuminates the deepest darkness, the light which cannot be overcome, the luminous glory of God himself, the star that guides everyone who looks to him in faith. Christmas proclaims: the Light is here, and here to stay.

We bask in his light when we pray. It is in his light that we stop groping in the darkness and discover where we are standing. Our prayer is joined to his (don't we pray "through Christ our Lord"?), for he gives to the many events and circumstances of our lives the warm light of hope, peace and strength. The Lord has come to us.

His light is here to stay, to re-create creation, to sustain and nourish what he first created before time began.

The important thing about understanding prayer as basking in the light of Jesus is that we do not turn to prayer only in times of need. Daily, spontaneous, simple prayer — prayer for no "reason" at all, if you will — is the way to grow in our relationship with Jesus. His light is here to stay, to re-create creation, to sustain and nourish what he first created before time began.

He is also here to re-create us. It is ironic that when the trees and lights are taken down, we sometimes feel sad that Christmas is over, as if we must now return to a former, less satisfying life. But the Light who is Christ cannot be extinguished. He is to be carried within as a torch, flashed as a beacon, prayed as if basking in the sun, lived as a new life … throughout the year.

Would that our homes would shine with his light all year round, and even more so after the Christmas trees have come down.

Meteors flash
and vanish,
bulbs twinkle
and are extinguished,
but never The Light.

Shepherds, illumined,
return to field and flock.
Magi, enlightened,
go home on camels' backs.
Business as usual?
No, not the same,
ever again.

Invincible Light,
dawn in darkness,
seed of prayer,
warm and grow us
to Your image.
You pitched Your tent
in the sun
so no one could miss you.
You have come to stay,
— forever —
and we, with you.
Amen.

January 10, 2004

We hold many people close in our hearts

During Christmas dinner, my sister, Sally, did something I have heard her do many times: she called her son, Joel, "Peter." I would like to say she only calls him "Peter" when she's angry at him — a subconscious reminder of being angry at me when I was a kid — but that would not be true. I think it's simply force of habit. She's known me longer than she's known him, and there I am again, sitting at her supper table.

Some former parishioners have three children: Louis, Walter and Mary Margaret. Many times after Mass, as we gathered for coffee and donuts in the parish hall, I watched their mom round up the boys, either to make them behave or to prepare them for going home. "Louis Walter!" she would say, as if the two were one person. It was easier that way, I suppose, since they were typically up to something together.

I have noticed that many moms and dads do a kind of roll call before reaching the name of the child with whom they want to communicate. "Michael, Joseph, Katie, Brian, Anna," they hurriedly call out, usually in birth order, until they hit the name of the child whose attention they're seeking. The kids are used to it.

At a recent meeting with several priests and deacons, all of whom I know well, I repeatedly confused two of their names. We had a good laugh. Then one of them unwittingly started doing the same, and the laughter grew louder.

Force of habit, disciplinary technique, frustration, hurry,

simple confusion? Perhaps a combination of factors. But this past weekend, I began to wonder if there's not something else at play.

As a kind of annual finale to the Christmas season, I take another look at the cards I have received, enjoy the enclosed notes and photographs, and say a prayer for those who have written me. I smile as I see how the kids have grown, as I read how the wedding went, as I learn of prayers answered and new intentions to be lifted to the Lord.

What's interesting is that the experience is not like receiving news or information for my head, but rather like feeling memories and emotional ties well up from my heart. In other words, Christmas greetings bring forth from within something that is always there, very near the surface: love for family and friends. I realize that I am literally "filled" with the wonderful people God has placed in my path. Though they may be far away, and though I may not have seen them for years, they are always close, in my heart and prayers.

I realize that I am literally "filled" with the wonderful people God has placed in my path.

It seems that my experience as priest and bishop is like that of St. Paul, who maintained close ties to the people he encountered in traveling and preaching. His letters to communities and friends are clear evidence of those ties. He writes to the Christians at Philippi, "It is right that I should think this way about all of you, because I hold you in my heart, you who are all partners with me in grace." (Philippians 1:7) And to the Romans, "God is my witness, whom I serve with my spirit in proclaiming the gospel of his Son, that I remember you constantly, always asking in my prayers that somehow by God's will I may at last find my way clear to come to you." (Romans 1:9-10)

He begins and ends letters with greetings to and from the "beloved," "co-workers," "fellow slaves," and "fellow prisoners"

— expressions of close relationships and common faith. He often mentions specific names of friends and loved ones: Timothy and Titus, both "my true child in faith," "my child Onesimus, whose father I have become in my imprisonment," Tychicus, "my beloved brother, trustworthy minister, and fellow slave in the Lord," Aristarchus; Mark; Justus; Epaphras, "one of you, a slave of Christ," Luke, "the beloved physician," and Demas. Strange names, perhaps, to us; but not to Paul. They rolled effortlessly from his tongue, the names of family members and friends who filled his heart. No matter where he traveled, they were never far from him in Christ.

I think we sometimes confuse the names of loved ones because God has made our hearts so expansive that we hold them very close all the time. It doesn't take much for them to burst spontaneously from our subconscious and into just about any conversation.

I unplugged my Christmas lights on the evening of January 11, the feast of the Baptism of the Lord, but not my Christmas memories or fondness for those who fill my heart. With Paul, I say:

"And this is my prayer: that your love may increase ever more and more in knowledge and every kind of perception, to discern what is of value, so that you may be pure and blameless for the day of Christ, filled with the fruit of righteousness that comes through Jesus Christ for the glory and praise of God." (Philippians 1:9-11)

There's a final expression that comes to mind, this one uniquely Southern in style. Several of my aunts are fond of saying, "Tell your mama and them hell-o." Names are not necessary here, and there is no confusion. I know well who they're talking about. We hold "them" close, always in our hearts.

January 17, 2004

SEASONS OF THE CHURCH: LENT-EASTER

What is at stake for Catholics this Lent?

A s I prayed the opening prayer at Mass for the first Sunday of Lent, I realized once again how much I have to learn.

"Father, through our observance of Lent,
Help us to understand the meaning
Of your Son's death and resurrection,
And teach us to reflect it in our lives."

The liturgical year continuously exposes us to every aspect of the mystery of Christ — not because we best understand his life, death, and resurrection in chronological order, but because by being continuously exposed to Christ, we allow him to enter more deeply into our lives. The same lesson I learn this year can be deepened next year, both because I have had new experiences, and because I have allowed Christ to help me understand them in his light.

I would like to offer a "Lenten Primer" in this and next week's column, to outline what is at stake during this season. It seems to me that such a primer would include the following elements:

■ The reality of evil and of the Evil One: Satan was at first a good angel, created by God. But by free, deliberate choice, he and the other demons radically and irrevocably rejected God. He is a liar who wants to draw us away from friendship with God, and it was through him that sin and death entered the world. We must face the truth that Satan exists, that he is ever on the prowl, and that we are targets of his seductions.

To forget that he exists, or to reduce him to a mere literary personification of evil, is to open ourselves wide to his tricks.

■ The recognition of original sin: We cannot tamper with the revelation of original sin without undermining our understanding of the mystery of Christ. Adam was given original holiness and justice by God — and not for himself alone but for all human nature. He and Eve lost that grace by preferring themselves over God. By giving in to Satan's seductions, they committed a personal sin, which affected the human nature they would then transmit to their descendants in a fallen state. Original sin is "contracted" and not "committed" — it is a state and not an act. This state in which we are born leaves us subject to ignorance, suffering and death, and inclined to sin.

■ The reality of personal sin: Baptism imparts the life of Christ's grace, erases original sin and turns us back toward God. However, the consequences of original sin (our weakened nature and inclination to sin) remain, and we confront our sinfulness in concrete situations. Lent invites us to face ourselves squarely in the mirror and admit that we have sinned — that by deliberate choice, we have at times turned away from God. We cannot say, as Adam and Eve did, that "the devil made me do it." He tempted us to sin, but we take responsibility for the wrong we have done and humbly ask God and those we have offended to forgive us.

■ Human persons are fundamentally good: Original sin has wounded human nature but has not totally corrupted it. All of us are made in God's image and likeness — created in freedom for freedom, created in love for love. All that God created is good, and God never falls out of love for us.

■ The power of Satan is not infinite: Satan is only a creature and cannot prevent the building up of God's reign. He is the cause of great harm, but he cannot overpower God, whose strength and gentleness guide human and cosmic history. It is a mystery that God permits diabolical activity, but "we know that all things work for good for those who love God."

(Romans 8:28) We are to fiercely avoid the ways of Satan, wisely recognize his temptations for the lies they are, and humbly cling to God. We are not equipped to battle Satan alone, and we should not try. Like Jesus, we look to our Heavenly Father for strength in the fight against evil. He will keep us safe.

We are not equipped to battle Satan alone, and we should not try.

■ The Son of God saves us: God promised a redeemer to humankind, but he went beyond all expectations in sending his own Son. Jesus is the "second Adam," because in him human nature was restored to its original holiness. "Just as through one transgression, condemnation came upon all, so through one righteous act, acquittal and life came to all. For just as through the disobedience of one person the many were made sinners, so through the obedience of one the many will be made righteous." (Romans 5:18-19) By his death on the cross, he put an end to death's power over us.

■ The call to conversion: By announcing and ushering in God's reign, Jesus won back what was lost by original sin — that original holiness first enjoyed by Adam and Eve. By his death and resurrection, he set us once again on the path of God and invites us to renounce the seductions of Satan, and to give glory to his Father in all things — in heart and in action.

These are basic Christian themes, which must be grasped in order to comprehend the meaning of Christ's death and resurrection, and to begin to understand how to reflect it in our lives. Next week I will explore how life gives us many opportunities to do so.

March 15, 2003

Becoming powerless, humble, forgiving

M y father used to joke about the response he would receive after finding a shattered glass in the garbage can. "What happened to the glass?" he would ask us kids. "It broke," one of us would answer. No one claimed responsibility. It just broke.

Last week, I began this "Lenten Primer" by explaining that Lent highlights what is at stake in our salvation. It is not pleasant to write about Satan, evil and sin; but if we do not confront those realities — the brokenness of humanity — we will not understand the blessedness of salvation. Lent invites us to grasp the magnitude of Christ's victory over sin, but it also invites us to come to terms with our personal battle with evil. This week, I would like to focus on some practical ramifications of that battle.

Every genuine intention to grow spiritually is a response to God's grace. In other words, we don't come up with such desires on our own. If we discover in ourselves a desire to be better persons, the source of that desire is God, already at work — and what God inspires in us, he will bring to completion. All we need do is cooperate with him.

That is why Lent is a time of hope: our yearning to be better is a response to God's mercy already at work in us. His merciful love, ever-present, attracts us. Our sorrow for sin is at the same time an attraction to the Lord Jesus, who desires that we share in his victory: "I have told you this so that you might have peace in me. In the world you will have trouble, but take courage, I have conquered the world." (John 16:33)

Quoting an early Christian hymn, Paul reminded the Colossians that "all things were created through him and for him. He is before all things, and in him all things hold together… He is the beginning, the firstborn from the dead." (cf. Colossians 1:15-20) All humankind is included in Christ's act of atonement, because he is the new Adam, the head of humankind. What he has done "for the world," he has done "for us." And what he has done "for us," he asks us to do "for one another."

It is not unusual to have a sense of powerlessness when trying to combat sin. That is a good thing, for if we think we can do it on our own, we will never submit our weakness to God.

We do not focus on our weakness for its own sake, but so that we may submit it to the power of God.

Paul prayed three times for the Lord to remove his thorn in the flesh, and the Lord responded, "My grace is sufficient for you, for power is made perfect in weakness." Paul wrote, "I will rather boast most gladly of my weakness, in order that the power of Christ may dwell with me." (2 Corinthians 12:8-9) We do not focus on our weakness for its own sake, but so that we may submit it to the power of God.

The recognition of our powerlessness does something extraordinary in us: it makes us humble. When we recognize that every good inspiration comes from God, when we admit that we are freed of sin not by our own effort but by him, we begin to realize that we have judged others harshly. "Why do you notice the splinter in your brother's eye, but fail to perceive the wooden beam in your own eye? Remove the wooden beam from your eye first; then you will see clearly to remove the splinter from your brother's eye." (Matthew 7:3-5)

Humility also involves letting go of the need to cast blame.

When something goes wrong, it is important to guard against the tendency to presume the guilt of others without evidence, to obsessively search out "who done it," while neglecting our responsibility to be instruments of healing. Sometimes it simply doesn't matter who did it. Perhaps no one did it. Sometimes things "just break." We are all among the guilty, but the Lord Jesus never sought to cast blame. Instead, he brought healing.

While original sin caused divisions in humankind, Christ came to make us one again. Thus, if we have recognized the power of God's mercy, we are called to be reconciled with one another, to forgive. Learning forgiveness is not optional for disciples of Jesus — it is a commandment. Jesus' command of forgiveness often becomes another occasion to recognize our powerlessness, for true forgiveness is not easy. We must forgive, but we cannot forgive on our own; therefore we submit ourselves to God's grace. "Lord, I cannot forgive him. I do not want to forgive her. May your mercy flow through me, so that I may forgive."

We have frequent occasion to join in arguments, to be sarcastic in speech or to gossip. We should never underestimate the harm done through divisive, contentious behavior, even on the smallest scale. Run from petty conflict! Refuse to engage in any conversation designed to divide, accuse or draw up sides. Otherwise, we simply demonstrate that we have not yet recognized, or have forgotten, our personal need for mercy. We have forgotten that Satan likes to tear apart what Christ has brought together.

Jesus took upon himself our guilt, our blame, and in their place, he left love. This Lent, may we drop the stones we were about to cast at others and receive God's mercy with open hands, that we might become merciful.

March 22, 2003

Peeling back layers of sinfulness to find God

E very Lent in the monasteries of the Orthodox Church, a seventh century work titled "The Ladder of Divine Ascent" is read aloud to the monks. It was written by St. John Climacus (literally, John of the Ladder, after the name of his book), while he was abbot of the Monastery of St. Catherine, which sits at the foot of Mount Sinai. In the Eastern Orthodox Church its popularity equals that of The Imitation of Christ in the Roman Catholic Church; and with the exception of the Bible, there is no book in Orthodox Christianity that has been studied, copied, and translated more than The Ladder of Divine Ascent.

John Climacus presents holiness as a ladder of 30 steps which each of us must ascend. Each rung of the ladder reflects a lesson, virtue or grace encountered as one follows the footsteps of Christ. John takes us from Renunciation through Obedience, Penitence, Anger, Slander, Falsehood, Lust, Insensitivity, Fear, Pride, Simplicity, Humility, and Prayer to the 30th step, Love.

I was introduced to the Ladder about 15 years ago. Taking my copy off the shelf recently, I noticed how many passages I had marked for special emphasis. One passage in Step 5, "On Penitence," has always stayed with me: "Repentance is the renewal of baptism and a contract with God for a fresh start in life... [It] is the daughter of hope and the refusal to despair."

Contrition is called "perfect" when its motive is love for God above all else. Confession of one's sins is at the same time confession of faith in the mercy of God. Repentance is both turning away from sin and turning toward God. Conversion involves looking back at where one has been and forward to where one is headed.

I bring out these points because we Christians dare to look at our sinfulness only in the light of God. To examine the wrong I have done, to delve into the reasons for acting as I have, and to resolve to do better can be helpful psychological exercises; but they are not the same as repentance. In fact, dwelling on my faults can be demoralizing and paralyzing if I have no higher purpose than to define some psychological category under which I fall. Moreover, if I think the way out of sinfulness is simply greater effort on my part, I will soon be filled with either pride at my success or frustration at my failure. The opposite of sin is not my effort or virtue, but the grace of God.

Dwelling on my faults can be demoralizing and paralyzing if I have no higher purpose than to define some psychological category under which I fall.

Repentance involves looking at myself through the eyes of God, with the goal of giving myself totally to him, step by step. Repentance is a way of marveling at the greatness of God, which I can discover by admitting my smallness; it is a way of discovering God's infinite love for me, a sinner; it is the path to love-in-practice, as I learn to be as merciful to others as God is to me. In other words, repentance is not about self-improvement. It is about growth in God.

That is why St. John Climacus wrote, "Repentance is the refusal to despair." Through repentance, we give ourselves to God, who forgives the unforgivable debt, searches out the lost sheep, and never tires of welcoming home the wayward son or daughter. Jesus said that is the way of our heavenly father! For the Christian, then, sorrow for sin goes hand-in-hand with joy in God.

Recognizing all of this, we embark on a life of conversion.

Conversion means letting God draw us closer to himself, leaving behind those sins, attitudes, perspectives, false gods, false beliefs, and hurts that have obscured our view of life's true purpose; it means embracing a new way of living according to the truth. Conversion unmasks the deceit of temptation and the folly of sin, and reveals the goodness of God. It leads to spiritual growth and peace. It is a life-long process.

How does God draw us to himself? Through the teaching of Jesus, prayer, the guidance of the Church, the gentle prodding of those who love us, the inspiring witness of others, remorse over our sinfulness, even feelings of utter helplessness when faced with a problem — in other words, any way he can grab our attention. We discover the surprising truth that our sinfulness occasioned the outpouring of God's love in Jesus Christ, we grow in hope that we are on the way to a better life, and we commit ourselves to that way.

It should not discourage us when we find ourselves retracing the same steps over and over again, when we discover new sins or layers of sinfulness we did not know existed. Discovering the depths of our sin helps us see the heights of God's love. The fruit of conversion is that we begin to notice that being near God and living the life of Christ brings us the fulfillment we have been unable to find any other place.

St. John Climacus knew God can overcome any flaws we uncover in our lives; in fact, it is only through his light that we uncover them. The task is to be humble enough to admit our powerlessness to heal ourselves, then let God take charge. It is never too late to renew our baptismal promises and make a fresh start. Repentance is the daughter of hope, the refusal to despair. Conversion is the way home, and the father's longing for us literally draws us there.

March 24, 2001

Are you in the game or watching from your seat?

"If you build it, he will come." For those who have seen "Field of Dreams," these words evoke a fantasy about an Iowa farmer who builds a baseball diamond in the middle of a cornfield.

Hearing a mysterious voice whisper them, he feverishly embarks on the baseball project, then travels the country looking for clues to its meaning. When he returns home, he discovers long-deceased baseball heroes playing in his field. The movie is about folks finding their way in life ("Go the distance"), relationships between fathers and sons ("Ease his pain"), and charges of corruption ("Say it ain't so, Joe"), set in a cornfield where ghosts practice baseball.

"Win one for the Gipper."

Notre Dame fans will recognize this famous line from the pep talk given by Knute Rockne to his 1928 team and immortalized in "Knute Rockne: All American." Plagued with injuries and about to take on Army, the Irish huddle with Rockne in the locker room, where he gives his legendary speech. He tells them about George Gipp, the greatest player he had ever coached, who died in 1920 of a severe case of strep throat.

Near death, Gipp had said, "I've got to go, Rock. It's all right. I'm not afraid. Some time, Rock, when the team is up against it, when things are wrong and the breaks are beating the boys, tell them to go in there with all they've got and win just one for the Gipper. I don't know where I'll be then, Rock, but I'll know about it, and I'll be happy."

The Irish defeated Army, 12-6, stirred by Rockne's moving account of Gipp's deathbed request. "This is the day, and you are the team," he told them. Rockne knew that if they could not win by talent, they could win by inspiration and passion.

Many lines from sports movies are memorable because they evoke images of discipline and drive, goal and gumption. Whether the stories are true or not, they entertain and motivate us.

St. Paul often used sports images to teach the meaning of Christian discipline:

"Do you not know that the runners in the stadium all run in the race, but only one wins the prize? Run so as to win. Every athlete exercises discipline in every way. They do it to win a perishable crown, but we an imperishable one. Thus I do not run aimlessly; I do not fight as if I were shadowboxing. No, I drive my body and train it, for fear that, after having preached to others, I myself should be disqualified." (1 Corinthians 9:24-27)

"But you, man of God … pursue righteousness, devotion, faith, love, patience and gentleness. Compete well for the faith." (1 Timothy 6:11-12)

"An athlete cannot receive the winner's crown except by competing according to the rules." (2 Timothy 2:5)

"I have competed well; I have finished the race; I have kept the faith. From now on the crown of righteousness awaits me, which the Lord, the just judge, will award to me on that day, and not only to me, but to all who have longed for his appearance." (2 Timothy 4:6-8)

Teaching about the discipline needed to condition oneself for the kingdom of God, early Christian writers borrowed a term from the world of Greek sport: askesis — "practice," "bodily exercise," and "athletic training." The English word "asceticism" is derived from askesis.

Christian asceticism includes bodily conditioning — fasting and abstaining from meat, for example. It trains us to reach beyond the satisfaction of our appetites to the fulfillment of our deepest hunger. But as Paul taught, asceticism also includes the spiritual and emotional conditioning of shedding whatever is incompatible with Christ (bickering, envy and slander, for example) and practicing virtues like patience, gentleness and devotion. Anyone who has put Paul's teaching to work knows that doing so requires discipline and prayer. Grace is the essential requirement.

> *It trains us to reach beyond the satisfaction of our appetites to the fulfillment of our deepest hunger.*

The goal of Christian asceticism is to bring every aspect of life into conformity with the ways of God. Long ago, Abram left the land of his kinsfolk and bravely set out in obedience to God's command. The Israelites abandoned the relative comfort of Egypt to undergo the hardships of a desert journey, prodded by the promises of God.

Athletic training strives to put the body in such shape that it appears and performs optimally; it is an end in itself. Christian asceticism strives to put the whole person into such shape that he or she allows God to work his marvels; God, therefore, is its "end."

I am writing this column a few hours before the start of Super Bowl XXXVIII, a game famous as much for its television commercials as for its athletic competition. I'm tempted to reflect on another famous sports movie line — "Show me the money!" — but I won't.

This afternoon's hype suggests askesis of another plane. Do I devote all I have to God? Have I surrendered all my goals to him? Am I training for the kingdom?

Christian asceticism is not a spectator sport. It is characterized by the disciplined determination of Paul, the gutsy obedience of Abraham, even the meandering attention of the Israelites. Neither is it its own origin or its own end. Its purpose is inspired and fulfilled only by the sacrificial love of Jesus, whose crown was made of thorns — and whose prize is everlasting.

February 7, 2004

Applying wisdom can be clumsy, messy

Last week I had the pleasure of joining a Little Rock family for dinner. The food was delicious, and the company could not have been more delightful.

Present were mom and dad, their four small children and dad's parents. We enjoyed stories of soccer games and patron saints, of parenting tips and favorite recipes, of dance recitals and violin lessons. The 5-month-old demonstrated his acrobatic skills, and there was even an impromptu concert.

We began the meal with adults and baby in the dining room and the other three kids in the play room, but the separation did not last long. One by one, the little ones joined us — chicken nuggets, French fries and all. Peter, who is "almost three," was second to come to the table to ask his mom if he could eat with us. "Sure," she said.

Within seconds, he appeared at the door of the dining room, sporting a huge smile — and his plate full of food flat against his chest. He had been careful and resolute; he was not going to drop any of his supper on the floor. We watched as his dad gently peeled the plate from the front of his T-shirt, revealing a huge ketchup stain, flat fries and smushed nuggets.

We all had a good laugh, and no one was angry. Peter had done exactly as he had been told, and with great care and determination. What better way to protect your supper than to hold it tight to your chest?

Life is full of opportunities to learn how to put important lessons into practice. At times we misunderstand a lesson altogether, while at other times we understand it but ignore it. At times we mistakenly assume we have already mastered the lesson, while at other times we are frustrated out of fear we will never get it right.

Most of the time, however, we do understand, or at least we want to understand. And with the best of intentions, we try to apply what we've learned, with grit and determination. Still, the results can be embarrassing, and we may feel as though we're all thumbs.

I think God smiles lovingly at our clumsy attempts to learn his wisdom and apply it to life. Scripture often shows how God deals with us patiently, as a mother or father cares for a child. One of my favorite biblical images comes from the prophet Isaiah.

> Fear not, I am with you;
> be not dismayed; I am your God.
> I will strengthen you, and help you,
> and uphold you with my right hand
> of justice…
> For I am the Lord, your God,
> Who grasp your right hand;
> It is I who say to you, 'Fear not,
> I will help you.'
> Fear not, O worm Jacob,
> O maggot Israel;
> I will help you, says the Lord.
> (Isaiah 41:10, 13-14)

Odd as it might seem, "worm" and "maggot" are terms of endearment in this context. This section of Isaiah refers to the return of Israel's exiles from Babylon to Jerusalem, and how God will clear the road for them.

Just as we might call the baby squirming in our arms a "little worm," or an energetic toddler a "monkey," God tenderly looked upon Israel, in need of his protection, love and guidance.

Easter is that time when we mark our return from the exile of sin and resolve to follow Jesus, the Way. The Christian road is not easy, nor are our footsteps always sure. We trip and skin our knees, lose our clothes and waste our food, forget hard-learned lessons and get discouraged by our weakness.

How often does your heart go out to your children, and in how many ways? Probably beyond counting.

But God reads our hearts, smiles on our efforts and says, "Fear not, I will help you." He stretches out his hand to lift us up.

Whether they realize it or not, mothers and fathers possess an instinctive insight into the mind and heart of God. How often does your heart go out to your children, and in how many ways? Probably beyond counting.

So it is with God — only his heart goes out to us even more often, more deeply, and more patiently.

As you love your kids, so do you taste the love of God. And like you, he doesn't mind at all when we end up with supper on our T-shirts.

"See what love the Father has bestowed on us that we may be called the children of God. Yet so we are." (1 John 3:1)

May 17, 2003

When contrition becomes less about me

My favorite Act of Contrition is the one I learned as a child. "O my God, I am heartily sorry for having offended thee..." It's the one I pray every evening before going to bed.

I cannot remember a time when I did not experience remorse after having done something wrong. That claim is not as noble as it sounds, since the motives for my remorse, and the offenses for which I have felt it, have passed through many stages over the years. In fact, the Act of Contrition actually refers to the developmental stages of my contrition.

"... and I detest all my sins because I dread the loss of heaven and the pains of hell." I learned very early that misbehavior had unpleasant consequences. Whether it was a spanking, or a silent trip to my room, or grounding when I would have preferred playing with my friends, punishment proved to be a very effective deterrent to misbehavior in my case. As a youngster looking down the long road to eternity, I definitely did not want to find out what "the pains of hell" were all about. It was easy to be sorry for my sins because I did not want to go to hell.

At some point I began to realize that there were better reasons to be sorry for my sins than the avoidance of hell. I pondered the next words in the Act of Contrition, "... but most of all because they offend thee, my God, who art all good and deserving of all my love." To be honest, there was a long period when I prayed those words but did not feel the reasons for sorrow they expressed. I wanted to feel sorry for my sins just because I loved God and did not want to offend him, but I was not there yet. I continued to pray the words and added a parallel prayer that God would help me feel sorrow for that "most of all" reason that eluded me.

Gradually — I cannot say when — God answered my prayer. I began to understand sins as offenses against "someone." I noticed that lies were not only wrong in themselves, but that they could hurt people. I noticed that selfishness was not only against the rules of my family, but that it deprived someone else of his or her share. I learned that not doing my duty (homework or housework) meant not only a bad grade or a stern reprimand, but that it made me less than I could be and forced others to unhappily carry my load. And that was just the beginning.

In other words, I discovered the personal nature of sin — "personal" in the sense that I am personally responsible for the wrong I do, but "personal" also in the sense that my wrongdoing hurts, offends, or disappoints "someone." I suppose this development took place as I became aware of relationships as give-and-take propositions, when I stopped insisting on my place at the center of the universe. I also quietly observed that my parents' love did not end when I offended them; I saw that my teachers did not give up on me when I failed a test.

However, I did not yet measure up to the "most of all" words of the Act of Contrition. There was still significant selfishness in my motives. Yes, I was sorry for my sins because they offended someone — but I still thought of him or her as someone who had a relationship to "me."

Was it a high school Search weekend? Was it during prayers one night? Was it listening to a sermon or reading a book? I don't know, but a time came when I experienced God's personal, perfectly selfless love for me, and then I knew I wanted to love him back. "... but most of all, because they offend thee, my God, who art all good and deserving of all my love." My sins not only offended a host of people; most of all, they offended God, who loved me despite my sin. God, whom I wanted to love with all my heart. The motives for my remorse had begun to mature, as the reasons for my contrition flowed from my love for God. This was all God's doing, in answer to my prayer.

The maturing of my own contrition helped me understand that God patiently takes what he can get from us. In other words, if the only reason I can muster to avoid evil is that I don't want to be punished, so be it. At least I am avoiding evil, and that pleases God. But God knows that in order to be happy and at peace, we eventually need purer motives than fear, since the avoidance of evil simply out of fear can quickly turn to anger and apathy. For those open to it, God's grace can refine mixed motives into one pure motive. Love. Then love reveals that there is a lot more to being a Christian than avoiding evil.

But God knows that in order to be happy and at peace, we eventually need purer motives than fear, since the avoidance of evil simply out of fear can quickly turn to anger and apathy.

When contrition becomes less about "me" and more about "thee," it becomes genuine. Then it can mature into repentance. And then we have begun the path of conversion.

"I firmly resolve, with the help of thy grace, to confess my sins, to do penance, and to amend my life." Next week I will reflect on the sacrament of penance as a sign and a means of repentance. The following week I will reflect on conversion as a way of life.

March 10, 2001

In the sacrament of penance, Christ repairs his body

The Mount of Olives offers a splendid view of Jerusalem, just across the Kidron Valley. The most imposing feature of Jerusalem today is the Moslem Dome of the Rock, with its royal blue tiles and brilliant roof. In Jesus' day, however, the Temple stood on that spot, having recently been rebuilt by Herod; and from the Mount of Olives Jesus would have enjoyed a prime view of its monolithic columns, its towers of precious marble, its gleaming bronze doors and statues, its ornamentation of gems and gold-leaf reflecting sunlight on every side.

As a child of 12, Jesus had visited the Temple with his parents, remaining behind to engage the teachers in discussion. Many years later, it was in the shadow of this magnificent sight, on the Mount of Olives, that he wept for Jerusalem.

"As he drew near, he saw the city and wept over it, saying, 'If this day you only knew what makes for peace — but now it is hidden from your eyes. For the days are coming upon you when your enemies will raise a palisade against you; they will encircle you and hem you in on all sides... because you did not recognize the time of your visitation.'" (Luke 19:41-44)

Near the spot where Jesus spoke these words is the chapel called "Dominus Flevit" ("The Lord Wept"). Built in 1955, it rests on the excavations of a Byzantine monastery, surrounded by tombs bearing Hebrew and Christian symbols. One wall of the chapel faces Jerusalem, and through its large, clear windows one has a panoramic view of the city.

Jesus wept because the people of Jerusalem did not recognize the one in their midst and the gift he had come to bring; they did not realize who and what they were rejecting. As he wept that day, I wonder if he also felt the burden of our rejection, if he anticipated the sadness we visit upon ourselves when we sin.

I mention this because we best understand sin in the context of grace. When we discover that God's love is freely given and that he desires nothing but our happiness, we unmask the folly and ingratitude of sin. St. Irenaeus once wrote that God created us so that he might have someone in whom to place his great gifts. Jesus knew the tragedy of sin in the face of his heavenly father's gifts, so he wept for Jerusalem and for us.

We also best understand sin in the context of truth revealed to us in Jesus. In addition to being an offense against the love of God, sin is also a deliberate violation of the law of God. The Ten Commandments, the Scriptures and Church teaching illuminate the difference between good and evil. There are such things as right and wrong, and sin is a transgression against what is objectively "right" and "good."

Finally, sin has consequences. Not only do we offend God, we also offend ourselves, others, and the Church. We injure the Body of Christ by our sin, because we go against the sacred Baptismal bond that links us to Christ and every Christian. This is a concept easily understood by any family who has suffered because of the sin of one of its members. The consequences of our sin spill over to those we love.

St. Paul questioned the Romans, "What profit did you get then from the things of which you are now ashamed? The wages of sin is death." (6:21, 23) In other words, sin is a bad deal! Temptation cannot deliver what it promises, because the only wage paid by sin is death. On the other hand, "the gift of God is eternal life in Christ Jesus our Lord."

God's love has triumphed over sin, and through faith and baptism we were snatched up, forgiven, set in a right relationship with God, and showered with his gifts. Sin is an offense against

God's love, a violation of God's law, and an injury to Christ's body; but we can be restored to our baptismal state through the sacrament of penance, confession.

"I firmly resolve, with the help of thy grace, to confess my sins." When we make use of the sacrament of penance, we confess both our sins and our faith in God's mercy, humbly admitting that we have offended God and injured Christ's body.

As with the other sacraments, God imparts a special, life-changing grace through confession. It is God who gives us a contrite heart in the first place, God who inspires us to confess our sins, and God who forgives us through the sacrament of penance. We never reach the limit of his mercy, for he never tires of welcoming the prodigal son.

> *We never reach the limit of his mercy, for he never tires of welcoming the prodigal son.*

We can conjure up many reasons for not going to confession: It's been so long, I wouldn't know where to begin. Father once yelled at me. Why ask forgiveness when I know I will sin again? Why confess to a priest? I don't know what sin is any more. I'm embarrassed at what I've done. I'm afraid God won't forgive me.

I offer a simple and sincere plea this Lent. Surrender yourself to the mercy of God in confession, no matter how long it's been. Knowing that contrition and forgiveness are gifts of God, why not receive them with a humble heart? This I know for sure, you will be unburdened as never before, and God will change you. He will give you the grace of conversion.

Among the Greek inscriptions found in the ancient ruins at Dominus Flevit was this one from the donor of a mosaic: "Simeon, Friend of Christ, has fabricated and decorated this oratory for the expiation of his sins and for the repose of his brothers ..."

Jesus wept, but they were tears of mercy.

March 17, 2001

Crucifix is also a reminder of the Father

Perhaps you're familiar with the Salvador Dalí paintings of Christ on the cross. He titled one of them, "The Christ of St. John of the Cross," because his inspiration had come from a sketch by the 16th century Spanish mystic and poet.

One day, while he was chaplain of the monastery of the Incarnation at Avila, John of the Cross was praying in a loft overlooking the church. Receiving a vision, he took pen, ink and grainy parchment and sketched what he had seen. The sketch, which survives today as the only example of John's drawings, is quite small, about 4 inches by 3 inches, with an oval border. I have a reproduction hanging in my chapel at home, and it is one of my prized possessions, though it cost about 50 cents.

It depicts Christ crucified, his cross hanging in space, leaning toward his people. The perspective is unique — Christ is seen from above, from the viewpoint of the Father looking down on his beloved Son. Try to imagine the scene from above, as John did. The Father sees the Son, his lifeless and contorted body hanging heavily forward with the weight of our sins, held to the cross only by the nails in his hands. Though the sketch is simple, John is able to give the impression that the light is coming from above and behind the cross.

To understand the meaning of the sketch it is helpful to read the poetry of John. For example, in Romance 7, "The Incarnation," he relates a conversation between the Father and the Son. Christ says,

> I will go and tell the world,
> spreading the word
> of your beauty and sweetness
> and of your sovereignty.
> I will go and seek my bride
> and take upon myself
> her weariness and labors
> in which she suffers so;
> and that she may have life
> I will die for her
> and lifting her out of that deep,
> I will restore her to you.
> (Romance 7, 9b-11)

Had not Jesus told parables about heartsick fathers racing down the roads to fetch their wayward sons? Parables about sheep lost, found and joyously carried back to the flock on shepherds' shoulders? About merciful masters who forgive impossible debts?

Had not Jesus forgiven the sins of the woman cowering in fear of those about to stone her? Had he not healed the blind and the lame, the leper and the lunatic? Had he not raised little children and friends like Lazarus from the dead, and restored them to their families?

Had not Jesus given himself so completely to others, so lavishly sacrificed himself for our sakes that he gave his all, to the end?

Had not Jesus given himself so completely to others, so lavishly sacrificed himself for our sakes that he gave his all, to the end?

And had he not said, "Whoever has seen me has seen the Father?" (John 14:9)

Looking upon Jesus, we see the very image of the Father, and we are brought into union with him. In a sense, the cross tells us that Jesus has traveled the distance we sinners have strayed from the Father in order to reclaim us and bring us home. He comes out searching for us — no matter how far we have strayed — and finding us, he restores us safely to the household of his Father. Thus, when we fix our gaze on Jesus crucified — for the cross bridges the painful distance he has searched for us — our eyes and the Father's eyes meet.

On Good Friday, we will go to church to meditate on the Lord's Passion. We will walk in quiet procession to his cross and kiss it. Perhaps this year, when we look on the cross and see God's eternal, boundless love poured out for us in sacrifice, we will be mindful that we are also looking to the Father, who sent his Son to find us and bring us home. After all, is he not looking down at his Son?

Lord, send your abundant blessing upon your people who devotedly recall the death of your Son in the sure hope of the resurrection. Grant us pardon. Bring us comfort. May our faith grow stronger, our wonder grow deeper, our love grow more sincere. Teach us to fix our gaze on the cross of Christ so that our eyes and your eyes will meet, eternally. We ask this through Christ our Lord. Amen.
(Adapted from the Good Friday Celebration of the Lord's Passion)

March 23, 2002

Slowing down enough to notice what we've lost

Until March 6 I had not worn a ring since my first year of college, when I lost my high school class ring (a few years later the person who found it offered to sell it back to me. I declined). Since then I never had a desire to wear another ring.

However, I have found that the episcopal ring holds great meaning for me. As he placed the ring on my finger at ordination, Archbishop Beltran said, "Take this ring, the seal of your fidelity. With faith and love protect the bride of God, his holy Church." Its weight and feel are a constant reminder of my vocation to be faithful to God and to you, the Church of Little Rock. The ring bears my coat of arms and motto, "Of You My Heart Has Spoken"; it was the gift of my cousins, the Pooles.

Holy Thursday afternoon I thought I lost it.

Before getting ready for the Mass of the Lord's Supper at the Cathedral, I decided to take a 15-minute "power nap" in my recliner; I leaned back and rested the back of my head in my hands. Very soon I realized I did not feel the ring on my finger.

I jumped from the chair and began searching the house for where I might have left it: the night stand, the desk, the sink. I knelt momentarily in my chapel and prayed for help.

I considered calling the people with whom I had eaten lunch but couldn't remember taking the ring off at any point during the day.

Embarrassed and frustrated, I ruminated about my carelessness, my cousins, and especially about the spiritual and sentimental value of the ring placed on my finger at ordination. I prayed some more, took deep breaths, and thought back through the day.

Then I remembered opening a package containing a gift secured with hundreds of Styrofoam pellets. I had placed all the pellets back in the box before throwing it away. Out to the garbage cart I went, thinking to myself, "How could the ring have possibly gotten into that box?" As I removed the pellets from the box, something shiny and heavy rolled to the bottom. Thank you, God. As I placed the ring back on my finger, I noticed how easily it slipped on — too easily, in fact. Better check the size.

The rest of the day I had a feeling of great relief and even greater affection for my episcopal ring and what it symbolizes. I also had an interesting feeling of gratitude that I had noticed the absence of the ring. Wearing a ring is quite new to me, but already it has become part of me; even trying to take a nap I became aware of its absence.

Good Friday morning I reviewed the chapter in the "Ceremonial of Bishops" about how a bishop conducts the Celebration of the Lord's Passion (the "Ceremonial" gives instructions, among other things, about how a bishop vests for the liturgies he celebrates throughout the year). I was stunned to read that on Good Friday "the bishop uses a simple miter, but not the ring or pastoral staff."

I had grown accustomed to the ring, but on the day of the Lord's death I am not to wear it.

That makes sense. Holy Thursday evening we stripped the altars and sanctuaries of our churches and removed the Blessed Sacrament from its usual place, as we do not celebrate the sacraments on Good Friday or Holy Saturday. The Triduum slowed us down to reflect on the Lord Jesus in the sleep of death, and we felt his absence.

What was it like for Jesus' followers in the hours and days after his death?

When she found the tomb empty, Mary Magdalene anxiously reported to Peter, "They have taken my Lord, and I don't know where they laid him." (John 20:13) She was lost without her Lord.

Even before his death, Jesus had given a foreshadowing of what was to come. When the disciples of John the Baptist asked Jesus why they and the Pharisees fasted but his disciples did not, Jesus responded, "Can the wedding guests mourn as long as the bridegroom is with them? The days will come when the bridegroom is taken away from them, and then they will fast." (Matthew 9:15)

The "Ceremonial" says, "In contemplating the cross of its Lord and Bridegroom, the Church commemorates its own origin and its mission to extend to all peoples the blessed effects of Christ's passion that it celebrates on this day in a spirit of thanksgiving for his marvelous gift." The utterly selfless gift of his life for his bride, the Church.

Doesn't all grieving contain a heavy measure of gratitude for the "marvelous gift" of the ones we've lost? It's their absence we notice, because they've become part of us.

Good Friday is a day that can be appreciated especially by husbands and wives who have lost their spouses. Doesn't all grieving contain a heavy measure of gratitude for the "marvelous gift" of the ones we've lost? It's their absence we notice, because they've become part of us.

After reading the "Ceremonial," I didn't wear the ring again until the Easter Vigil. I keenly felt its absence from my hand.

Thank you, Lord, for helping me lose my episcopal ring, and helping me find it. You taught me something about fasting, and dying, and grieving, and slowing down to pay attention on the day the world felt lost while its Savior slept in death. May I never lose sight of you, Lord, or of our bride, the Church.

April 29, 2000

Recognizing your travel companion, Jesus

Not long ago the Carmelite nuns in Little Rock gave me a book about St. John of the Cross, "The Impact of God," by Iain Matthew. They know of my affection for the writings of John and Teresa of Avila and thought I would enjoy it. I began reading it on a day spent mostly in transit, on airplanes and in airports.

Airports are places of paradox — tens of thousands of people pass through them each day, yet they can be the most impersonal and alienating places we visit. For some reason, however, traveling alone by air I experience a kind of solitude that appeals to me. Usually gregarious and the first to initiate conversations, when traveling I often sit quietly and read. After a long flight many years ago, the woman sitting next to me said, "You must be in the military." When I asked why she thought so, she said, "Because military people are always secretive." I had noticed that her husband was not in a talkative mood, so I had gone out of my way to speak to her, but apparently I had been much less talkative than she had hoped.

When on a layover, I often take the corner seat in the waiting area, or look for a gate where no one is sitting, to watch, listen and read. Children cry, announcements roar from the public address system, news flashes on a TV monitor, business people talk on cell phones, traveling companions laugh and make plans. Ironically, in such noisy settings I do some of my most concentrated and fruitful reading.

During two flights and in two airports, I read "The Impact

of God." John of the Cross was a master poet and writer, who was able to express the paradox and mystery of the spiritual life with great effect — and great affect. Painful solitude and intimate friendship, chilling dark nights warmed with God's hidden presence, "the silence of music, the mighty sound of solitude," hindrances and passageways, imprisonment and freedom, wounds and healing, deprivation and feasting — all were a part of John's experience of life and of God. It was his profound desire to be one with God which sustained his dogged spiritual quest. God's love is so sublime, he intimated, that poetry could offer only a hint of it.

John once spent nine months in prison, and it was then that he experienced a different kind of poverty, the seeming absence of God. Dragged to the limit of his personal resources, he cried out to God, "Where have you hidden?" Gradually he began to experience the presence of Christ in his imprisonment.

One of the ways he describes this emerging awareness of Christ is very appealing to me. John says it is as if we enter a dark room and sit for a few moments by ourselves, only to realize after a time that there is someone with us, someone who has been there all along, in silhouette but increasingly clear. He speaks of "a kind of companionship... which walks with the soul and gives her strength."

This image of John is helpful to me in many ways, and I often think of it when I look at the second chair in my chapel, the tabernacle and the vigil light. God is there, and he invites me to join him; as I quiet myself in prayer his peaceful presence emerges.

God is with us, a companion on the journey. Our time of prayer gives the eyes of our soul time to grow accustomed to his light and thus gradually enables us to perceive the presence of our companion and rest in his love. Perhaps our awareness of God's presence does not clarify into anything more than a silhouette — perhaps at times we do not perceive his presence at all — but in prayer we always grow in his strength.

John's image is also helpful when I find myself in the

surprising solitude of bustling airports and over-booked airplanes. Christ's presence emerges in the tense faces of passengers rushing to catch their planes, in the loving voice of a mother calling to check on her kids far away, in the ethnic features and dress of travelers from another country, and in the evident sadness of one whose life has been turned upside-down by tragedy. At such times, Christ, my traveling companion, points to his presence in others and reminds me to keep watch over them.

The Easter season is a time to allow the risen Christ to show himself to us, perhaps in unexpected ways and unsuspecting persons. A weeping Mary Magdalene first thought he was the gardener, but when he spoke her name, she cried, "Rabboni!" On the road to Emmaus, two despondent disciples failed to recognize him until he revealed himself in the breaking of bread. After Christ had risen, his disciples encountered him in many new ways, and after Pentecost they continuously discovered his presence in the Church.

There is no crowd we pass during the day that does not reveal him somehow, somewhere, in someone.

Most especially you and I have the opportunity to meet Christ in the sacraments and in prayer, for the 50 days of Easter call us to continue what we began in Lent. But this is also the time to meet Christ in his other manifestations. There is no schedule of appointments that does not include several opportunities to encounter him. There is no crowd we pass during the day that does not reveal him somehow, somewhere, in someone.

In "Sayings of Light and Love" (47), John wrote, "Lord, my God, you are not a stranger to him who does not estrange himself from you. How do they say that it is you who absent himself?"

April 21, 2001

Lean unto the Lord
for comfort this season

The "disciple Jesus loved" is an intriguing figure in the Gospel of John. He is never given a name, but it is clear that he had a profound friendship with the Lord. John refers to him directly or indirectly only about 10 times, but the significance of his presence cannot be ignored. In art, he is often shown leaning into the side of Jesus, a sign of their closeness.

At the Last Supper (John 13), after Jesus announces that one of the apostles will betray him, Peter nods to the beloved disciple (who is "reclining at Jesus' side"), signaling him to ask who the betrayer will be. When Mary Magdalene found Jesus' tomb empty (John 20), she reports the news to Peter and the beloved disciple. They hurry to the tomb themselves, but the other disciple outruns Peter. It is interesting to note that while he arrives at the tomb first, he allows Peter to enter first. John is indicating the chief place of Peter in the early Church.

After the resurrection, Jesus appears to his disciples at the Sea of Tiberius one morning at dawn, but they do not recognize him (John 21). Although they have caught no fish all night, he tells them to cast to the right side of the boat, and doing so, they haul in a great catch of fish. The beloved disciple then recognizes Jesus: "It is the Lord," he tells the others.

There is a particularly significant appearance of the beloved disciple in John 19. At the crucifixion, Jesus gives the beloved disciple to Mary as a son, and "from that hour the disciple took her into his home." By linking Mary with the beloved disciple, John is telling us something very important. Mary has been at the side of Jesus from the beginning of his public ministry at the wedding in Cana, embracing his mission and sharing his suffering. Now John shows that Mary is given a role as the mother of all Christians, who are represented by "the one whom he loved." In that sense, Mary is a symbol of the Church itself.

Mary and the beloved disciple remind us of the importance of intimate, faithful discipleship of the Lord. Jesus' profound love for them, and theirs for him, awakened in them such insight ("It is the Lord!") and fidelity ("Do whatever he tells you!") that they never left his side, even at his darkest moments. They loved him and supported him, but it was from him that they drew their strength.

They loved him and supported him, but it was from him that they drew their strength.

The Easter season is a time to enter the home of Mary and the beloved disciple and quietly savor with them what the Lord has done for us. What might they have talked about during those early days? Whatever the topic, we know it must have been stirred by their love for the Lord. There can be no doubt that their active discipleship after his death and resurrection was grounded in prayer.

In the same way, artistic depictions of the beloved disciple leaning into Jesus' side give us a beautiful image of the source of our strength for daily discipleship: prayerful friendship with our Lord. One of the early Church fathers, Evagrius, wrote: "The Lord's breast: the knowledge of God. Whoever rests on it will be a theologian." He was referring not to the scholarly study of theology but to its original meaning — "speaking about God." In other words, our faith in the Lord Jesus is best fed by intimate familiarity with him, the kind that has its origin and sustenance in prayer.

When he was incarcerated in the Tower of London, St. Thomas More asked for the grace to "lean unto the comfort of

God." (from "A Godly Meditation") I have always wondered if he was seeking to be like the beloved disciple, who drew his strength from the Lord.

St. Anselm of Canterbury once wrote, "O God, let me know you and love you so that I may find my joy in you; and if I cannot do so fully in this life, let me at least make some progress every day ... While I am here on earth let me learn to know you better, so that in heaven I may know you fully; let my love for you grow deeper here, so that there, I may love you fully." (from "The Proslogion")

I hope to spend the Easter season in the house of Mary and the beloved disciple. I want to learn to do whatever the Lord tells me. I want to lean unto his comfort at the Eucharist. I want to recognize him everywhere, however he chooses to come to me. I want to run breathlessly to his side, wherever that may be. I want to stay there, faithfully sharing his mission with Mary, Peter and the beloved disciple. I want to know and love him so well that I will always speak clearly of him, that others may also come to be his beloved.

I have so far to go, but I know the risen Lord is near, in the Church. He is my strength, and he will help me make some progress, every day.

April 24, 2003

Jesus is always waiting, thinking of us

The Sea of Galilee is a magnificent fresh-water lake, encompassed on several sides by towering mountains. The surrounding landscape is different from the rest of Israel in a number of ways. In contrast to the hot, dry desert, it has a more temperate climate and boasts an impressive array of plants and flowers. When touring the Holy Land as a seminarian, I noticed how the temperature gradually cooled as we neared the lake in our dusty un-air-conditioned bus.

This captivatingly beautiful area was a favorite of Jesus and many others of his day, including the Roman governors, who built villas there. The sixth chapter of the Gospel of John begins on the hills that gently slope upward from the sea to the mountains, where Jesus had stopped with his disciples to rest. It was springtime, and they relaxed in the lush, green grass, enjoying the sweet fragrance of orange blossoms carried aloft by cool winds blowing off the sea.

It was a perfect place to unwind, and from this perch on the hill there was an entire horizon of things for Jesus to observe — boats gliding across the water, their sails capturing the powerful breeze; fisherman paying out and pulling in nets, their catches wriggling free as they fell into the hold; clouds floating silently past, their clear reflection visible in the blue depths.

It was not long before he spotted a large crowd coming his way, drawn by the signs he had performed on the sick. Everyone had watched closely as he embarked in a boat with his disciples at Capernaum, and with an unobstructed view across the lake, they knew the boat had landed at Tiberius. They followed on foot. From the hills Jesus saw them coming, and he knew they were coming to see him.

This was no accidental meeting: they had watched him disembark and climb the mountain, and from his high resting place he saw and anticipated their approach. A crowd of more than 5,000 would have been hard to miss! As he watched and waited, Jesus thought about their aches and their hungers, their hopes and their needs. I wonder if the disciples did not watch the procession in disbelief, annoyed that they had been found.

John writes that after the thousands gathered around Jesus on the grass, he fed them until they were completely satisfied, and there were leftovers enough for anyone else who would ever be hungry. Then he slipped further up the mountain alone, for during the meal he had overheard talk of crowning him king.

When I read this passage, my reflection always returns to Jesus and the disciples resting on the beautiful mountain, bathed in the sunlit colors of a beautiful spring afternoon. Perhaps the disciples dozed, or joked around, or picked oranges. Jesus prayed and thoughtfully studied the landscape of nature and human need. For him this was all about encountering his flock and showing them the way to the Father.

It was all about the encounter — Jesus anticipating the folk irresistibly drawn to him, they letting their hunger lead them to him. Finding him, they were not disappointed, for he fed them beyond their expectations.

It is still that way. It is still all about encountering Jesus.

As we continue our Easter reflections, I would like to focus on a particular aspect of Christ's risen life. The Letter to the Hebrews teaches that Jesus lives forever to intercede for us. He holds us eternally in his heart, fixing his gaze on us, lifting us up to his Father in praise and intercession, always ready to encounter us in prayer, in the sacraments and in love. Perhaps it helps to picture his heavenly resting place as that beautiful spot high above the Sea of Galilee, but now we must keep in mind that there was also another vantage point from which he observed us — the cross. And even as our eyes are raised to heaven, we must keep in mind that in his risen life Jesus is still with us — and, because of our baptism, within us.

I often think of the risen Christ as the contemplative Christ, particularly in the reserved Blessed Sacrament. Contemplation, after all, is about love. Forever united with his Father and the Holy Spirit in love and praise, Jesus is also forever united with us, in love and grace. It is his contemplative intercession for us in the Father's presence that draws us to him, whether we realize it or not.

Perhaps we unwittingly approach prayer as a matter of calling upon God to hear us, when in fact it is the other way around.

Perhaps we unwittingly approach prayer as a matter of calling upon God to hear us, when in fact it is the other way around. We are drawn to Jesus in prayer, whether it is born of simple faith or of panicked desperation, precisely because he is forever lifting us up in prayer. He is always awaiting an encounter with us, no matter its purpose. Before we utter a word or make our way toward him, he sees us coming and waits patiently, contemplating our aches and our hungers, our hope and our need.

Just as he stretched his gaze across the vast expanse of sea beneath and watched the crowds make their way toward him, just as he saw his disciples wide-eyed with fright as he walked toward them on the water, just as he looked down at his mother and the apostle John from the cross, Jesus is always thinking about us and lifting us up to the Father.

No encounter with him is ever accidental.

May 5, 2001

Pray for persecutors, don't seek revenge

"**I**s it over yet?" When we hear those words, we often picture someone with hands cupped over eyes, shielding himself or herself from a frightening scene in a movie. Eyes remain covered until the scene is finished.

"Is it over yet?"

Such voluntary blindness is very different from turning a blind eye toward real evil, when its devastating aftermath is in plain, terrifying sight. In the first instance, we are protecting fragile emotions from images on a screen. In the second, we are face to face with evil but pretend it does not exist — as if ignoring it gives us a certain immunity to its consequences.

I wonder if we haven't blurred the distinction between images on a screen as entertainment, and real evil with real effects. For example, so much violence appears in movies and television shows that we can be seduced into believing either that all violence is imaginary, or that it is perfectly acceptable. When violence is thought to be imaginary, when it ceases to frighten us ("Is it over yet?"), we turn a blind, bored eye; and when it is deemed acceptable, it perpetuates itself in an uncontrollable spiral. Violence begets violence begets violence.

Jesus lived in a violent society, and when he told his disciples to expect hostility to the Gospel, some of them urged him to fight sword with sword. "They said, 'Lord, look, there are two swords here.' But he replied, 'Enough!'" (Luke 22:38)

Later, as he was urging his sleeping disciples (Luke says they were "sleeping from grief") to join him in prayer in the Garden of Gethsemani, a crowd arrived with Judas in front.

"His disciples realized what was about to happen, and they asked, 'Lord, shall we strike with a sword?' And one of them struck the high priest's servant and cut off his right ear. But Jesus said in reply, 'Stop, no more of this!' Then he touched the servant's ear and healed him." (Luke 22:49-51)

Jesus was sent by the Father to put an end to the unbridled reign of evil. Many of those who followed him thought it only natural that he should be a warrior Messiah, the kind who would forcefully usher in God's kingdom; they pressed him to fulfill their fantasies of conquest. But Jesus would have none of that. He knew that fighting evil on its own terms only gives it control, so he said, "Enough! Stop! No more of this!"

He knew that fighting evil on its own terms only gives it control, so he said, "Enough! Stop! No more of this!"

This demanding teaching has very practical implications. "Blessed are you when they insult you and persecute you and utter every kind of evil against you falsely because of me." "But I say to you, whoever is angry with his brother will be liable to judgment." "Settle with your opponent quickly while on the way to court with him." "But I say to you, offer no resistance to one who is evil. When someone strikes you on your right cheek, turn the other one to him as well." "But I say to you, love your enemies, and pray for those who persecute you." (cf. Matthew 5)

It was clear to those who listened to his preaching that Jesus demanded an entirely new way of thinking, an utterly new approach, a complete change of heart. It was clear to those who watched him, particularly those who witnessed his passion and death — when he bore the full, violent assault of our sin — that he practiced what he preached. It was clear to those who encountered him after the resurrection that he had not the slightest inclination to seek revenge for his death. There was only peace.

Is it clear to us who have been redeemed by God's unbridled forgiveness that violence is not God's way (and therefore not to be our way)? Do we remember that God chose not to hold our sins against us, not to respond in kind to our assaults on his love? Perhaps we have lost a sense of the incalculable dimensions of salvation. We owed a debt that could not possibly be repaid, but God paid it with the blood of his Son. We deserved condemnation, but he gave us peace.

Easter calls us to survey the unfathomable depths of God's love and ponder its incomprehensible ramifications, all the while recalling that it is this very love that saved us.

In this context, I have been pondering the recent publicity surrounding the approaching execution of Timothy McVeigh, and particularly the decision to broadcast the execution over closed-circuit television. McVeigh is guilty of an unspeakable crime, an act of violence impossible to comprehend. Equally difficult to comprehend is how the victims and their families must feel, how inconsolable their loss must be. They need and deserve our prayers.

Still, Jesus' words haunt me. "Enough! Stop! No more of this!"

It frightens me to think of what might proceed from televised executions, no matter how selective the audience. We should never turn a blind eye toward evil; crime deserves punishment, and the government has a responsibility to protect citizens from violent criminals. But the more we champion vengeance as the legitimate response to wrongdoing, the farther we travel from the way of Jesus, the Savior of the world.

April 28, 2001

Your life should be changed with Christ

A parishioner who had undergone serious surgery once showed me a letter the doctor had written his wife indicating that he had been officially released from medical care. It went something like this: "Dear Mrs. Smith, I am happy to inform you that your husband has completely recovered from surgery. There are no restrictions on his activity, except for one thing. He should never be asked to vacuum the floors. Sincerely yours, Dr. Jones." Guess who dictated the letter.

I once ran into an old friend at a picnic. He had been laid up for months after a near-fatal heart attack. "You look great," I said. "Yep," he responded, "and I feel great, too." "Has the doctor placed any restrictions on your diet?" I asked. With a mischievous smile he said, "He told me I could eat anything I want. It took me a long time to find that doctor."

It is not unusual for doctors to give patients habit-breaking, life-altering advice, particularly after recovery from serious illness: lose 20 pounds; stop smoking; get some exercise; stay away from fatty foods; cut down on alcohol consumption; no caffeine. The advice is given with a view toward maintaining and improving the patient's health — and preventing an even worse recurrence of the illness.

As hard as we try to make excuses, as much as we'd like to eat what we like and do what we like, as much as we'd like to find a doctor who will tell us what we want to hear, we know that something must change after we have recuperated from serious illness. With health comes responsibility for healthy living.

Several Gospel passages report incidents when Jesus healed or forgave and said, "Go, and sin no more." As a result of his gift, the healed and forgiven were to take up a new life. Early Christians had a similar understanding of the duty handed those who had been healed from sin and saved from death in baptism. As a result of this healing of healings, this return from the dead, Christians were to live a new life.

This is the message Paul sent to the Colossians. In a passage that reflects an ancient custom of taking off old garments and putting on new ones after being united with Christ in baptism, he wrote: "If then you were raised with Christ, seek what is above, where Christ is seated at the right hand of God. Think of what is above, not of what is on earth. For you have died, and your life is hidden with Christ in God …

"Put to death, then, the parts of you that are earthly: immorality, impurity, passion, evil desire and the greed that is idolatry … Now you must put them all away: anger, fury, malice, slander and obscene language out of your mouths. Stop lying to one another, since you have taken off the old self with its practices and have put on the new self, which is being renewed in the image of the creator.

"Put on then, as God's chosen ones … heartfelt compassion, kindness, humility, gentleness, and patience … as the Lord has forgiven you, so you must also do. And over all these put on love, that is, the bond of perfection. And let the peace of Christ control your hearts … And be thankful." (see Colossians 3)

In a number of places, Paul teaches that as we recognize the new life given us by the death and resurrection of Christ, we must also recognize that life-altering adjustments are in order. Things must change because things have changed! We have been healed — why would we want to be sick again? We were dead in sin but have been brought back to life in Christ — why would we want to fall back into old lethal habits? We have been found — why would we want to get lost again? We were slaves but have been set free by Christ — why would we want to go back into slavery?

We have been healed — why would we want to be sick again? We were dead in sin but have been brought back to life in Christ — why would we want to fall back into old lethal habits? We have been found — why would we want to get lost again?

The Easter season is prime time to ask whether the lives we lead, the words we say and the priorities we set give witness to our baptism in Christ. During Lent we took time to examine our need to repent, to "put off" the old person. Easter offers us the opportunity to "put on" the ways of Christ, to preserve and strengthen the health — the life — he has restored to us.

Those healed and forgiven by the Lord often became instant evangelizers. The crippled walked, the mute spoke — it must have been a joyous, incredible sight, one not soon forgotten. "Look what he did for me!" they must have exclaimed. Undoubtedly some onlookers were more fascinated by the miracles than the message, but there was no denying the "before" and "after."

Still, as marvelous as Jesus' miracles must have appeared, it must have been even more marvelous when those who had been healed by him began to live as he lived.

Christians are signs that the kingdom of God is here. There was a "before," but we are a people of the "after." May everything about us point to the presence of the Risen Christ.

May 10, 2003

LOVING FROM
THE CROSS

Painting shows me another view of cross

Joseph-Jacques Tissot was born at Nantes, France, in 1836. He studied at the Academy of Fine Arts in Paris and began a celebrated career as a painter and illustrator. He won a name for himself through a series of watercolors, first about Paris, then about London. While working on a painting about a woman singing in church, he regularly attended church services, and it was there that he found inspiration for another painting, which he titled, "Christ Appears to Console Two Unfortunates in a Ruin."

This painting marked the beginning of a new stage in his art and, ultimately, a new stage in his life. So attracted was he to the figure of Christ that he was unable to put him out of his mind. He decided to spend a year in the Holy Land studying the geography and culture of the area. He then spent 10 years painting a series of watercolors, which he eventually published in a book titled "The Life of Our Lord Jesus Christ" — 865 drawings of Gospel themes and accompanying notes.

I had never heard of Tissot until April of last year, when I visited Assisi, the birthplace of St. Francis, during my retreat in Rome. Walking Assisi's hilly, cobbled streets, I passed a small, half-empty shop selling antique drawings and prints. Eyeing several religious prints in a window display, I decided to go inside. After browsing a few minutes, I came across an old colored lithograph titled, "What Our Saviour Saw from the Cross," by J. J. Tissot. Hoping that I would buy the print, the shopkeeper assured me that Tissot was famous.

I was immediately drawn not just to the drawing, but also to its theme. It is a downward view of a crowd from the cross, through the eyes of Jesus. The viewer stares directly into the eyes of Mary and other grieving women, and the scene is filled with a motley assembly of characters: a Roman soldier standing defiantly at guard; shepherds squatting with staffs in hand; three men on luxuriously saddled horses; official-looking elders off-handedly observing from the rear; simple people, men and women, caught up in the somber events; casual passersby gawking merely out of curiosity.

One of the most captivating features of the drawing is that its focal point is outside its borders; in fact, one quickly gets the feeling that every character is looking at you. What or who is the focal point? Is it Jesus? Or is it I? I found myself asking whether I would have understood what the drawing is about had Tissot not given it a title.

I think I would have understood, because Tissot offers clues to the identity of the assembled crowd. The sad faces of the four women in the foreground (one by herself, three others nearby), a tomb hewn into the rock (open and at the ready), the Roman soldier (surveillance, lest trouble erupt), three men (three Kings?) on horseback — these and other artistic touches point to the presence of Jesus, though he does not appear in the drawing.

What emerges is a kind of identification of the viewers with Jesus: he gazes from the cross at those for whom he gave his life, and we see them through his eyes.

Jesus is, in fact, the focal point. But with brilliant subtlety, Tissot makes the viewers the focal point as well, because the crowd seems to be staring at us. What emerges is a kind of identification of the viewers with Jesus: he gazes from the cross at those for whom he gave his life, and we see them through his eyes. At the same time, because we naturally picture ourselves in the crowd, it dawns on us that we are looking at ourselves through his eyes.

Each time I study the drawing, I discover new details in Tissot's careful artistry. And now, each time I study a crucifix, I catch of glimpse of Jesus' loving embrace of those for whom he died. Every Christian who sees a crucifix can be consoled and strengthened by the Savior's sacrifice; but seeing a crucifix, we are also called to imitate his selfless love.

Thanks to God's grace, the Scripture, prayer before the Blessed Sacrament, ministry among God's people, and a 100-year-old drawing by a French illustrator, I have begun to understand in a new way how as priest and bishop I am to serve you, in Jesus, from the cross. In his recent apostolic exhortation, "Pastores Gregis" ("Shepherds of the Flock"), Pope John Paul II wrote:

"At the daily celebration of Holy Mass, the bishop offers himself together with Christ … The bishop's love of the Holy Eucharist is also expressed when in the course of the day he devotes a fair part of his time to adoration before the tabernacle. Here the bishop opens his heart to the Lord, allowing it to be filled and shaped by the love poured forth from the Cross by the great Shepherd of the sheep, who shed his blood and gave his life for them. To him the bishop raises his prayer in constant intercession for the sheep entrusted to his care." (no. 16)

We are all embraced by the gaze of Jesus from the cross. We are all being formed by his love flowing from the cross. Each of us, in his or her unique way, is called to bear the cross. I promise that every day, you — the sheep entrusted to my care — are in my prayers of intercession before the tabernacle. Pray for me, that I will accept the grace to make my identification with Christ complete.

February 21, 2004

Pray for more laborers to join in harvest

"To live means to be desired and loved by God, moment after moment." (from a Vatican document about the consecrated life)

Of all the ways one might define human life, that brief and startling statement says everything. I wonder what kind of definition each of us would write were we asked to define "to live." I have a suspicion that many of us would begin, "To live means that I ..." Our definitions would continue with a list of things that "I" would accomplish, achieve, feel, think, know, do.

But the true definition does not begin with anything "I" set as a goal for myself. Instead, it begins with recognizing that the only reason I am alive is that I am "desired and loved by God." By desiring and loving me, God brought me into being and sustains me. I am neither the source nor the goal of my own life. I am one who is desired and loved by God, moment after moment, and therefore I am alive. My existence is evidence that God exists!

For most of us, taking that definition seriously means letting a revolution happen in our hearts. If the reason I am alive is that I am a desire of God, the beloved of God, a thought of God, an object of God's favor, then nourishing a relationship with God brings me even more to life. Making myself the center, the point of it all, only lessens me. The self-centered husband or wife quickly sours a marriage.

It is the revolutionary irony of the Gospel that in forgetting myself I find myself, that in surrendering myself to God as his instrument I come alive. That upside-down logic is at the core of the Beatitudes, and it is emphasized by all four Gospels as a key to Jesus' teaching: "For whoever wishes to save his life will lose it, but whoever loses his life for my sake will save it. What profit is there for one to gain the whole world yet lose or forfeit himself?" (Luke 9, 24-25)

One obstacle to serious consideration of a religious vocation for some today is that they begin their discernment by asking, "Should 'I' do this?" In other words, some approach a vocation as they would a career change, when, in fact, it has much more to do with one's willingness to leap into God's arms. It has to do with surrendering oneself to the truth — even though I do not fully understand it — that no matter what I have already accomplished, the reason I am living is because I am desired and loved by God.

"Is God calling me?" That is the proper question to ask oneself when contemplating a vocation. Discerning a vocation means allowing myself to be defined by God's desire and love for me, to want to become an image of God's love and desire for everyone. In this age of "self-fulfillment," that is no easy task, but that is precisely what the Church — the world — needs.

Am I too weak? Yes, but God is strong. Will I miss my former life? Probably, but I will gain something more. Will I abandon what I have built up? No, I will give it to God.

Discerning a vocation means putting myself at God's disposal, so that when he calls I will not respond, "I have something better to do."

Am I afraid of falling? God will catch me. Am I too weak? Yes, but God is strong. Will I miss my former life? Probably, but I will gain something more. Will I abandon what I have built up? No, I will give it to God. Will I limit my future choices? Most definitely yes, but in giving myself to God I will gain everything.

May 2 is the 41st World Day of Prayer for Vocations, and Pope John Paul offers this prayer:

"We turn to you, Lord, in trust! Son of God, sent by the Father to the men and women of every time and of every part of the earth! We call upon you through Mary, your Mother and ours: may the Church not lack in vocations, especially those dedicated in a special way to your Kingdom. Merciful and holy Lord, continue to send new laborers into the harvest of your Kingdom! Assist those whom you call to follow you in our day; contemplating your face, may they respond with joy to the wondrous mission that you entrust to them for the good of your people and of all men and women. You who are God and live and reign with the Father and the Holy Spirit, forever and ever. Amen."

Please join me in prayer for those in our diocese who are considering a vocation to the priesthood or consecrated life (and for those who are not considering a vocation but should be!). Pray that they will come alive in God's desire and love for them, that they will give their "I" to God for his sake and ours. Pray that they will have the courage to stake their lives on what it means "to live." Pray that they will hear his call and answer, "Yes!"

I would like to make a request of everyone who reads this column — lay, religious and priest. Think of at least one young man or woman who you believe would be a good priest or religious; pray the Holy Father's prayer for that person's intentions; and mail a copy of this article to him or her, with your personal words of encouragement.

Part of your vocation is to extend the call of God.

May 1, 2004

Altar server lives life by taking up his cross

Tobías Ferrer, 34, has been my altar server for the past five days. Originally from San Miguel de Epehan in the Mexican state of Michoacán, his family now lives in Fresno, Calif. The two of us are spending time at the Mexican American Cultural Center in San Antonio for intensive language study; I am studying Spanish to better serve our Hispanic parishioners, and he is studying English to prepare for vows next year as a member of the Marianist order.

Our conversations are in broken English and broken Spanish, as both of us put our studies into practice. After Mass the other day, we had an extended chat with two sisters and a laywoman, all Mexican; when the women left, Tobías motioned that he wanted to speak privately for a few moments. After closing the door, he gently gave me several lessons in avoiding common mistakes; apparently I had been teetering dangerously on the edge of using bad language! I told him he was to be my "vocabulary guard" from now on.

Tobías can be seen walking enthusiastically around campus throughout the day, toting his backpack full of textbooks to the next class. A little shorter than I, he has a ready and infectious smile, and everyone is happy to greet him. He serves at the altar with a quiet reverence that has a calming effect on all who attend daily Mass in the small chapel.

I have learned more about him with each passing day. He is the third of 14 children, four of whom, including Tobías, have been deaf since birth; a sister and brother died very young because the family had no access to medical care. In Mexico the Ferrer family was poor, and from the age of 5 Tobías worked with the crops and animals in the fields and scavenged the hills collecting wood for the fireplace.

He attended school for five or six years and continued to work in the fields in the afternoons and on weekends. Since he could not hear or read lips, he did not understand what his teachers were saying; but he learned to read and write by watching others. By the time his family migrated to the United States in 1981, his father was disabled because of an arm injury. When his older brother and sister married, Tobías decided to make his family his life. He quit school and started working full-time with his mother in the California fields, picking oranges, lemons and grapes.

The nine children younger than he attended school, and Tobías made a personal commitment to provide them with everything he never had and ensure they received a good education. In effect, as he puts it, he became the "manager" of the household. He organized their home life and paid the bills, and it was to him that the younger children came when they needed something. He insisted that they work with him and their mother in the fields on weekends, because he wanted them to know the value of hard labor.

The Eucharist became the center of his life — as he says, a "vitamin for life," the most important thing in the world to him.

In 1983, Tobías joined his parish youth group, began serving Mass, and helped others in a variety of ways. The Eucharist became the center of his life — as he says, a "vitamin for life," the most important thing in the world to him. He continued managing the household and looking after his nine brothers and sisters.

It was not until 1985 that he and his deaf brother and sisters acquired hearing aids and began to hear sounds which before then had been mysteries to them. For the first time they heard their native Spanish spoken; their speech improved and a new world opened up. Although he does not know sign language, Tobías intends to learn it — after he masters English.

At a certain point, he sensed that a "theme" was emerging for his life, one taken straight from the Gospel: "Take up your cross and follow me." Realizing that these words fit him like a glove, he made them his own. He has a secondary theme as well, from the Stations of the Cross — "Jesus falls a third time" — but "Take up your cross and follow me" is always at the center of his heart. Although as a young person he had never considered a vocation, several years ago he decided to enter religious life. But before doing so he made sure his commitment to the family was fulfilled — he paid off the bills and watched with pride as his little sisters and brothers finished high school and college. In May of this year they all became American citizens.

Tobías told me that his grandparents taught him the value of a close family, and it was for that reason that he made a personal, life-giving commitment to his; even now the entire family gathers every Sunday at his parents' home in Fresno. As a priest he hopes to work with engaged and married couples, particularly those facing trials.

"El que quiera seguirme, que renuncie a sí mismo, cargue con su cruz y me siga." (Luke 16:24)

Now beginning his "second life," Tobías realizes that everything has happened to him for a reason, and he relishes the idea of giving back what he has been given by God. I can't help but think that those who will someday come to know "Padre Tobías" will witness very quickly, with their own eyes and their own ears, the unsurpassed power of the cross of Christ.

September 1, 2001

Religious heroes are God's bait to reel us in

My family will attest to the fact that when I was growing up, I did not like to read. When reading was required, my sisters rightly accused me of reading the same book, "Grant Marsh: Steamboat Captain," over and over. I got a lot of mileage (i.e., book reports) out of Grant Marsh.

When finally I did begin to enjoy reading, I found most interesting books about people who decided to follow Jesus. I read "Lad of Lima," about St. Martin de Porres, my father's patron saint. I read "The Man Who Got Even with God," about the angry son of a tobacco farmer who eventually "got even" after he entered a Trappist Monastery. I read Willa Cather's "Death Comes for the Archbishop." I read "The Seven Storey Mountain," Thomas Merton's autobiography. In a multitude of ways, these books and others spoke to me and inspired me.

I was fascinated by their dramatic stories of conversion, discipleship and courage. They were a kind of bait God used to get my attention, the hooks he set in my soul, with which he began to reel me in. I gladly took bait and hook and let my imagination roam to places and accomplishments similar to those about which I read. These were people I wanted to imitate, people who did things and said things that made a difference, strong people whose strength supported many others.

But there was a problem: I was not like the people in those books. My life story was not dramatic, certainly not the stuff of exciting biographies, and I found myself in a quandary. I wanted to reach the same end point as those about whom I read, but I wondered if my starting point, so different from theirs and so ordinary by comparison, was a good enough place to begin.

Looking back, I realize that, while I had taken the bait God left for me, I was concentrating more on it than on him. In other words, I had compiled a list of heroes. No doubt about it, they were good models; but I had to get beyond hero worship to worship of the One who made them into everything I so admired.

Eventually — and providentially — I recognized that there was one crucial thing I had in common with my heroes: I was known to God.

Eventually — and providentially — I recognized that there was one crucial thing I had in common with my heroes: I was known to God.

That might seem like so basic a truth as to go without saying, but it was necessary for me to grasp it fully. No less than Martin de Porres, Thomas Merton, or Cather's fictional Fathers LaTour and Vailant, I was known to God. He did not know me through them (as I had come to know him through them). He knew me personally and directly.

Matthew's account of the call of the disciples is typical of the Gospels. Seeing the fishermen Peter and Andrew casting their nets, "Jesus said to them, 'Come after me, and I will make you fishers of men.' At once they left their nets and followed him." Then, eyeing James and John in a boat with their father, "He called them, and immediately they left their boat and their father and followed him." (Matthew 4:18-22)

What made their call dramatic was not their personal history (the evangelists give us very little of that), but the fact that it was the call of Jesus. Their immediate abandonment to him was an inspirational act of courage, but it was only the beginning.

Recently I re-read one of the conversion stories that had been particularly inspiring to me as a young man. Someone left everything to become a priest. It struck me that now, years later, I am what he once aspired to be, what reading about him had inspired me to be. It also struck me that like all the heroes of my childhood, he had not yet arrived where he was truly heading, nor have I.

Heroes come and go. They can fall flat on their faces, stumble with their clay feet, and become bloated with pride in their accomplishments. Through no fault of theirs, they can fail to meet my exalted expectations. Though real they can also be projections of my ego, of my need to be known for having done great things. Heroes can be an inspiration, a hook, God's bait — but they are only that, and not the prize or end point.

God, who knows me, calls me, and he will never fail me. He will give me strength to do what he needs me to do, and as I learn to rely on him alone, I will also work along with him more and resist his ways less. It would make no sense to take the bait and run with it away from him. Those true champions of God were such not because they led lives more interesting than mine, but because no matter who they were, they surrendered everything they had — grand or plain as it might have been — to him.

I cling to the truth that I am known to God, known from the womb, known to the tips of my toes and the depths of my soul, known today and to eternity. The important thing is that I abandon all to him, that he might use me as he needs me.

I guess you can tell I went fishing last week.

July 12, 2003

25 years as a priest: God has molded me

To borrow a favorite phrase from my good friend, Carlo Pirani (who borrowed it from Ricky Ricardo), in the past 25 years God has had to "splain" many things to me. That is not because God owed me any explanation — to the contrary, it is I who need for him to explain things to me, for left to my own devices and my own logic, I would certainly have misunderstood just about everything.

I am blessed with a wonderful spiritual director. During one of our sessions several months ago, I told him what was on my heart, where my struggles lie, how overwhelming my faults can seem, how I need to grow in prayer and love, and about my hopes for the Diocese of Little Rock. When I finished, he responded, "Sounds like God is making you into a bishop." He was right, of course, for through it all God is calling me to give myself to him completely, so that everything I do will come from his hand.

My spiritual director's remark is a good way to frame what God has been doing for me since my ordination to the priesthood 25 years ago: he has been making me into a priest. In that process, he has had to explain many things to keep me on the right path. Let me give several examples.

I enjoy preaching. I enjoyed public speaking and communications courses in college, and I enjoyed homiletics in seminary. Learning to speak is not the same as learning to preach, however, and through the years God has had to explain that difference to me over and over again.

I have lost track of the number of times through the years that, as I prepared a Sunday homily, I have come to a sort of mental or spiritual block and found myself "speechless." I could not find what I considered the right words to open up the Scriptures for my parishioners. Gradually, it began to dawn on me that the problem was that I was concentrating on speech, on technique, on style, and not on the Word of God. God explained to me, "It matters not that you are speechless. What matters is that you speak my Word. My Word will do its work."

The prophet Jeremiah told God (1:4-9) he was not qualified to be a prophet. "I know not how to speak. I am too young." And God responded, "Say not, 'I am too young.' To whomever I send you, you shall go; whatever I command you, you shall speak ... See, I place my words in your mouth!"

I found out quickly that I did not know the answers, nor was I a magician or miracle worker.

As he did for Jeremiah, God has had to explain to me that I am to concentrate less on my speech and more on his Word. As St. Paul wrote to the Corinthians, "We do not preach ourselves, but Jesus Christ as Lord." (see 2 Corinthians 4:1-7)

Here's something else God has had to "splain" to me:

After ordination, tuned up and fresh out of the seminary, I assumed that I was to have answers for the questions folks brought me, that I was to know how to fix what spiritually or emotionally ailed them. I found out quickly that I did not know the answers, nor was I a magician or miracle worker. My unskilled, fidgety hands were empty. My feet were clay.

Again, God explained things to me. It was good that I recognized my emptiness, he said, because then I could begin to allow myself to be filled with him. It was good that I trudged along on feet of clay, because the contrast between my frailty and his strength would teach me about his mysterious love.

Paul wrote, "We hold this treasure in earthen vessels, that the surpassing power may be of God and not from us." (see 2 Corinthians) God had to explain to me that I had to empty my hands of dependence on skill and allow him to fill them with the gifts his people truly need.

Then I began to understand that the hopes, dreams, worries, longings, sins, aches, sorrows, joys and thankfulness of the people I am sent to serve (not to mention my own!) are to be the offering I make, along with bread and wine, at Mass each day. Moreover, God explained that it is not "my" offering, but Jesus' offering — for on the cross, with arms outstretched, he offered all of that and more, making of himself and of us a perfect sacrifice to his Father. Precisely because we could not make the kind of offering that would save us or atone for our sins, Christ made it for us.

"My" priesthood is his priesthood, and only his. You and I are the offering he made on Calvary and eternally makes in the kingdom of heaven. Only his perfect offering — for he held nothing back from his Father — could save us. That is why he joins our sacrifice to his in the Eucharist.

Perhaps the most important thing God has had to explain to me is that it is not enough to admit that I am speechless, that my hands are empty, that my feet (along with the rest of me) are clay, that "my" priesthood is his. There is something more.

He has explained to me:

■ "Strive to be even more 'speechless' — most especially in prayer, but also in preaching. What matters is not your speech. What matters is my Word.

■ "Strive to be even more empty-handed. The less you focus on what you think you should have to offer, you will face your emptiness and let me fill you with my very life, which knows no limits. Then, without your even knowing it, through your hands I will give my people everything they need. See how Jesus has taken you and your people to the cross with himself, and give all that you have to him. He will bring it to me.

■ "And as for your clay feet, remember that you are an earthen vessel filled with an eternal treasure. That is the way I want it to be. You may feel like a lump of clay, but I am molding you into a priest and bishop. Let my fingers and thumbs do their work. I will water your clay to make it malleable, and the fire of my love will strengthen you.

■ "See my love for your flock, and watch over them through my eyes. Love them, as I have loved you, to the end."

Thank you, Lord, for "splaining things" to me. In the next 25 years, day by day and more and more, may I decrease, and may you increase.

July 26, 2003

We often overlook the blessings received

Bishop Sartain delivered this homily during the Chrism Mass at the Cathedral of St. Andrew on March 25, 2002.

Many Christian churches celebrate a Seder supper during Holy Week. "Seder" means "order" and refers to the ritual followed during the Passover meal celebration.

The Seder meal is a joyous, family celebration. When I was the pastor of a parish, I usually played the guitar and led the singing during our Seder meal, and everyone's favorite song was "Dayenu." Even though its tune is playful and rhythmic, when you sing it you can't escape asking serious questions about your attitude toward God and his blessings.

Dayenu was written in about the sixth century, and its author is unknown. It calls to mind the divine favors, especially God's loving covenant with his people. The Passover Haggadah is the telling of the story of the Exodus in prayer and proclamation. To demonstrate all the positive consequences of choosing God, the Haggadah lists all the good God has done for the Jewish people throughout history.

Therefore, how much more so do we owe abundant thanks to God for all the manifold good he bestows upon us. He brought us out of Egypt, he executed justice upon the Egyptians and their gods. He slew their first born. He gave to us their wealth. He split the sea for us, led us through it on dry land and drowned our oppressors in it. He provided for our needs in the wilderness for 40 years and fed us the manna. He gave us Shabbat, led us to Mount Sinai and gave us the Torah. He brought us into the Land of Israel and built for us the Temple to atone for all our mistakes.

The song "Dayenu" has 15 stanzas, corresponding to the 15 blessings of God in the Haggadah. The genius of the song is that it makes us stop to give thanks for each — "If God had only divided the sea for us and not brought us through it dry shod, Dayenu! — that alone would have sufficed, and we would have been grateful ... Had God helped us 40 years in the desert and not fed us with manna, Dayenu! — that alone would have sufficed, and we would have been grateful ... Had God brought us to Mount Sinai and not given us the Torah, Dayenu! — that alone would have sufficed, and we would have been grateful."

When we of the 21st century think of the sweep of salvation history, perhaps we perceive it as one action of God. Dayenu reminds us that God deserves thanks for each stage of that history, for each of his blessings.

God knows us well. Give us an inch and we'll expect a mile!

If God had "merely" split the Red Sea in two for us and not brought us through on dry land — he would still deserve our thanks.

Would it have been enough to accomplish the full liberation of his people? Probably not. But that is not what Dayenu — "it would have been enough" — means. Dayenu means that this act alone would have sufficed to bring upon us the obligation to thank God.

God knows us well. Give us an inch and we'll expect a mile! As a friend of mine likes to say about the way we sometimes treat God, "It's not, 'what have you done for me'; it's, 'what have you done for me lately?'"

Dayenu invites us to savor each and every blessing and to

thank God for each. Its attitude is that even if God never does any more special favors for me, this favor alone would have been reason enough to give thanks. But we can't gain that attitude if we haven't first savored the blessing.

A few years ago I heard a rabbi tell a wonderful story at an ecumenical Thanksgiving service.

Once there was a grandmother who doted on her grandson's every whim.

She bought him the best clothes, the best toys. She took him to fancy places and on grand vacations, so much did she love him.

One day, tragedy struck. Dressed in their finest, the two went for a walk by a lake. The grandson slipped and fell in. Desperately he paddled and paddled but could not swim to shore. Bystanders jumped in the water to rescue him. It was only a few seconds, but it seemed like an eternity.

The grandmother looked up to heaven and prayed, "God, help us! Save my grandson from drowning!"

Sure enough, within just a few moments, the rescuers emerged triumphantly from the water and pulled her grandson to safety. She hugged him and hugged him again, then carefully straightened out his sopping wet clothes. But something was wrong.

After a few moments of tense silence, she looked up to heaven indignantly and said, "He had a hat!"

Perhaps at times, when our prayerful expectations are not met, we fail to thank God for the marvel he has done. One reason we do not always appreciate the blessings of God is that we are accustomed to them — they are so much a part of the atmosphere we breathe that we take them for granted.

Dayenu teaches us to celebrate each one, for each is the loving action of God for us.

Tonight we remember God's blessing to this diocese in the ministry of our priests. They have been anointed with the Spirit of God to bring good news, to act in the person of Christ, to continue Christ's saving work among us. They were chosen and ordained by God, in repeated acts of blessing for this diocese.

I wonder if we take enough time to thank God for our priests, who selflessly pour out their lives for the Lord and for us. Particularly in these days, when we are all deeply saddened by the tragic behavior of a few, it is good for us to remember — in the spirit of Dayenu — each and every priest, each and every blessing the Church of Arkansas has received through them.

"For that one alone we would have been grateful." Would only one have been sufficient to carry on the work of the Church in this diocese? No, not in the physical sense — though we need to recognize that many of these men are doing the work of three!

To tell the truth, God never gives us simply "enough," and we know it.

My point is that each priest is a reason to give thanks, each one a blessing not to be overlooked — from our senior priest, Msgr. John O'Connell (ordained in 1933), to our junior priest, Father Joseph Marconi (ordained in 2001), to Deacon Jack Vu, who will carry the Oil of Chrism this evening, and who will be ordained a priest June 8.

We are called to live in the spirit of Dayenu. To tell the truth, God never gives us simply "enough," and we know it. Jesus' parables speak again and again of the largesse of God, who goes beyond every expectation and even beyond comprehension. But do we give thanks for each blessing? And do we imitate God's largesse in our care for others?

Dayenu! For each and every blessing we are grateful. No new blessings lately? Then go deeper into the last one. No doubt we'll find something we missed the first go-round.

During Lent, we have prayed so as to be in union with God.

We have fasted so as to demonstrate to ourselves that God alone satisfies.

And we have given alms because we know without doubt that God's blessings have been more than enough for us.

Every Holy Week, we mine the depth of Jesus Christ. For in him God has given us everything.

He continues to minister among us, in more ways than we notice or can count — particularly in the ministry of priests. There is no greater blessing than the Lord our Savior.

Thank you, Lord Jesus Christ, for all the benefits and blessings which you have given me, for all the pains and insults which you have borne for me. Merciful friend, Brother and Redeemer, may I know you more clearly, love you more dearly, and follow you more nearly, day by day. Amen.

— St. Richard of Chichester (1198-1253)

March 30, 2002

Mysteries come together at Chrism Mass

Bishop Sartain delivered this homily at the Chrism Mass at the Cathedral of St. Andrew Monday, April 14, 2003.

In our own way, each of us has had a glimpse of what Peter, James and John experienced on the holy mountain (Matthew 17, Mark 9, Luke 9). Their time with the transfigured Jesus, in the presence of Moses and Elijah, was so luminous that they did not want it to end. Fumbling for words as usual, Peter interjected, "Lord, it is good that we are here. If you wish, I will make three tents here, one for you, one for Moses, and one for Elijah." In other words, "Lord, this is too much for us to take in — don't let it end. Let us stay here, breathing in your glory."

Perhaps it was during a retreat, a quiet moment of prayer, at Sunday Mass, or at the birth of your children — by the grace of God, everything essential and important seemed to come together in an instant, brilliantly but without a sound, and you recognized the presence of God. You wanted to stay right there, to capture the moment, because it was difficult to take it all in.

It happened to me just a few weeks ago, on retreat. I spent a day in Assisi, the birthplace of St. Francis. After dark, I climbed to the roof terrace of the place where I was staying and prayed the rosary with the beautiful Basilica of St. Francis in full view. A crystal clear sky, a cool breeze flowing across the Umbrian hills, the brightly lit rose-colored stones of the Basilica, and a group of pilgrims making the Stations of the

Cross by candlelight on the narrow medieval streets below. In an instant, many things came together — the love of God, the passion of Jesus, the poverty of Francis, the gift of faith, the call to prayer, my vocation. Though it was getting late, I didn't want to go back down to my room. I could have built a tent there, like Peter, James and John. I wanted to capture the moment and savor it all night.

Glimpses and hints, foretastes and intimations — in this life, that is what we see of the glory of God, that is what we can consciously "take in." After those experiences, however, life soon gets back to normal, and like the three apostles we are disappointed to see a cross on the horizon. But does that mean that the glory was somehow not really there, that the experience was somehow a mirage? Does the re-appearance of the cross mean that Christ's victory was incomplete? No, far to the contrary.

It is true. We cannot take it all in.

But this, too, is true: we have all been taken in by Christ.

That is exactly what happened at Bethlehem, on the mountain, on the Sea of Galilee, at Calvary, in the upper room, at Pentecost, and in Jesus' solitary prayer — he "took us all in" his arms of love and lifted us up to the Father. With arms always outstretched, as a hen gathers her brood under her wings, Jesus has taken us all in. It is there that we abide, in the shadow of his wings, under the victory of his cross — whether we "know" it or not, whether we "feel" it or not.

We have been taken in by the Son to the bosom of the Father, and it is to celebrate that truth that we have come here tonight — for you see, instead of those flimsy tents we would have built on the mountain, Jesus has built the Church. Filled with the Spirit, the Church proclaims and imparts the grace of the risen Christ. The glorious, risen Christ is at work in the Church and in her sacraments.

This happens most perfectly of all, of course, when we

celebrate the Eucharist. And of all the times we do so during the year, a Chrism Mass holds special place:

For in a wonderfully tangible way, everything about the mystery of the Church converges on this celebration and goes forth from here. The bishop offers Mass with his priests, deacons, and the priestly people of God. The saving death and resurrection of the Lord is made present to us — and from this sacrifice, the fruits of the redemption flow to every corner of creation. As a particularly significant expression of the coming together of the Church, tonight I bless the oil to be used in the sacraments for the people of our diocese.

For in a wonderfully tangible way, everything about the mystery of the Church converges on this celebration and goes forth from here.

As soon as tomorrow, in towns many miles from this cathedral, the oil of the sick will bring the solace and healing of Christ to the sick, and on Saturday night the newly baptized will be anointed with the Spirit through sacred Chrism. The risen Christ, glorious and alive in the Church, takes us into his saving embrace. The fruits of this celebration will flow to your parishes and beyond through the ministry of our priests, who serve you, the body, in the person of Christ.

When Jesus took the scroll of the prophet Isaiah and read the passage about the anointing of the Spirit, he told those present that the prophecy was fulfilled in him. Everything promised by God through the ages was answered in him — and not just for a moment, not just in a glimpse or a hint, but fully and forever. Peter, James and John saw it for a moment, but because they had not yet seen their Lord on the cross they were apt to misunderstand it.

But we who have seen his cross and have carried it in our own lives know the high price Jesus paid and what it means. His arms outstretched on the cross, he has taken us all in, never to let us go. The astounding difference between now and then is that unlike those privileged apostles, on this side of the resurrection we know fully what he has done for us. We know that a tent would just not do — only the Church, the Body and Bride of Christ, through which he works unceasingly and unfailingly.

At ordination, we priests received that anointing of the Spirit which conformed us to Christ in a way far beyond our understanding. The Lord Jesus joined himself to us so completely, that through holy orders he fulfills his nuptial promises to the Church. Believe me, that astounding truth can make us priests shake in our boots! To know that through our ministry the promises of God are fulfilled is something that is difficult to take in, beyond our comprehension, humbling beyond words.

And yet that is what our risen and glorious Lord has done by anointing us with his Spirit. We will renew our priestly promises this evening because our place in the Church is the place of Christ — the servant, the Son, the spouse, the shepherd. No one would ever dare take such roles upon himself. All that we have and are comes from him, for he is the great and only High Priest.

Yes, it is good that we are here! But if we have pitched a tent, it is time to fold it for the journey. Someday, when we see God face-to-face, we will grasp fully what he has done for us. In the meantime, although we cannot take it all in, we rejoice that we have all been taken by Christ into the Church. From here flows the oil of gladness to anoint the people of God with freedom, forgiveness, healing and the loving embrace of the Father.

April 19, 2003

Priests should focus everything on prayer

Bishop Sartain delivered this homily for the jubilee Mass for priests at the Cathedral of St. Andrew in Little Rock May 27, 2003.

Among the jubilarians we honor tonight are a former seminary rector and pilot, a celebrated Scripture scholar and author, a musician, teachers, spiritual fathers and pastors. They are more than deserving of an evening of tribute, for they have done remarkable and inspiring things for the Lord.

When I read the Gospels, the Acts of the Apostles, the lives of the saints or the stirring stories of courageous Christians, I often find myself praying, "Lord, make me like them. Use me that way. Make me courageous, even heroic." The circumstances in which these friends of God lived out their faith are equally astounding: earthquakes and iron shackles; uncharted, untamed territory among people hostile to the faith; furious persecution and political oppression; desperate poverty and disease. "Help me to be as fearless and untiring as they, Lord," I find myself praying.

Then I read those passages — almost asides — which jump from the pages of Scripture. There was one tonight, from Acts (16:25):

"About midnight, while Paul and Silas were praying …"

The dank atmosphere of the prison was first warmed by prayer before it was liberated by an act of God.

"While they were praying …"

The vocation to the priesthood, which we celebrate tonight by honoring jubilarians who have given a combined 385 years of service, finds its source and goal in prayer. When we are in faithful touch with God through prayer, we allow ourselves to be filled with his grace, which in the end is everything and all we have to offer.

I have no power to save anyone. I have no power to heal anyone. I have no word of my own whose worth is greater than the morning headlines. What I have to offer comes from God, who alone saves, who alone heals, who alone sets free, whose Word alone abides forever. But as the old Latin dictum reminds us, "Nemo dat quod non habet" — one cannot give what one does not have. It is for us to be receptive to God's loving kindness, so that we might be his instruments in what we say and do. That receptivity comes about most fruitfully in prayer.

What I have to offer comes from God, who alone saves, who alone heals, who alone sets free, whose Word alone abides forever.

Before we priests step into the pulpit to preach, before we close the door of our offices to offer counsel to a parishioner, before we stand at the altar to offer Mass, we must be fed on a steady diet of nourishing communion with God in prayer. Otherwise we run the risk of appropriating to ourselves both the success and the failure of our ministry, and — much worse — fall under the delusion that we have something of our own creation to offer. Prayer makes us humble, receptive, contrite, patient, nonjudgmental and joyful.

It is in prayer that God tells us who we are. "You are my beloved. I have chosen you. I desire you to be my priest." Yesterday (May 26) we celebrated the feast of St. Philip Neri, a great evangelizer and servant of the poor. The day's Gospel passage came from the 17th chapter of John, often referred to as Jesus' "High Priestly Prayer." In an ingenious and engaging way, John shows us Jesus voicing to the Father a prayer that the disciples (and we) overhear.

As I read that prayer, a line jumped to me from the Scriptures. "I pray that the world may know that you loved them even as you loved me." (see John 17: 23) The Father loves us as he loves the Son. And he wants the world to know it. The Father loves us as he loves the Son.

This High Priestly Prayer, then, is in part Jesus' prayer for you and me. But because we are his priests, it is also our prayer for the people we serve. "Lord, may they know that you love them as you love me." The knowledge of such love, and the giving of it to others, comes through prayer.

As we feat these jubilarians, we reflect again on the astounding truth of God's love for us and for his people. Are these priests heroes? Untiring? Unfailing? Courageous? Fearless? Whatever folks say of us when we are gone, no better epitaph could be offered than this: "Faithful in prayer."

Luke says the earthquake came and shackles were loosed "while they were at prayer." May everything we do, happen, and whatever we say, be heard, while we are at prayer. It would be wonderful if one day they could write of us:

"He received the emergency call from the hospital … while he was at prayer."

"He prepared his lesson plans and wrote his books … while he was at prayer."

"He counseled the couple about to be married … while he was at prayer."

"He spoke with the disgruntled parishioner … while he was at prayer."

To my fellow jubilarians, I say with joy and admiration, "Ad Multos Annos!" Thank you for your generous priestly ministry, your love for the Lord, your untiring efforts for his people.

And most of all, thank you for the time you spend on your knees.

June 7, 2003

FAMILY, FRIENDS, MENTORS AND MODELS: A CLOUD OF WITNESSES

FAMILY, FRIENDS, MENTORS AND MODELS: A CLOUD OF WITNESSES

Perseverance can inspire others, give hope

March 5 will mark the 60th anniversary of the premiere of Symphony No. 7, sometimes referred to as the Leningrad Symphony, of Russian composer Dmitri Shostakovich. The circumstances of its composition and first public performances inspired many during a dark period in Russian history.

September 8, 1941, the Nazi army began its infamous 900-day Siege of Leningrad, which caused the deaths of almost a million people through bombing, starvation and exposure to the harsh Russian winters. It is difficult to imagine the suffering endured by the people of Leningrad during the horrifying Siege. Shostakovich, a native Leningrader, helped in the war effort as a volunteer fireman, doing what he could to slow the disastrous fires ignited in the fierce fighting. In his spare time, he worked on Symphony No. 7. Before completing it, he was evacuated to the far-away city of Kuibyshev, where the symphony premiered on March 5, 1942. It soon became a favorite of many, even in America, who regarded it as a musical tribute to the struggle against fascism.

Performances followed in Moscow and, eventually, in Leningrad. Leningraders had decided that the symphony should be performed in the city which gave it birth and to which it was dedicated, but arranging the performance was no easy task. First it was necessary to find able-bodied musicians and bring them home to Leningrad; the military assisted by granting leave to professional musicians, some of whom came directly from the front. The first rehearsals of this demanding work lasted only a few minutes — the exhausted and malnourished musicians had no stamina, some were so weak they could not lift their instruments, and the brass players' lips froze to metal in the unheated hall.

When at last the musicians had regained enough strength and skill to perform publicly, the Soviet army ordered its gunmen to prevent Nazi shelling of the city while the symphony was played. The performance of the Leningrad Symphony in Leningrad was an important and inspiring victory at the height of the Siege, which finally ended on January 27, 1944.

This was a victory achieved not by the high and mighty, but by the weak and powerless.

Undoubtedly, there were many motives at play in the heroic struggle to perform the work; some were political, others philosophical, others musical, others religious. Clearly it was a brave symbol of resistance to the Nazi army, but Shostakovich later said it was also a requiem for the victims of the Stalinist regime. What inspires me about the symphony and its performance is the single-mindedness of those involved and their refusal to accept defeat at an incredibly hopeless time. A musical performance in a besieged city was a significant declaration of victory over hatred. This was a victory achieved not by the high and mighty, but by the weak and powerless. They kept their eyes fixed on a goal, and in their suffering they both found and gave hope.

The author of the Letter to the Hebrews writes of an ancient "cloud of witnesses," who offer hope through their witness of faith. "Faith is the realization of what is hoped for and evidence of things not seen," he writes. (Hebrews 11:1) As examples he gives Abel, Enoch, Noah, Abraham, Sarah, Isaac, Jacob, Joseph, Moses and others. They persisted through great calamities and responded affirmatively to God's will against all earthly odds. "The world was not worthy of them." (v. 38) Of some, he writes, "these died in faith. They did not receive what had been promised but saw it and greeted it from afar." (v. 13) They had hope — hope based on God's promises — and they kept their eyes fixed on God, whom they knew to be faithful.

The greatest of these witnesses was Jesus.

"Therefore, since we are surrounded by so great a cloud of witnesses, let us rid ourselves of every burden and sin that clings to us and persevere in running the race that lies before us while keeping our eyes fixed on Jesus, the leader and perfecter of faith. For the sake of the joy that lay before him he endured the cross, despising its shame, and has taken his seat at the right of the throne of God. Consider how he endured such opposition from sinners, in order that you may not grow weary and lose heart." (12:1-3)

Catholics love crucifixes, because the body of Jesus on the cross is a sign of hope. In his agony, against all odds and against insurmountable opposition, Jesus kept his gaze on the Father's unsurpassed love. On the cross he was weak and powerless over his oppressors, but his trust in the Father enabled him to "see from afar" and endure the agony for our sakes. When in the midst of suffering we fix our eyes on him, he guides our gaze to the Father of all promises, who is worthy of trust.

Almost 60 years ago, a weary, ragtag collection of musicians took a stance against hatred and gave hope to a besieged city. Perhaps the author of Hebrews would number some of them among his "cloud of witnesses." We have been inspired by others who have persevered similarly through the pain and suffering life brought them.

But Lent reminds us that the leader and perfecter of faith is Jesus. If we keep our eyes on him, no matter what life gives us, we will persevere with hope in the promises laid out before us. Our perseverance will then give hope to others.

March 2, 2002

Blessed Karl: Witness for holiness, vocations

Karl Frederick Wilhelm Maria Leisner, prisoner 22356, died at age 30 on August 12, 1945, barely three months after the liberation of the Dachau concentration camp. He had been imprisoned for five and a half years.

Born at Rees, Germany, in 1915, Karl was the eldest of five children. He was bright, adventuresome, athletic, energetic and faith-filled, a natural leader. At age 12 he was asked by his pastor to head the parish youth group, and his teenage years were spent leading prayer, pilgrimages and camping trips. He was eventually tapped by his bishop to serve as diocesan youth director.

Sensing a call to the priesthood, he entered the seminary, hoping to shepherd Catholic Germans to a more intimate relationship with Christ. His seminary formation was interrupted by six months' compulsory government service in a labor camp, which entailed back-breaking work in murky swamps. Despite Nazi opposition, he arranged trips to Sunday Mass for fellow Catholic workers.

Serious about all he undertook, Leisner went through intense soul-searching before petitioning ordination to the diaconate. He was particularly troubled about whether he was called to marriage or the priesthood, having become enamored of a young woman whose family he knew well. It was she who ultimately encouraged him to seek ordination as a deacon.

Six months after diaconate ordination, Leisner was diagnosed with tuberculosis, most likely contracted in the damp swamps. He was sent to a local sanitarium and gradually regained his health. After hearing of a failed attempt on Hitler's life, he made an off-hand comment in a group of patients and was reported to the local police as anti-Hitler. He was taken directly from the sanitarium to jail, and thus began five and a half years in the hands of the Nazis, first at Freiburg, then at Mannheim and Sachsenhausen, and finally at Dachau.

Youthful but frail, Leisner quickly became a favorite of other prisoners. Though sick and deeply affected by the desperate environment of the camps, he always presented a joyful exterior and offered encouragement to fellow internees. He scrounged bits of food for the hungriest and sickest and shared his own meager rations — much to the dismay of companions, who knew he needed food as much as anyone.

Leisner lived as a deacon at Dachau, and everything he did was for the sake of Christ. He had been imprisoned just months before his ordination to the priesthood, and fellow prisoners shared the unlikely hope that he could be ordained a priest, even in the camp. The unthinkable became possible when a French bishop was sentenced to Dachau for his collaboration with the resistance.

Since everything had to be done according to Church law, the necessary documents were smuggled in and out of the camp. At great personal risk, a 20-year-old woman living in a local convent became an underground courier, using the alias "Madi." In early December 1944, Leisner received a letter from one of his sisters, in the middle of which were these words, written in another's hand: "I authorize the ceremonies requested provided that they are done validly and that there remain of them definite proof." The words were followed by the signature of Leisner's bishop.

Everything having been authorized, many prisoners

participated surreptitiously in an intricate plot to prepare for the ordination. Vestments were tailored for the bishop and Leisner, a bishop's ring was crafted by a Russian communist, and a crozier (bishop's staff) was carved by a Benedictine monk. Inscribed into the curve of the staff were the words, "Triumphant in Chains."

Still weak with tuberculosis, his face red with fever, Leisner was secretly ordained a priest at Dachau on December 17, 1944. He secretly celebrated his first Mass on December 26, the only Mass he would ever celebrate.

He secretly celebrated his first Mass on Dec. 26, the only Mass he would ever celebrate.

When the allies liberated Dachau on April 29, 1945, the gravely ill Leisner was taken to a hospital, where he died on August 12 in the presence of his family. For most of his life he had kept a diary, and the last entry, dated July 25, echoed the final words of St. Stephen: "Bless my enemies, too, O Lord. 'Lord, lay not this sin to their charge.'"

Pope John Paul II beatified Karl Leisner in 1996 in the Olympic stadium in Berlin, built by Hitler for the 1936 games. Holding the crozier used at Blessed Karl's ordination, the pope said, "Karl Leisner encourages us to remain on the way that is Christ. We must not grow weary, even if sometimes this way seems dark and demands sacrifice. Let us beware of false prophets who want to show us other ways. Christ is the way which leads to life. All other ways are detours or wrong paths."

Present for the beatification were Blessed Karl's brother and family, former inmates of Dachau, and an elderly Sister Josefa Imma Mack, once known as "Madi." Fifty-two years earlier, she had risked her life so that a young man she never met could be ordained a priest in secret.

Blessed Karl, pray for us! Like you, we want to love in imitation of the Lord Jesus. We want to be holy. We want to bring joy wherever we are. We want to learn to forgive. Blessed Karl, pray for those whom God is calling to the priesthood and religious life, that they might be courageous and generous, like you and Madi.

August 14, 2004

Patron for young adults is 'man of the eight beatitudes'

This past Sunday about 30 young adults, married and single, traveled from Memphis to Little Rock for a day of recollection at St. John Center. I celebrated Mass for them in the morning, and Father John Antony gave several talks in the afternoon on the Eucharist. They are part of The Frassati Society of Young Adult Catholics, a group which formed last year at the parish I served as pastor. Similar groups are springing up all over the country.

The goals of the Frassati Society are three-fold: to help young adults grow in their relationship with God; to help them increase their knowledge of the Catholic faith; to help them put their faith into practice. The group is named for Blessed Pier Giorgio Frassati, who was beatified by Pope John Paul II in 1990; the pope referred to him as "The Man of the Beatitudes" and offered Frassati to young adult Catholics as their model and patron. Parishioners of St. John in Hot Springs have noticed that Father West named their youth activity room "The Frassati Room."

I first became acquainted with the life of Pier Giorgio Frassati quite by accident. As a seminarian in Rome I would frequently pass a 12th century church on the way to St. Peter's but always found that the church was locked. I happened by one afternoon and noticed that the door was open, and young people were coming and going; I took my cue from them and entered myself. I enjoyed seeing the starkly beautiful interior of the church — the only time I ever found it open — but was just as captivated by the exhibit it hosted on the life of Frassati. There were photographs and other memorabilia of the young Frassati, an avid outdoorsman and athlete, participant in Catholic youth groups, and man of prayer. These young people were engaged in spreading the word about his life and teachings, so I decided to learn more.

Frassati was born in the northern Italian city of Turin April 6, 1901, the son of a prominent journalist and a painter; he had one sister, Luciana, who lives in Rome today. His father was the founder of *La Stampa*, a daily newspaper still published in Turin; for a period of time he was a senator and later served as the Italian ambassador to Germany. Frassati grew up in a cultured, well-to-do Italian home; he loved literature and the arts, was popular among his peers, loved to ski and hike the mountains and was recognized as a leader. His marks in school were often average and below, however, and his interests did not seem to lie in making a fortune or a name for himself like his father before him. Frassati eventually entered the Royal Polytechnic University at Turin to study mining, because as he told his friends he wanted to "serve Christ better among the miners," a group known to suffer under oppressive working and living conditions.

His marks in school were often average and below, however, and his interests did not seem to lie in making a fortune or a name for himself like his father before him.

Frassati spent his free time with the poor and sick, in prayer before the Blessed Sacrament, and in active involvement in groups of young Catholics. Some thought he frittered time away and considered him a disappointment to his prominent parents. On July 4, 1925, he died only six days after the onset of acute poliomyelitis, which doctors later surmised he had contracted from the poor he had been visiting. He had once said, "Jesus visits me each morning in holy Communion, and I repay him in my very small way by visiting the poor."

At his funeral his parents expected to see their colleagues, family and friends; but they were astounded to find the streets of Turin lined with thousands of poor people who knew Pier Giorgio as the young man who had always been there to help them. It was only after his death that his family learned the full extent of the impact of their son and brother. In fact, it was the poor of Turin who asked their archbishop to open Frassati's cause for canonization. His sister has been the prime force behind the publication of his letters, speeches and stories of his life.

At his beatification on May 20, 1990, Pope John Paul II said, "With him the Gospel turns to welcome solidarity, intense truth seeking, as well as demanding commitment to justice. Prayer and contemplation, silence and reception of the sacraments give tone and substance to his varied apostolate; and his whole life, enlivened by the Spirit of God, is transformed into a wonderful adventure."

"Entirely immersed in the mystery of God and totally dedicated to the constant service of his neighbor, he is a man of the eight beatitudes. Thus we can sum up his earthly life."

Since my first exposure to Pier Giorgio Frassati in the mid-70s, he has become one of my personal patrons; my episcopal coat of arms bears an allusion to him, and I included him in the litany of saints at my ordination. His feast day is July 4.

He is an extraordinary model for all young adult Catholics. From the earliest days after I learned of my appointment as your bishop, I have asked him to intercede for the young members of the Catholic Church in Arkansas.

Blessed Pier Giorgio Frassati, pray for us!

July 29, 2000

The challenge of climbing to the summit

B lessed Pier Giorgio Frassati (Italian, 1901-1925) loved the outdoors and was an avid skier and mountain climber. He once told a friend that he had "left his heart" on a mountaintop and looked forward to retrieving it on a climb to the summit of Mont Blanc. Since prayer and the Eucharist were the integrating factors of the many spheres of activity in his busy life — family, social, political, and service to the poor — it was his custom to make a visit to the Blessed Sacrament after each climb.

Frassati climbed his last mountain on June 7, 1925, less than a month before his sudden death of acute poliomyelitis. On one of the photographs taken of him that day, he wrote, "Verso l'alto" — "Toward the top." Those simple words have become a posthumous emblem of his brief life, during which he climbed toward the summit of Christian discipleship through prayer, the Eucharist, and active love for the poor.

I am struck by the ironic contrast of Frassati's "Verso l'alto" with Pope John Paul's favorite reference to the Latin translation of Luke 5:4, in which Jesus commands the fisherman, Peter, to "put out into deep water" — "Duc in altum." Peter has caught nothing all night, but because of Jesus, he casts his net one more time and pulls in a great catch.

"Verso l'alto" — "Duc in altum." "Toward the top" — "Put out into the deep." I like the juxtaposition of the two phrases, because it expresses the scope of our calling as Christians. We are to reach for the heights and plumb the depths of faith.

St. Paul marveled at his groundbreaking call to preach "the inscrutable riches of Christ" to the Gentiles. He longed to delve more deeply into Christ, and he longed for his communities to do the same. From prison, he wrote to the Ephesians:

"… I kneel before the Father (praying) … that Christ may dwell in your hearts through faith; that you, rooted and grounded in love, may have strength to comprehend with all the holy ones what is the breadth and length and height and depth, and to know the love of Christ that surpasses knowledge, so that you may be filled with all the fullness of God." (Ephesians 4:14-19)

Paul groped for the proper language to explain how God's plan of salvation affects the universe in all its dimensions — "toward the top" and "into the deep." He longed for us to be "filled with all the fullness of God" and knew that no Christian will reach that fullness if he or she stands still. The Christian life is about growth in Christ. But first we must want to grow.

Msgr. Charles A. Kelley, a priest of the Diocese of Richmond, was vice-rector of the North American College when I was a seminarian; he died last year, in his early 60s, of cancer. Blessed with a keen intellect and a gift for preaching, he could convey key points in sharp, memorable phrases. He once said to us, "The temptation to mediocrity is great." He meant that we must watch for the trap of "getting by" in ministry by reaching a certain level in pastoral skill, prayer and study — and remaining there. If we rely on seminary formation alone as the basis for a lifetime of ministry, if we do not strive to grow in our relationship with God, we will never fully taste the fruit of faith and will eventually cease to offer the nourishment for which our parishioners hunger. Mediocrity is not the path to happiness.

Msgr. Kelley's advice is equally true for all disciples of the Lord. It is a great temptation to settle into comfortable and ordered, but mediocre and unfruitful, lives of faith. Baptism opened for us the inexhaustible riches of Christ, and we will spend our lives climbing his heights and plumbing his depths. If we rely solely on the formation we once received in a Catholic school or Parish Religious Education Program, we risk stagnation — or worse, we risk letting go of Christ altogether. If we are not striving forward, we are being lulled backward.

If we are not striving forward, we are being lulled backward.

It is never too late to grow in faith. Folks are often surprised at how little it takes to begin re-discovering the riches of Christ. A few minutes spent in daily prayer, attending an extra Mass during the week, taking part in parish Bible study or adult education (or starting them!), volunteering to serve the poor, participating in Cursillo, reading a few pages of a spiritual book each day — such simple efforts open us anew to the world of faith. The more we grow, the more we will want to grow. The more we get to know the Lord, the better we will want to know him.

In his "Life of Moses," St. Gregory of Nyssa wrote, "To find God is to seek him unceasingly. To seek is not one thing and to find another. The reward of the search is to go on searching. The soul's desire is fulfilled by the very fact of its remaining unsatisfied, for really to see God is never to have had one's fill of desiring him."

"Verso l'alto!" "Duc in altum!" We climb to the Summit and plunge into the deep Fullness Who made us. The road out of mediocrity is taken by following our hunger and thirst for God. The fulfillment that awaits us is greater than we can possibly imagine, because the mystery of God is inexhaustible.

November 2, 2002

Being Christian and being Christ in world

I just finished reading "Five Loaves and Two Fish," a little book by Archbishop François-Xavier Nguyen van Thuan, president of the Pontifical Council for Justice and Peace. It is the archbishop's spiritual memoir of imprisonment under the North Vietnamese. Because his appointment as coadjutor archbishop of Saigon in 1975 did not meet the approval of communist authorities, he was immediately placed under house arrest; seven months later, he was formally arrested and spent almost 10 years in a variety of prisons and reeducation camps, often in solitary confinement.

He begins Chapter 5 with this brief account:

"One night when I was sick, in the prison of Phú Khánh, I saw a policeman walk by and I shouted: 'For goodness' sake, I am very sick; please give me some medicine!' He responded: 'There is no goodness here, nor love; there is only responsibility.'"

The policeman had made his perspective clear: the sole arbiter of his actions was responsibility. Reflecting on the tense atmosphere of his relationship with the guards, the archbishop pondered his response. He writes, "One night, a thought came to me: 'Francis, you are still very rich. You have the love of Christ in your heart. Love them as Jesus has loved you.' The next day I began to love them, to love Jesus in them, smiling, exchanging kind words." He soon began to notice that the tense atmosphere changed dramatically for the better.

Retired Vice Admiral Edward W. Cooke is a close friend whom I hold in the highest regard. His life has been a succession of distinguished careers — Navy, business and Church. While reading Archbishop Nguyen van Thuan's book the other day, I called Ed to discuss a conversation we had more than 10 years ago. If my memory serves me correctly, I had asked him what single word he would use to describe the driving force behind each of the careers he had chosen. He thought for a moment and said, "For the Navy, it was 'duty.' For business, 'expedience.' For the Church, 'hope.'"

Whether we recognize it or not, each of us allows some driving force to arbitrate our attitudes, words and decisions. It is the perspective out of which we live, out of which our sense of well-being and fulfillment is ultimately determined. Although the influence of such driving forces can be subconscious, there comes a time when we must deliberately choose one as the most important. To avoid choosing, to remain indifferent and without purpose, is to suffocate our own spirit. To choose one that is selfish and narrow is to ignore the lives of others. To choose an immoral one is to walk the road of death.

The distinguishing mark of Christian faith is that it offers the only driving force, the only arbiter, which integrates and fulfills all others: hope in the love of Christ. The archbishop had been schooled in Christian hope since childhood, but consciously deciding to make it the driving force behind his tension-filled prison existence, he discovered its depth and power. In the most dramatic days of imprisonment, unable to pray and on the brink of utter exhaustion, he would repeat to himself, "I am the living testament of the love of Jesus." Not only did his life begin to change; the lives of others changed as well.

There is a vast difference between applying Christian principles to life and choosing hope in the love of Christ as our driving force. In the former, we pick and choose, treating faith as one among many available codes of conduct; in the latter, we choose to be transformed entirely as living testaments of the love of Jesus. It is the difference between saying, "I will be a

Christian businessman" and "I will be Christ in the world of business." The significance of such a shift in perspective is immense. The archbishop could have been nice to his captors as a means to an end, and perhaps they would have responded with occasional favors. He chose instead to be a living testament of the love of Jesus, and through him they encountered the Lord.

It takes great courage and humility to offer oneself as a living testament. The way of the Lord is not always the most expedient, and the conventional wisdom of our corner of the world may consider his way foolish or naíve. But when we courageously choose hope in the love of Christ as our driving force, we soon find that our sense of responsibility is expanded; duty is ennobled; and expedience is never achieved at the expense of others.

The way of the Lord is not always the most expedient, and the conventional wisdom of our corner of the world may consider his way foolish or naíve.

The reason I hold Ed Cooke in such high esteem is that he has always allowed hope in the love of Christ to ennoble and integrate every aspect of his life — family, Navy, business, Church. He is a man at peace, and surely it is the peace of Christ.

On August 16, 1975, under house arrest in Cây-Vông, the archbishop prayed, "If I am awaiting the opportune moment to do something truly great, how many times in my life will similar occasions present themselves? Jesus, I will not wait. I will live the present moment, filling it to the brim with love. The road of hope is paved with small steps of hope."

Jesus said, "Where your treasure is, there also will your heart be." When we choose him as our treasure, our only driving force and arbiter, every step we take paves the world with hope.

February 2, 2002

Giving yourself during the Eucharist

In last week's column I mentioned a book by Archbishop François-Xavier Nguyen van Thuan, "Five Loaves and Two Fish," which chronicles his 10 years in North Vietnamese reeducation camps. In Chapter 4, the archbishop reveals how he secretly celebrated Mass with wine and hosts smuggled into the camps. After his arrest, he had been allowed to write a note to friends requesting things he needed most — clothes, toothpaste, etc. But he added, "Please, could you send me a bit of wine, as medicine for my bad stomach?" They sent him a small bottle of wine, labeled "stomach medicine," and some hosts concealed in a torch.

As the years went by, he celebrated Mass every day, but instead of a chalice he used the palm of his hand. He prayed the Eucharistic prayers from memory. At times he celebrated Mass curled up on his bed at night after the lights were out, encircled by other Catholic prisoners, and distributed Communion under the mosquito netting. During solitary confinement, his Mass was at 3 p.m. daily, the hour of Jesus' agony. "They were the most beautiful Masses of my life."

He closes Chapter 4 with a prayer: "Once I used to celebrate with a gold-plated paten and chalice, now your blood in the palm of my hand... Once I used to celebrate Mass in front of thousands of faithful, now in the darkness of night, giving Communion under mosquito netting... If you were to permit me to choose, I would not change, because you are with me! I am not afraid anymore, I have understood, I am following you in your passion and in your resurrection."

About 10 years ago I read "Martyr of Brotherly Love: Father Engelmar Unzeitig and the Priests' Barracks at Dachau." The concentration camp at Dachau, set up less than two months after Hitler came to power, has been called the "biggest monastery in the world"; nearly 3,000 clergyman suffered there, all but 500 of them Catholic priests. Only 32 years old when arrested, Engelmar Unzeitig was among them. He spent four years in Dachau, only to die of typhoid shortly before the end of the war, having volunteered to care for infected prisoners.

Clergyman at Dachau were housed in Barracks 26, 28 and 30, surrounded by barbed wire, because the SS considered them dangerous. Barracks 26 had a chapel where daily Mass was celebrated; the altar was constructed of crate slats, the chalice was a metal bowl, and the tabernacle was crafted of tin cans. At times priests clandestinely celebrated Mass on the campgrounds, using a tin can or water glass as a chalice. Prisoners stood around a flowerbed or squatted in the corner of a greenhouse, keeping a watchful eye for the SS.

Because Polish priests were not allowed to take part in religious services for most of the time Dachau was in operation, other priests would try to bring them Communion. One wrote, "Often I took a second host in my hand, carried it with me in a clean piece of paper to the plantation in order to be able to bring Communion to the poor Polish priests who had to do without this comfort. I had my tabernacle in a small fir tree."

Such accounts of Christian witness and heroism always inspire me to reflect on the gift of the Eucharist and celebrate Mass with even greater devotion. Archbishop Nguyen van Thuan and the priests of Dachau went to extraordinary lengths to maintain the Eucharist as the center of their lives, to continue their sacramental ministry among other prisoners, and to bring the Gospel to those who did not know the Lord. The archbishop calls the Eucharist, "my only strength."

There is a great danger of taking the Eucharist for granted by reducing our understanding of its spiritual benefit to "what I got out of it," in the same way we casually evaluate many experiences in daily life. The Catholic prisoners of Vietnam and Dachau, however, never lost sight of its true meaning; perhaps their appreciation of the Eucharist was even heightened because of their identification with the suffering of Christ.

> *There is a great danger of taking the Eucharist for granted by reducing our understanding of its spiritual benefit to "what I got out of it," in the same way we casually evaluate many experiences in daily life.*

When the Eucharist is celebrated, we are not simply remembering an important event in history; instead, the mystery of the Lord's death and resurrection is made present and contemporaneous to the Church — to us! We are joined to Christ's "once for all" sacrifice and receive its inexhaustible benefits. We actually take part in the eternal liturgy of heaven, where Christ intercedes for us and presents his sacrifice to the Father.

Priests have a solemn responsibility to celebrate the sacraments prayerfully and to prepare nourishing homilies. Lectors should be suited to their task and well prepared to proclaim God's word. Musicians should devote the time it takes to plan and practice. The congregation has a responsibility to participate with attention and reverence.

No doubt, there will be times when some aspect of the particular Mass we attend does not meet our expectations, but in such a case did the Lord Jesus hold something back from us? Is he any more present at one Mass than another? Could he offer himself to the Father for our sake more completely at one Mass than other? The answer to those questions is a resounding, "No!" Just ask Archbishop Nguyen van Thuan and the priests of Dachau. They never lost sight of the gift.

Christ could not possibly give himself more completely to us than he does at every celebration of the Eucharist, but perhaps we could make a better gift of ourselves. Ash Wednesday is a good time to start.

February 9, 2002

'Instinctive mercy' that brings healing

I'm told that my Uncle Ed used to say of my mother, "Katie is so tight-lipped she could have a million dollars in her pocket and no one would ever know." Having been her son for almost 50 years, I can testify that Uncle Ed was right (and there are plenty of folks who would testify that I am just like her in that respect).

Mom is that way naturally, but it is a quality that fits well with her vocation as a mother. Every mother observes and listens as children test the waters of life, sometimes sure, sometimes frightened, sometimes foolish, sometimes off-course. They watch with joy and pride, but there are certainly those times when they watch with worry and dismay. What should I do for him, what should I say to her, they ask themselves.

How many times do mothers simply overlook our faults and failings, with an instinctive kind of mercy that brings healing and peace to a family? And how many times do they simply store things quietly in their hearts, praying over them and thus exposing them to the light of God's love?

St. Luke writes that after the shepherds had been told by the angels of the birth of the Savior, they visited the manger and saw the newborn Jesus. "Mary kept all these things, reflecting on them in her heart." (Luke 2:19) Already she had been stunned by the angel's announcement of her pregnancy, and to her amazement the whole world was now being brought in on the secret. As the years unfolded she would store up many other thoughts and observations, reflecting on them in light of God's promises to her people and to her.

Mothers do that. The love with which they give birth serves their whole lives as a secure repository of the living biographies of their children, where secrets are "kept," where questions are pondered, where faults are forgiven. Every mother's vocation entails not only the privilege of being an instrument of God's creation of a new life — it also entails the mystery of his re-creation through his Son's cross and resurrection. Mary observed and pondered as Jesus grew and preached and healed and suffered. All mothers watch and wonder as their children's lives unfold.

> *Every mother's vocation entails not only the privilege of being an instrument of God's creation of a new life — it also entails the mystery of his re-creation through his Son's cross and resurrection.*

Although my mom would never let on about her imaginary million, there are many things in her keeping which are always quietly on display — most especially her love for God and her love for our family. The Catholic faith was the atmosphere we breathed at home — beliefs that formed us, evening rosary in the living room, daily Mass when school was not in session, confession on Saturday. One vivid memory from my early childhood is of a Saturday afternoon (I could not have been more than 5 years old) when I literally put my nose into a wasps' nest at a neighbor's house and suffered multiple stings. I can well remember the pain; but I also remember that within a few hours we were at St. Thomas Church for confession, my faced caked with soothing calamine lotion. There were priorities, and God was Number 1.

Our home's atmosphere was also built of family love — meals, games, and songs together; homework done nightly on the dining room table; chores delegated and shared, sometimes begrudgingly. Mom was in her forties when I was in high school, the last of the five kids. I was amazed that someone her age (!) could still remember what she had learned in high school and help me with Latin homework. As the five of us struck out on our own, we were lovingly set free, though we knew we would always be welcomed back.

When I was in high school and my father was ill, mom went to work as the secretary to our parish grade school, where she still serves as a volunteer. After more than 35 years, her children number in the thousands; and I have often heard stories from kids-turned-grownups who thought of Mrs. Sartain as their in-school mom. Now some of their kids' kids see her in the office most school days. The adventures of our family alone certainly give her enough to ponder and "keep," but she also stores carefully the wonder years of several generations of St. Paul grade-schoolers.

She is "Mother," "Mama," and "Mom" to me and my sisters; "Miz Sartain" to the kids of St. Paul; "M-I-L," "Kate," and "Katie" to sons-in-law; and "Mimi" to grandchildren. She can keep a secret better than the best CIA agent. And she knows how to turn things over to God, even as she keeps them tenderly in her heart.

This year I couldn't be with you physically on Mothers' Day, Mom, but my thoughts, prayers, love — and thus these simple words — were.

May 18, 2002

Becoming closer to fathers even after death

Thirty years ago this past February 1, Father Thomas called me to his office at the seminary to tell me that my father had died.

I remember with fondness his gentle hesitation, his respect for my silent response. The task that fell to him that day would bind us together until his own death 13 years later. No, not just "until" — even "beyond." I say that because death does not put the final limit on relationships or what one can learn from them.

I have witnessed this extraordinary truth in ordinary ways, and perhaps as an adult I can appreciate it better than I did as a college student. I know my father better now than I did the day he died.

My childhood memories are filled with images of my pharmacist dad, a man with a mysterious fiction-like past; himself the son of an east Tennessee pharmacist, motherless at age two yet mothered to adulthood by three Jewish spinsters from the house next door and a rarely-spoken-of stepmother.

On Saturday afternoons, I would sometimes accompany him back to our drug store (he had been home for lunch and a nap) and sit high atop the swivel stool edged close to the table in the back room, making up games or doing homework. When as a family we traveled to Jackson or Nashville to visit relatives, we played "The Disease Game" in the car — a test of one's skill at naming diseases corresponding to each letter of the alphabet. Needless to say, the pharmacist always won. In an earlier column I wrote about my father's love for opera, baseball and his family's secret recipe for fiery (and fatty) chili.

He did not always understand me, nor I him. But my childhood memories are punctuated with laughter and song, sacrifice and love. I thought I knew him then, but I know him better now.

Chance meetings with friends and acquaintances of my father have provided me with new memories, for they have been eager to share a story once they knew my name. One such encounter gave me a particularly poignant memory, especially since the hero of its story had been an entirely nameless one for the teller until he and I met in 1985.

After the Sunday afternoon baptism of the newborn son of friends, I joined the extended family for a reception at their home. The proud grandfather and I met for the first time, and he asked about my background. I told him of our now-demolished drug store at the corner of Bellevue and Lamar, across the street from the now-abandoned bank building. "I know exactly where it was," he said. Then he told me a story.

> *"I know exactly where it was," he said. Then he told me a story.*

One memorable day 45 or so years ago, he left work early because he was not feeling well. As he drove east on Lamar, he felt worse and could drive no further. Pulling to the curb he stopped, left his car, and walked dizzily up the concrete-and-stone steps leading to the nearby drug store. Once inside, he collapsed. The white-jacketed druggist behind the counter hurried to his side to offer help, but he replied that he would be fine if he could get home.

The druggist reached unhesitatingly for his keys, locked up the store, and drove the man home, making sure before he returned to work that the man's wife was there to care for him.

Thirty years later the proud grandfather still did not know who had driven him home that day, but I knew it was my father.

Other such encounters have taught me that the kindness of my father was not occasioned only by the misfortunes of others; it was a way of life — perhaps a way of survival — and a way I hope to imitate. I know him better now than I did the day he died, and I will probably get to know him even better in coming years.

Father Thomas did not know him at all, yet now in death he knows him better than I. Death does not pronounce the final verdict on life. Jesus won that victory when death died on his cross. And newfound memories of my father prove it true.

Happy Father's Day to all the dads of Arkansas. May our Heavenly Father strengthen you to lead your families with love and faith put into action every day.

June 15, 2002

New insight into communion of saints

Msgr. Patrick J. Lynch died the morning of August 8, one day before his 78th birthday. Known simply as "Father Pat," he was everyone's priest, everyone's friend, everyone's hero. There was good reason.

Ordained a priest of the Diocese of Nashville in 1950 with his identical twin brother, Tom, he served his entire priesthood in Memphis. Those who knew the twins comment about their vastly different personalities, their extraordinary closeness and their intuitive "sixth sense" of how the other was doing. When Tom was killed in an automobile accident in 1961, Pat was devastated, but he moved forward, committed as ever to his vocation.

I got to know him well when I entered the seminary, since he was director of vocations. He became my confidant, confessor and primary priestly example. He was the gauge many of us used to measure how we were doing as priests. When he was diagnosed with Parkinson's Disease in 1977, he kept going. Gradually the disease worsened, and a few years ago he moved to Chattanooga, where his sister cared for him until his death.

I was privileged to preach for his funeral Mass at Sts. Peter and Paul Church in Chattanooga on August 11. I told stories of tough kids straightened out, shy kids who walked tall with his encouragement, perplexed parishioners who found clarity in his counsel, priests and religious who persevered through his direction, and the elderly given hope in their infirmity by his inspiration.

He was short at 5 feet 6 inches but packed with thunder, a feisty coach who loved a good fight and fought his mightily. He was strong as an ox but alert to his weakness. He could have been anything he wanted to be, and he wanted to be a priest. He would have been the best of husbands and fathers, so God made him father to thousands. He could have had the world but took up the cross.

He could have had the world but took up the cross.

Traveling back and forth to Chattanooga, I had time to think of Father Pat and why he had such profound influence on so many lives. How did he touch people so deeply, especially those in trouble or heading in that direction? I think it was because he continually allowed God to purify his heart.

The "pure of heart" keep their focus on God, through prayer and surrender. They know his guiding hand, because it has nudged them back on the path when they have wandered. They know his mercy, because they have confessed their sinfulness. They have learned his wisdom, having been tried and refined in the fire of life's inevitable trials.

Most of all, they have allowed God to teach them how to see. Keeping their eyes fixed on him, they have developed an intuitive sixth sense of their kinship with all God's children, especially the poor and suffering. Seeing, they love. St. John Cassian (fifth century) wrote that purity of heart helps us climb, step by step, to the perfection of charity. As he climbed each rung of that ladder, Father Pat's heart was purified, and he saw more and more with the eyes of God. He loved us and then we, too, could see.

The afternoon before his funeral, I drove to South Pittsburg, my father's hometown, 30 miles outside

Chattanooga. I passed the house where he grew up, the church his family helped build, and the site of my grandfather's drug store — now a clothing store, where the tile floor of the display window still reads, "Sartain Drug Company." Then I visited the cemetery where my grandparents and uncles are buried.

I never met any of them. My grandmother, Josephine Marie Reilly Sartain, died in 1914 at the age of 34; my grandfather, Luther, died in 1930 at the age of 53; two of my uncles died as toddlers in 1908 and 1911. My father remembered little of his mother (he was barely 2 1/2 when she died), except the day she was taken by wagon to Chattanooga, where she died in the hospital of an "abscess of the appendix."

After I had walked the cemetery for a few minutes, I was taken aback and deeply moved to find that someone had left flowers on my grandmother's grave. We no longer have relatives in the area. Though I never knew her, I smiled and thought of her photographs, of the house around the corner where she once lived, and of my grandfather, father and uncles for whom she cared.

My quick trip to Chattanooga last weekend was a time of grace, for God brought me closer to Father Pat and my grandmother, and he gave me new insight into the communion of saints. Faith in the Lord Jesus and a pure heart enable us to see our communion with all God's children, living and dead. That gift of sight is a call to love, a call Father Pat accepted gladly. He recognized God's "little ones" as his and embraced them with fatherly care.

The gift of sight also gives us hope in the life to come, where we will be perfectly, visibly one in Christ forever. Flowers on my grandmother's grave were a sign of the lingering beauty of one who, now with the Lord, loves and prays for me.

"Blessed are the clean of heart, for they will see God."
(Matthew 5:8)

Purify my heart, Lord, that I may see … and love … and come to the perfection of charity in your kingdom.

August 23, 2003

Welcoming the 'strangers' among us

Uncle Charlie passed away last week. He wasn't actually my uncle, but the uncle of a close friend. I knew him for so many years that he seemed like my uncle, too, so I simply began referring to him as family. Uncle Charlie, his brother and his sisters were the children of Sicilian immigrants who made it to this part of the country at the turn of the century. Like many of their fellow Sicilians and Italians they worked hard to establish themselves in the United States, and later they opened a neighborhood grocery where the whole family worked. The parents spoke a Sicilian dialect and broken English, and their children learned enough of the dialect to understand what was being said to them or about them.

Their growing-up years were not easy. They worked hard and scrimped and saved; they endured the prejudice immigrants often experience; and they sacrificed so their children could have a solid foundation on which to build their futures. The surviving children keep constant watch over one another to this day.

Uncle Charlie eventually served as a food broker at the Scott Street Market, where he helped his "paesani" sell the produce they grew on the "truck farms" which dotted the highways leading out of town. Uncle Charlie was a natural salesman and became a fixture at the market, renowned especially for the poetry he composed to describe the quality of his produce. Always congenial and full of faith, he brought a smile to my face whenever I saw him. As I write this column I wish I could recall a few words of one of his famous poems, but I can't remember even a line. Suffice it to say they were good. And funny.

Uncle Charlie's interaction with his brother and sisters was always colorful, at times hilarious. They fussed and fumed, counseled and scolded, laughed and cried with one another. There was no doubt about their love for one another, their willingness to go more than an extra mile for one another, but their way of expressing love and concern was quite unique.

One of Uncle Charlie's sisters, Mary, had four children, two girls and two boys, To the consternation of her daughters, she would often say, "I have four children. Two sons."

When Mary died, it happened that another of her sisters had a stroke the day of the wake. As I arrived at the funeral home to lead the service, I noticed that two other sisters were walking toward their car with serious expressions on their faces. I asked what was the matter, and they told me about their sister's stroke; one of them added, in a stern indictment of her ailing sister, "And we found McDonald's coupons in her coat pocket!" The nerve of her, to eat stroke-causing hamburgers the day before the funeral.

They had more than their share of heartache, but through it all their faith and love strengthened them.

Uncle Charlie, his brother and his sisters were as close as any family could be. They raised families of their own and proudly passed along what they had learned from their immigrant parents. There was a quality to their faith that was at once fierce and tender, the kind that epitomizes both faith's life-and-death seriousness and God's gentle care. They had more than their share of heartache, but through it all their faith and love strengthened them.

In many ways they are like all the immigrants and descendants of immigrants who have built this country. Last weekend I visited Tontitown during the 102nd annual Grape Festival and learned about the Italians who first settled there well over 100 years ago, and whose descendants make up most of the membership of St.

Joseph Parish. Their story is now being repeated in their own backyard, as thousands of Hispanic immigrants make their way to northwest Arkansas to begin a new life.

A few days ago I met with one of our seminarians, who in 1991 immigrated to the United States from Vietnam; given the political constraints of their homeland, the members of his family could not all leave at the same time; this past July they were together for the first time in 20 years.

The other day at St. Mary's in Helena I met a beautiful family from Sudan, recent arrivals to our country and our diocese.

These immigrant stories come to mind this week because I just celebrated Mass for the faculty and board of Mount St. Mary Academy at the end of a workshop titled "Faith and Culture," which was conducted by staff from the Mexican American Cultural Center in San Antonio. The purpose of the workshop was to help the faculty explore the many facets of living and teaching in an increasingly multi-cultural community. I applaud Sister Deborah and the school for undertaking such an important task.

Uncle Charlie, his brother and his sisters, the Italians of Tontitown, the Mexicans all across Arkansas, our Vietnamese seminarian and his family, and the new Sudanese parishioners in Helena remind me of one of our responsibilities as the Church — in the name of Jesus Christ, to welcome the newcomer. We Catholic Americans have a critical obligation in this regard, for we are an immigrant Church; our own diocese is rich in more than 150 years of immigrant history.

I'm reminded of some beautiful words of St. Edith Stein:

"For the Christian there is no such thing as a 'stranger.' There is only the neighbor — the person who happens to be next to us, the person most in need of our help. Whether he is related to us or not... doesn't make a difference. Christ's love knows no boundaries, stops at no limits."

August 26, 2000

Relationship with Jesus brings joy, sorrow

Louis (pronounced "Louie"), a longtime friend, died a few weeks ago. I first met Louis in the late 1970s, when I was his associate pastor. Like many parishioners, he was the son of Italian immigrants whose "truck farms" once punctuated the highway on which the parish was located. They were proud of their heritage, their families and their Church. It was a pleasure to be among them.

Louis was also an active member of the St. Vincent de Paul Society, and each Sunday after early Mass I joined him and the others for breakfast at the Bonanza Steak House. All of them were old enough to be my father. We laughed, chided one another and solved the world's problems over bacon and eggs. They became my good friends.

After I moved to another parish, we still kept in touch, and seeing them always brought a smile to my face. I last saw Louis in March, when I was in Memphis to give a talk; he and our mutual friend, Tony, waited around afterward to say hello. We laughed as in the old days and reminisced about our other friends; some had died, others were in poor health. Little did I know that it would be our last meeting.

Louis' son called my office the day his father died. Unbeknownst to me, Louis had left written instructions that I should be asked to preside at his funeral. I was saddened that because of an unchangeable commitment I was not able to do so, but I promised to offer Mass for the repose of his soul.

A week or so later, Louis' son sent me a photocopy of a handwritten letter he had found among his father's personal effects. Dated Oct. 20, 1996, it read,

Dear Jesus,

Today I heard a talk from one who turned his back on you and found courage to seek you again. I too turned my back to you, but returned to my faith and love of you.

With this letter I again ask forgiveness for my past sins and ask you to give me strength to never sin again. Help me do the things expected of me, be more tolerant of my fellow-man and love all people.

Teach me to pray more and to give more of myself to you, my family, Church, and friends so I may have a happy death.

I pray I will see you in heaven.

Louis

A jumble of emotions for the Lord — love, sorrow, joy, longing and gratitude.

Louis and Jesus were on a first name basis. The tenderness of the letter did not surprise me, because Louis' love for the Lord was readily apparent. That love motivated his goodness to others, made him sad and sorry for his sins, filled him with joy and endeared him to so many of us. A jumble of emotions for the Lord — love, sorrow, joy, longing and gratitude. It's what the early Christian monks of the Egyptian desert called "compunction."

When it dawns on us that we are sinners and that God has forgiven us, we are filled with a mix of emotions: contrition for our misdeeds and gratitude for God's mercy; embarrassment for our selfishness and wonder at God's generosity; sorrow for our small-mindedness and joy at the freedom God has opened for us.

The effect of compunction is beatitude. St. John Chrysostom wrote, "It is possible to be in mourning for one's own sins and in joy because of Christ."

St. Nilus wrote, "Lamentation over one's sins brings a very sweet sadness and a bitterness which tastes like honey, being seasoned with a marvelous hope. That is why it nourishes the body, causes the depths of the soul to shine with joy, enriches the heart and causes our whole being to thrive. How right David was to sing, 'Tears have become my bread day and night.'" (Psalm 41:4)

And Abba Isaiah wrote, "Sadness according to God… is a joy, the joy of seeing yourself in God's will… Sadness according to God does not weigh on the soul, but says to it, 'Do not be afraid! Up! Return!' God knows that man is weak, and strengthens him."

Compunction is the amazement of a desperately ill person at the news that he has been cured. He never forgets the disease, and thus he never forgets the cure. That's what Louis wrote to Jesus — he would never forget the sinfulness, and he would never forget the forgiveness. He saw himself in God's will — thus he was a man of hope and joy.

Dear Louis,

I'm sorry I couldn't come to your funeral, but I sure appreciate the fact that you wanted me there. It would have been my honor. I would have talked about breakfast at Bonanza, about my calling you 'Luigi,' about your toughness and tenderness. I would have even thrown in a few Italian prayers to honor your parents! I remember how your eyes welled up with tears when you spoke of them.

But most of all, I would have talked about your love for Jesus and your gratitude for his mercy. He gave you hope, and you never forgot what he did for you.

Pray for me, too, Louis, that we will meet again in heaven.

Your friend,

Father Pete

October 12, 2002

Teachers witness 'how everything fits together'

This spring I have been taking part in a number of high school graduation ceremonies, including that of my nephew, Will Alexander. There is a certain predictability to graduations, but there is also something unique to each, depending on the philosophy of the school and the personalities of its students and teachers.

At the end of one graduation (St. Joseph in Conway), I noticed a faculty member wiping a tear from her eye as the graduates exited the church. I do not know her, but I assumed she was both proud and sad that the young people she had taught are moving on. It probably wasn't always easy to teach them.

Several Sundays ago, I had breakfast with one of my former high school teachers, George Beck. George coached basketball and football and taught one section of senior religion. Although he has lived in Dallas for almost 30 years, his daughter, son-in-law and granddaughter now live in North Little Rock, and he and his wife visit our area frequently. It has been a pleasure renewing our acquaintance after all these years, particularly because George had a significant impact on my life when I was 17.

The section of my high school class with whom I spent most of each day was composed of kids I had known since first grade. We were like brothers and sisters, who knew one another's strengths and quirks, who could play off one another's antics as if following a script. Apparently teachers considered us a handful. Years after we graduated, one of the priests who taught us told me he used to spend 10 minutes in a dark room each day before he faced our class. If only we had known ... I'm afraid we would have been worse.

Enter George Beck, a few years older than we were, recently married, just out of college. Young guy, new husband, new coach, new teacher — ordinarily this would have been a recipe for classroom disaster, but that is not at all how it turned out. What I remember about George is not the course he taught, but the witness he gave. He was a man of faith, comfortable talking about God with kids just beginning to find their way. He took us seriously, he treated us with respect, and he taught us how to be Catholic adults in our corner of the world. This he did primarily by example, not by lesson plan.

> *What I remember about George is not the course he taught, but the witness he gave.*

He recently told me over breakfast that he had felt woefully unprepared to teach us religion that year. I said we learned a great deal from him nonetheless. Students don't often think of teachers as "having a life" outside the classroom, but George showed us how everything fits together in faith, and he had no problem letting us know he was still a work in progress. We took note and remembered his class in the ensuing years.

George also shared with me some behind-the-scenes anecdotes of his time at our high school. The non-Catholic head football coach who gave him the job of making sure the team got to Mass on holy days, and the pastor who didn't appreciate their showing up in shorts. The assistant principal, Sister Inez, who kept him out of hot water with the principal when he blundered through inexperience. His weekend job managing the neighborhood Catholic Club in order to make ends meet. The squabbles, sometimes physical, he had to referee between parents of competing teams. We didn't hear those stories when we were seniors, but it was clear to us that George did have a life outside the classroom, and we saw through his eyes how everything fit together, through love, faith, commitment and responsibility.

When I saw the teacher at St. Joseph wipe a tear from her eyes at graduation last Saturday, I couldn't help but think she probably had a powerful impact on the graduates.

I wonder how many Catholics in Arkansas are teachers? I hazard a guess that their number is very large. They teach kids of all ages and abilities in public, private and Catholic schools. They challenge the bright students, light fires under the lazy ones, and ache with the struggling ones. They have more homework to do each night than they give the kids. They often accept more extracurricular responsibilities than they should because they want to give young people a variety of opportunities. They take summer courses because they want to be better teachers. They have families — "lives" — of their own and try their best to be good spouses and parents.

And whether or not they realize it, they hold a power few people hold — the power to inspire a young mind and a young heart. When Catholic teachers deliberately approach their job as a God-given vocation, when they consciously live their faith in the classroom, they also allow God to inspire young souls. It matters not whether they're allowed to speak a word about Church in their lessons; by example their faith speaks volumes.

George Beck is now a grandfather, and he hasn't taught in a classroom for years. I have no doubt that God used him in the late 60s to help me grow up and to inspire me to follow my vocation. And I have no doubt that the Catholic teachers of Arkansas are having just such an impact on their students, an impact more powerful than they will ever know.

May 25, 2002

Families are at the core of the Church

My close friends, Sherry and Dick Orians, recently celebrated their 33rd wedding anniversary. Dick has been principal of St. Louis School in Memphis for 30 years, and Sherry is guidance secretary at Christian Brothers High School. Their three children, a daughter and two sons, are grown, but they often come together as a family.

Both Sherry and Dick have hobbies and leisure interests, but to tell the truth, Dick has more than Sherry — fishing and duck hunting chief among them. Sherry will not go hunting (too early, too cold, too dirty), but occasionally she goes fishing with Dick. Through the years, she has had no objection to his hunting and fishing almost whenever he wishes, but when the kids were small, there was a simple rule:

"One child minimum."

In other words, "Fish, hunt, coach, play golf, but you must take at least one of our children with you."

The rule is a common-sense approach to a potentially touchy situation, typical of Sherry's straightforward style. It has worked well. In fact, I have benefited from Dick's know-how on many fishing and hunting trips. Often one of the kids was with us.

Sherry's simple rule is just one example of the Orians' ability to keep the entire family in mind as they go about life. They instinctively view their schedule and their decisions in light of what's good for the whole family, even now that their children are well into their 20s. This consistent perspective gives their marriage strength.

Using an ancient expression, we often refer to the family as the "domestic Church," because the Church is the family of God. Families are schools of love, faith, Christian life and human development. In our families we learn the value of work, the joy of being part of a community, the protection and security of discipline, and the necessity of forgiveness.

Family life is at the core of the mission of the Church and forms our understanding of Church, community and world. When we say we are a "member" of a family, we don't mean that we have "joined" the family as we might an organization. Rather, we mean that our particular family is our origin, identity and first point of reference. Whether or not we realize it, our family profoundly affects the way we understand ourselves as part of society and the world.

Every one of us is part of a whole, and what we do always has an impact on someone else — or many "someone elses."

One reason I have always liked the Orians' rule is that its underlying philosophy could be applied to many situations. In how many of our daily contacts would it be of benefit to mark our words and make our decisions in light of "the whole" (the "whole staff," the "whole company," the "whole group," the "whole parish")? Every one of us is part of a whole, and what we do always has an impact on someone else — or many "someone elses." It is especially true that one person's selfishness and anger have an impact on others.

It seems to me that more and more people are losing a sense of their place in the family of God, meaning in this case both the Church and the world. Ironically, as the Church and world grow smaller because of mass communication and travel, there seems to be a growing philosophy of navigating through life as islands unto ourselves. Folks seem to be drawn increasingly into a posture that either insulates them from others or places them at the center rather than as part of a wonderfully diverse whole. They ask, "How will this affect me?" and not "How will this affect us?"

It is precisely here that we Catholics have a powerful gift to offer. The Church is "one" and "catholic." Unity is the very essence of the Church, because it has its origin in the Holy Trinity; there is "one Lord, one faith, one baptism." (Ephesians 4) At the same time, the Church proclaims the fullness of the faith, bears the full means of salvation, and embraces all time and every place. Our oneness and catholicity constantly teach us to remember our place in God's family. They stretch us far beyond parish and town, reminding us that there are no foreigners, only sisters and brothers.

If we take to heart these marks of the Church, we gain a new outlook on both our corner of the world and on those far-away places and people who are equally loved by our Heavenly Father, for whom he also sent his son as Savior. The Church is the sacrament of God's plan for everything and everyone he has created.

One evening this summer, I joined Dick and Sherry for dinner at a restaurant. As we were led inside by the hostess, we noticed a well-dressed, middle-aged man sitting alone at a corner table. Within a few moments, he started making small talk with us from across the room. As people filled the restaurant, a young family with a baby was seated at the table next to his, and he struck up a conversation with them as well. Everyone enjoyed watching the family and how they joyfully cared for their baby. After they left the restaurant, the man turned and said to us, "That could still be me, but when I was young I partied too much and thought only about myself."

God draws us to himself as a family. Blessed are we — and blessed is the world — when we take our family into consideration in all we do.

September 21, 2002

Physical healing is Christ at work

M y closest friend is a doctor of internal medicine. Many of
his patients were also our fellow parishioners, so a few
years ago we began making rounds together once a week. Since
he frequented the 6:15 a.m. weekday parish Mass, most
Thursdays we would meet after Mass in the hospital doctors'
lounge. I listened in as he exchanged medical updates with
other doctors and nurses: emergency admissions during the
night, patients' progress following surgery, test results, and
treatment protocols. After a cup of coffee, we started rounds. I
brought my list of parishioners, and he brought his list of
patients.

As a priest I had visited the sick countless times, but making
rounds gave me insight into medical care "from the inside." I
watched as the doctor cared for the sick, listened as he asked
and answered questions, and observed the complex process of
deciding and arranging proper treatment. I had been involved
for a number of years in the selection of health care plans for
diocesan employees, but making rounds helped me understand that world from the perspective of physicians and hospitals, and thus enabled me to give better advice to our bishop.

Before we left each hospital room, I gave a blessing to the
patients, Catholic and non-Catholic alike. After completing
rounds, the doctor and I would have a bowl of soup, then go
for a run in the neighborhood. During the run we solved the
world's problems.

This Thursday custom became not only part of our routine
— in a certain sense, it also became part of the hospital's routine. On other days when I visited patients by myself, nurses

would ask, "Where's Dr. Kraus?" And frequently folks would ask him, "Where's Father Pete?" After a few years we had discussed so many facets of medical care that he would quip, "You're almost a doctor"; and I would respond, "Well, you're almost a priest."

We knew there was a grain of truth in the kidding.

Any priest will tell you that when we visit hospitals, patients often call us "Doctor." Certainly part of the reason is that the hospitalized are dealing with doctors all day long, and it becomes an unconscious habit to add "Dr." to every name. But making rounds with Dr. Kraus I noticed that patients sometimes referred to him and other doctors as "Father." I'm sure we confused them with our "team visit"; but because both "Doctor" and "Father" had a significant role to play in their healing, the confusion was in some respects much more telling than the distinction.

Both vocations involve bringing the healing presence of Christ to the sick, for all healing comes from Christ. There is not one aspect of human life — the bodily — that God has placed in our hands, and another — the spiritual — that he has kept for himself; our entire lives are in his hands, and he uses a variety of means, and a variety of people, to heal us in body and soul. All healing comes from Christ, and he wants to heal the whole person.

It's that truth, and Jesus' reminder that "when I was ill you cared for me," that inspired our ancestors to found Catholic hospitals, and inspired saints like Martin de Porres to devote themselves to the sick. They saw the face of Jesus in the sick and were drawn to care for him out of love.

But there's something more. As he went about his healing ministry, Jesus was inaugurating his Father's kingdom and undoing the effects of sin. Those who bring healing to the sick — through medical care, pastoral care, spiritual care, domestic care, sacramental care, research, etc. — are participating in the Lord Jesus' work of re-creating the world in God's image, of undoing the damage done to humanity through original sin.

Jesus made it very clear that there is no cause-and-effect relationship between an individual's sin and his or her illness. But the damage done to the human race because of sin manifests itself in many ways, including illness, and ultimately it manifests itself in death. The Lord's own death destroyed death's power over us, however, and his healing extends through all who work to restore health to the sick.

> *Jesus made it very clear that there is no cause-and-effect relationship between an individual's sin and his or her illness.*

The fact that all healing comes from Christ is the reason the Church supports genuine advances in medical science but opposes any practices based on the assumption that we have ultimate control over human life (thus, for example, we oppose abortion, sterilization, in-vitro fertilization, human embryo research, and euthanasia). The authentic healing arts are truly the power of God displayed, and for that reason we always respect God's sovereignty over the healing process; moreover, God's power is all the more evident in loving doctors, nurses, or ministers who look for Christ in every patient. When they find that medicine is not up to the task of physical healing, they still bring hope that the mystery of Christ's own suffering is lovingly present in those they serve.

It is an awesome realization that those called to the vocation of healing work with Christ himself in re-creating the world. Let's pray that Christ may always be their inspiration, and that the Father's wisdom will always be their first and only guide.

By the way, I may have become "almost a doctor" after years of making rounds, but I never became "almost a marathoner," despite those energetic runs through the neighborhood after rounds. But I sure had a good time.

November 11, 2000

Have you thanked your parish secretary?

Among the many unsung heroines and heroes of the Church are thousands of parish secretaries.

They are a special breed, unique for their dedication and generosity, indispensable in the variety of roles they play. They are at once receptionists and counselors, intermediaries and managers, bookkeepers and social workers, detectives and confidants.

As I think of the parish secretaries with whom I have had the privilege to work, a flood of names and fond memories pop into my head: Ethel, Donna, Virginia, Sweetie, Louise, Shirley, Marge, Harriet, Joyce, Nancy, Judi and Peggy.

All of them bring a special gift to their parishes, and they are the backbone of parish life. Often, parishioners are unaware of the long hours they work and the countless behind-the-scenes tasks they perform to ensure that everything runs smoothly.

Usually they are a parishioner's or visitor's first contact with the parish. They shift gears constantly, because their service is linked directly to the lives of others. What has happened today in the life of a family in the parish often determines how the secretary's day will unfold. In a parish office, one never knows whether the next phone call will be from a grieving family, a newcomer, the bank or the plumber.

Believe it or not, sometimes there are complaints, and parish secretaries are posted at the front lines. They listen, explain, pass along the message, heal, repair and save the day — usually getting no credit for having done so. Daily they are confronted with a host of expectations (often conflicting), and they are subject to all manner of evaluation, but they take it in stride. Although it is not in their job description to read minds, they are expected to do so. Amazingly, they succeed.

Although it is not in their job description to read minds, they are expected to do so. Amazingly, they succeed.

There is tedium, too, and accuracy matters when counting the collection, recording sacramental information, assigning Sunday ministers, or making reports to the diocesan office.

Scheduling software notwithstanding, how do they keep track of the fact that altar server Harry should be assigned to the same Mass as his lector-dad, Miles, and his extraordinary minister-mom, Susan? How do they balance the checkbook while the phone is ringing and the doorbell chiming? How do they remember to tell Father, as he rushes from one appointment to the next, that Mrs. Smith is in the hospital and needs the anointing of the sick?

Church work is about Christian discipleship, but one must also have street smarts to be a parish secretary. As one recently told me, "Bishop, you wouldn't believe who comes to the door." I would believe, and I know that a good dose of holy skepticism and good humor makes the job easier. As pastor of the Church in Arkansas, I am proudly confident that whoever does come to our doors, each is treated as Christ.

Large parishes have multiple secretaries, each of whom carries out a delegated set of important tasks. Small parishes have one secretary (perhaps part-time), the jack-of-all-trades who runs the place with quiet competence. Rarely are parish secretaries paid a salary commensurate with their work, and in many cases they just volunteer, out of love for the Lord. What would we do without them?

When someone accepts the job of parish secretary, she is soon astounded at the sheer variety and volume of the work and says to herself, "I would never have guessed that so much goes on in the parish office."

She probably wonders how she will get it all done, probably works past closing time, and probably doesn't count the cost. Realizing both the amount of work and the amount of good accomplished, she responds with a generous heart. Her response is one of faith in the Lord, love for his people, and stewardship of her own gifts.

We don't thank our parish secretaries near enough. Why not give yours a call or write her a note to express your gratitude? No doubt she'll be busy when she receives it, but she'll welcome the break and smile that someone noticed.

September 20, 2003

TO LIFE!

We must first begin to change hearts against abortion

Bishop Sartain delivered this homily during the Mass for Life Jan. 21, 2001.

Several years ago I began doing some amateur genealogical research, and in the process of gathering family birth and death records I came across a number of newspaper obituaries. One in particular caught my attention: that of my uncle, William Riley Sartain, who died in the summer of 1911 at the age of eight months. I would like to share with you part of his obituary, which appeared in the July 11, 1911, issue of *The South Pittsburg Hustler.*

"On Monday morning of this week the death angel visited the home of Mr. and Mrs. L.B. Sartain on Holly Avenue and plucked from the garden to transplant amid the roses of heaven, little William Riley, their eight-month old son, who had suffered several days with an abscess of the head and who had undergone an operation by Dr. Steele, the celebrated Chattanooga specialist. But little hopes of the child's recovery were entertained from the beginning, yet everything was done it seems that could be, but the Giver of all good saw fit to take the little one unto himself and he departed this life as an angel and is now at the right hand of God beckoning the loved ones on this side to come over to him and the righteous evermore. Funeral services were conducted at the Catholic Church Tuesday morning at 10 o'clock by Father Devery of the Paulist Fathers, Winchester and interment followed in Patton cemetery attended by a large number of friends and relatives of the parents. To the bereaved, we extend condolence."

Reading the clipping I cannot help being touched by the pain my grandparents must have felt at the death of their little boy, the second son they had lost. That same summer of 1911 my grandmother was pregnant with my father, and she must have been drained by anxiety over the health of the little one about to be born as well as the health of her two surviving sons. Since my grandfather was the town druggist, I am confident that, just as the obituary stated, "everything was done ... that could be" to save my infant uncle's life.

Reading the obituary I am also struck by the gentleness of its words and the respect for human life they convey. It is as if the little boy who died was the reporter's own, as if the whole community had suffered a great loss. Even more, I am struck by the way the reporter wrote un-self-consciously about the spiritual meaning of this death; he acknowledged that "the Giver of all good saw fit to take the little one unto himself." God was in charge.

Those were simpler days in many ways, to be sure. One might say that the circumstances surrounding my uncle's brief life were very different from those with which we are concerned this afternoon. This child was treated with the utmost reverence and care — "Everything was done ... that could be done." And as it happened, my grandmother herself died only three years later, of a ruptured appendix, at the age of 35. Years later, a druggist like his father before him, my father often questioned whether his older brothers and mother would have died had they enjoyed the benefit of today's medical knowledge.

But there are also similarities between our gathering today and those sad circumstances of 1911. Anxious parents; a pregnant mother with many worries; a fragile infant; the need for good medical care; a passion to do absolutely everything possible to save a life; strained family relationships spawned by an unexpected turn of events; the need for God's healing.

Today is not about nostalgia, however; we do not ask to bring back the old days. I can tell you that my father would never have wanted to bring back the time when, as he used to say, "little boys died of earaches," and young mothers died of appendicitis. Instead, today we are about calling to mind the truth that binds us to that generation and every other.

In a few moments we will march in silent witness to what we know to be true: that every life, without exception, is sacred, from the moment of conception to natural death. Our brief walk will be a public proclamation that we believe life is God's gift. But now we are gathered at the Eucharist to pray and meditate on the truth we profess. I believe God is calling us to deepen our own acceptance of that truth, so that our witness might be unblemished and uncompromised.

1973 was a watershed year for our country, a tragic year, when abortion was legalized and protected under law. But we must remember that Roe vs. Wade did not appear out of nowhere; it was the by-product of a gradual erosion of values fueled by a torrent of wars, unchecked and unbalanced material success, depersonalizing technological development, centuries of bigotry and indifference, and an unthinkable holocaust of another kind. The circumstances which made it possible for the Supreme Court of the United States to legalize abortion came gradually and seductively. To be sure, most of the scientific and cultural advancements we have witnessed in our century are something to be celebrated; but along the way, as we cheered the progress, we did not always take time to make sure that the truths that never change were not lost in the shuffle. What's most seductive about our success is that we think we accomplish it on our own.

What's most seductive about our success is that we think we accomplish it on our own.

We believe that human life is sacred. Our task is to let that truth permeate every single aspect of our lives, every relationship, every decision we make, every success we enjoy, our every word and every action. Just as Roe v. Wade evolved from a gradual erosion of values in every aspect of society, so must the road to healing cover every track. An end to abortion on demand will not be secure if we do not examine our individual and collective consciences and let God teach us how to live and how to submit every facet of life and society to his sovereign wisdom.

You and I are here because we believe that we will be judged on how we treat the most innocent and most vulnerable, the unborn, the frail elderly, and the terminally ill. We know the commandment, "Thou shalt not kill," and we believe God calls us to do what we can to put an end to the killing.

I want to affirm publicly and clearly what we Catholic bishops wrote in our November 2000 statement titled, "Abortion and the Supreme Court: Advancing the Culture of Death":

"As religious leaders, we know that human life is our first gift from a loving Father and the condition for all other earthly goods. We know that no human government can legitimately deny the right to life or restrict it to certain classes of human beings. Therefore the Court's abortion decisions deserve only to be condemned, repudiated and ultimately reversed."

It is tragic that the further we advance in time from 1973, many in our nation have resigned themselves to the misconception that abortion is a "right" and will always remain so. To assert that anyone has a "right" to take an unborn human life is wrong, terribly wrong. If anyone's rights need protection, it is those of the unborn. You and I must speak for them. St. Paul's words to the Corinthians in today's liturgy are especially apropos:

"… there are many parts, yet one body. The eye cannot say to the hand, "I do not need you," nor again the head to the feet, "I do not need you." Indeed, the parts of the body that seem to be weaker are all the more necessary."

But let there be no mistake: even should a human life amendment be passed tomorrow, you and I have accepted an awesome responsibility to advocate for an even deeper change — not just change in the law of our nation, but change in the heart of our nation. And we must admit, openly and humbly, that such conversion must begin with ourselves.

Jesus taught that the commandment against killing has broad implications. Anger and abuse kill, too, in their own way. So does indifference to the poor Lazarus at the gate. And prejudice. And refusing to forgive. And violence in any form. The end of abortion begins with a change in each of our hearts and a resolve to do no harm to anyone under any circumstances. It ends when we reach out as a matter of justice to those women and men who feel trapped into considering abortion as a solution to a problem. If we are truly against abortion, we must extend a hand, and open our pocketbooks, to those who need material assistance in carrying a pregnancy to full term, who need love, and who need moral support in making truly moral choices.

Anger and abuse kill, too, in their own way. So does indifference to the poor Lazarus at the gate. And prejudice. And refusing to forgive. And violence in any form.

We must also offer a firm hand of compassion to women who by exercising a legal "choice" have become victims of abortion themselves. They are our sisters, our mothers, our own. To them we offer assurance of God's forgiveness and our pledge to help the healing. But won't our words of mercy ring even more true if we also ask forgiveness of them for any action on our part that contributed to the culture of death in which such desperate choices are made? Please forgive us for not noticing the pain in your eyes, for our selfishness, our unaccepting ways, our murmured gossip, the cold shoulder we turned to you in your time of need, for not going out of our way to offer you another choice. We need your mercy, too.

The world needs our public witness to the sanctity of unborn life. We have a responsibility to give it. But today let us ask the One who gave us life to shape our hearts and deeds in every way according to his will. Then will our witness be clear and unsullied. Then will we slow and even reverse the torrent that caused the erosion of values that led to Roe vs. Wade. Then our walk to the Capitol, though silent, will shout loudly of the life that only God can give ... and take.

Thank God the days have passed when little boys have to die of earaches, young mothers of appendicitis. And thank God for the advancements our century has made. But may the days soon return when everyone recognizes that all of life is sacred, when the culture of death has died, and when we are at peace because we have given to God everything we have and are.

January 27, 2001

Everyone's vocation is to live and praise God

Bishop Sartain delivered this homily at the Mass for Life Jan. 20, 2002.

When I was five months old my mother arranged for a family portrait of her and the five children as a Christmas gift to my father.

I have a copy of it in my living room, and when I look at it I often smile and shake my head. I have a look on my face not unlike a deer in headlights, and a little spot on the front of my white jumpsuit where mom's Kleenex had not quite caught the drool running down the front of my chin.

Every once in a while it dawns on me that the person in that family portrait is the same one I look at in the mirror every morning as I shave. Amazing.

By the same token, the person I see in the mirror each day is also the 7-year-old in my First Communion picture, the 9-year-old in the Cub Scout uniform, the 17-year-old dressed in tux for the prom, the 26-year-old being ordained priest, the 47-year-old being ordained bishop, and the 49-year-old standing before you today.

The same person appears in each photograph, yet in each I appear differently. Full head of hair, less hair. Beard, beardless. Suit and tie, Roman collar. Tuxedo, vestments. A few pounds overweight, a few pounds underweight. Tanned, pale. Three feet 5 inches, 5 feet 9 inches. Yet always the same person.

We have home movies, too, some taken before I was born. One in particular has always intrigued me, showing my mother pregnant with me. Me! The same "me" standing before you today.

But 50 years ago I was not big enough to survive on my own, so my mother carried me in her womb. For a while I did not have all my fingers or toes, and she did everything for me. I could not breathe because my lungs had not yet developed, so I shared the oxygen from her blood. I could not see because my eyes were young and my eyelids shuttered tight, so she was my sight.

At first I could not hear, but after a few months in the womb I heard my mother, father, sisters, aunts and uncles "oo-ing" and "ahh-ing" at the baby to be born. I probably even gave an excited kick every once in a while when I recognized one of their voices. Just ask my mom.

Come to think of it, were you to ask my mother who she was carrying in her womb in those old home movies, she would say, "Peter!"

She would be speaking the truth, because it was I in her womb, the same person who stands before you today. You see, I have been "me" since the moment I was conceived.

The Bible has a sure and uncomplicated sense of life in the womb. The psalmist David wrote, "Truly you have formed my inmost being; you knit me in my mother's womb."

Today we heard the prophet Isaiah say, "Now the Lord has spoken who formed me as his servant from the womb."

The prophet Jeremiah wrote that the Lord said to him, "Before I formed you in the womb I knew you, before you were born I dedicated you."

And when Mary went to visit Elizabeth, she proclaimed, "At the moment the sound of your greeting reached my ears, the infant in my womb leaped for joy."

This simple, direct way of speaking reveals God's perspective on life in the womb: from the moment of conception, God loves every human life. He loves each and every human person, no matter his or her stage of development or age, and he wants each to know and enjoy his love in fullness.

He wants each and every one to be with him for eternity. There are no exceptions! He desires loving communion with us all.

There is another aspect of human life we must never ignore. Woven throughout the Old Testament, the New Testament, and constant Church teaching is the undeniable conviction that "to live is to praise God."

I need not be old enough to understand that I am praise to God. I need not have the capacity to speak or walk or work to be praise to God.

Just by being alive I am praise to God! I need not be old enough to understand that I am praise to God. I need not have the capacity to speak or walk or work to be praise to God.

Just by the very fact that I am alive, I am praise to God.

The Lord Jesus teaches us to be clear and constant praise, to live in a way that is consistent with our "destiny of praise," for he knew that when we embrace our relationship with our heavenly Father — just as he has embraced us — we discover what it means to be alive. Only in God do we find life, because only God gives live.

To live is to praise! To praise is to live!

Only God can give life, and only God can take life. We must be very careful to remember as we navigate the 21st century that the origin and destiny of every human being is found in God alone.

We are creatures of God, not gods. Just as we depended entirely on the life and sustenance of our mothers while in the womb, so — and even more so — do we depend on God for all things in this life and the life to come.

Our mothers nurtured and sustained us as we developed, and it was only after years of benefiting from their love, and that of our fathers, that we gained independence.

It is a sign of growth and maturity when we realize just how dependent we are on God for absolutely everything, when we admit that only looking to him do we find life, that only by making our lives praise do we become fully alive.

It is here that my analogy stops short. Unlike our relationship with parents, our dependence on God never ends.

To separate ourselves from God is to die. In fact, it is a sign of growth and maturity when we realize just how dependent we are on God for absolutely everything, when we admit that only looking to him do we find life, that only by making our lives praise do we become fully alive.

You and I celebrate life today, and in a few moments we will join hundreds of others to Walk for Life.

Our strong conviction that abortion is killing innocent life comes from our belief in the sovereignty of God, the inviolability of human life, and the destiny of every human person. And that strong conviction urges us not simply to state our beliefs but to put them into practice, to work tirelessly, respectfully, and non-violently for an end to abortion.

It urges "individual Catholics and the many institutions and organizations of the Church to unite in an unprecedented effort to restore respect and legal protection for every human life — to be what the Holy Father asks us to be: a people of life and a people for life." (Pastoral Plan for Pro-Life Activities, USCCB, 2001)

What is frequently referred to as a matter of "choice" is in reality a matter of life and death. It is a matter of right and wrong. It is a matter of accepting our destiny and the destiny of every human person from the very hands of God, or of ignoring it.

It is a matter of recognizing that I am not a god who makes up rules for my world by "choice," but that I am a creature of God whose fulfillment is found in his wisdom alone.

You and I have the responsibility and the vocation — from the womb! — to be praise of God, to live as loving creatures of God, to love and protect every human person from the moment of his or her conception, and to do everything in our power to ensure that such is the law in our country.

Please God, with your help, may it be so.

January 26, 2002

Like pope, elderly can show the fullness of God's mystery

A local radio station recently asked if I would agree to an interview regarding the state of the Holy Father's health and the process for electing a new pope. I declined.

I do not think the gentleman who called had bad intent — the Holy Father's health is a topic of natural interest, and folks are always fascinated by a papal election. However, if we focus on the future election of his successor, we will miss the profound witness of this stage of his life: the holy Christian witness of those in their senior years, the courageous Christian witness of those who suffer with Christ.

There is an assumption inherent in casual speculation about the "next" pope that once one is ill or aged, the fruitfulness of his or her life is somehow diminished. In the particular case of Pope John Paul II, the assumption is thus that he is past his ministerial prime. However, a pope is not a C.E.O. — he is successor to Peter, first of the Apostles, a witness to Christ in every experience, and in every stage, of his own life.

We have much to learn from observing and listening to the Holy Father in his 85th year. His witness challenges us to reflect on the role of suffering and aging in our lives and the lives of those around us. Do we somehow look "beyond" them — or even ignore them — as if their time is past, as if there is nothing more for them to contribute? If it is we who are aged or ill, do we assume that we are past the age and state of health for "growing in wisdom and grace?"

The pope commented on March 20 that patients in what is commonly called "persistent vegetative state" (PVS) should be given food and water, even if supplied artificially, since those are ordinary means of preserving life.

Patients in the "vegetative" state have sleep/wake cycles and thus are not comatose, but they give no sign of awareness of themselves or their surroundings. The Holy Father's point is that to deprive these persons of food and fluids, even though they cannot feed themselves, is to deprive them of the ordinary, basic things they need and deserve for living. To withhold food and fluids from persons in PVS would be a kind of euthanasia by omission.

In framing his remarks, the Holy Father first commented on the term "persistent vegetative state." He wrote that no human being ever descends to the status of a vegetable or animal. "Even our brothers and sisters who find themselves in the clinical condition of a 'vegetative state' retain their human dignity in all its fullness. The loving gaze of God the Father continues to fall upon them, acknowledging them as his sons and daughters, especially in need of help."

It is a striking and crucial point that a human person, no matter his or her age or state of health, will never be a vegetable or simply "vegetate."

It is a striking and crucial point that a human person, no matter his or her age or state of health, will never be a vegetable or simply "vegetate." Human life is always human life, even if physically impaired by serious disease or advanced years. A human person at every age and in any illness bears God-given dignity as a child made in his image and likeness.

Illness and age do not extinguish the extraordinary power of a single human life to witness mightily to the mystery of God. One does not have to speak to be a witness. One does not have to run a race to show the capability of the human body. One does not have to be "productive" in a functionary sense to have worth.

Illness and age do not make one less human or less valuable.

In a sense, illness and age take us to the edge of our faith because they can be mysterious and even confounding to us; but in another, more important, sense, they take us to faith's center.

The Lord Jesus bore our infirmities and endured our suffering on the cross. When Jesus first predicted his suffering, Peter could not believe that suffering could somehow be part of God's plan. Later, at the Transfiguration, Peter wanted to remain looking "beyond" the present moment toward Jesus' heavenly glory, his preference being to ignore what Jesus had told him. But Jesus knew it was crucial that his followers learn the fullness of his mystery — suffering, death, and resurrection out of love for us.

Those who suffer are close to Jesus and share his suffering, and through him their suffering bears fruit for the world. They share the dignity of the Lord himself. Who of us would dare say that suffering made him of less worth than he would have been had he not suffered for us? Think of the power that comes to those who join their suffering to his.

John Paul II's wise and holy witness of suffering and advanced age is important to our generation — as a reminder that every moment of life is sacred to God, from conception to natural death, and that God's grace is ever at work. Every human person, imbued with God's own dignity, can proclaim his wisdom — even if they are not conscious of doing so! God shows the breadth of his fatherly care in Pope John Paul's untiring faithfulness to Christ and his unstoppable witness to hope.

In fact, the sick and elderly proclaim God's wisdom in a way the healthy and young cannot. They can show us the fullness of God's mystery, his mercy, his healing, and his triumph — and evoke from us depths of love that reveal his compassionate face.

September 18, 2004

Do you have an intention for Bishop Sartain's prayer? If so, send it to him at Bishop Sartain's Prayer List, Diocese of Little Rock, 2500 North Tyler St., P.O. Box 7239, Little Rock, AR 72217.

Additional copies of
"Of You My Heart Has Spoken"
are available from:

Arkansas Catholic
P.O. Box 7417
Little Rock AR 72217

(501) 664-0125

www.arkansas-catholic.org

Please contact us for more information.

SHOULD I SHOOT?

31 Deadly Force Scenarios That'll Sharpen Your Concealed Carry Instincts

Printed in the United States
ISBN 978-0-9967874-5-1
Should I Shoot?, First Edition, Ninth Printing, 2022.
Written by Ed Combs, Mark Kakkuri and Sammy Reese
Cover Designed by Dylan Hopf
Designed by Dustin Reid and Ken Wangler

The information in this book is for informational purposes
only and does not constitute legal advice. For specific
questions, you should consult a qualified attorney.

CONTENTS

SECTION 1: AM I READY?

Buying a gun is only the first step in keeping you safe. The wisdom and planning necessary to make the proper decisions — and the understanding of laws and the realities of violent encounters — are what can make the difference between righteous use of force and a crime you don't know you're committing.

SECTION 2: SHOULD I SHOOT?

There's nothing easy or simple about defensive gun use. It's imperative that you mentally run through as many scenarios as possible now, before you're forced to decide whether to defend yourself, in order to be as ready as you can be if you're ever forced to make that call.

INTRODUCTION

In the realm of physical force, just about the only absolute that stands up to analysis is this: When it comes to stopping a determined attacker, hits count and misses don't.

Everything else is open for debate and declarative statements often fall short when we introduce logic to the topic.

"It is better to avoid a gunfight than to win one."

Really? Even when that gunfight begins because a stranger decided to start executing your fellow grocery shoppers in service to his Jihad? I would like to believe that, if faced with such a circumstance, many of the people reading this book would elect to engage the rapid mass murderer with accurate gunfire.

"If you're going to hit someone, hit him with everything you've got. If you're not going to do that, just walk away."

Hmmm … that doesn't leave much room for intermediate force options, like pepper spray or a flashlight shined in the eyes, does it? We all know that we are legally allowed to use only the force necessary to stop the threat. If stopping the threat does not require the use of deadly force, it really pays to have other options.

"Anyone sets foot in my house, they're dead."

Well, that's an odd way of looking at it, because if it turns out that the individual who snuck into your residence is a neighborhood kid with a learning disability who got scared and ran into the wrong garage, you'll be regretting that attitude and your subsequent actions until the day you die.

Nothing about the use of deadly force is easy, and very rarely is it even simple. Though rare, occasionally there is a case of a machete-wielding madman who kicks in someone's front door and rushes forward, weapon held high over his head, and who later — after three rounds to the torso stopped him — admits on tape that his intention was to kill everyone in the house. Unfortunately, self-defense shootings often occur in that cloudy area where investigators must determine "intent." Their findings are based on what our American legal system calls "the totality of the circumstances."

What that means is investigators will assess and interpret everything you knew at the time; your levels of training, experience and physical ability; environmental factors that might impact or influence your decision-making ability; and any other evidence they can find to determine one thing: Were you left with no choice but to employ deadly force to prevent imminent death or great bodily harm to yourself or another innocent party?

After that can be adequately demonstrated, all but the most zealously anti-gun prosecutors will choose to allow you to walk free without criminal charges.

But how do you know when you're at the point of having no other choice?

The only way to prepare for the potential of a deadly force incident is to start thinking about how and why such incidents happen. Then ask yourself, "What would I do if...?"

The body can't go where the mind's never been, and if you think "training" for armed self-defense ends with putting a few leisurely rounds downrange at the local sportsman's club, you will almost certainly be in for a very fast, very unpleasant series of surprises if you're ever faced with a deadly threat.

Attacks seem to happen in the dark rather than the light. They seem to happen when we're tired rather than when we're wide awake. They seem to happen when we really, really don't want to think we have to shoot someone rather than when we're absolutely certain drawing and firing would be the wisest course of action.

As I mentioned above, sometimes the bogeyman smashes through your door swinging a sword, and the decision's made for you. Usually, it's not that simple.

This collection of scenarios and tutorials will serve as your guide through the kind of thought processes you will have to practice in order to be as prepared as you can to live your life as a responsibly armed American.

They're all designed to get you thinking more often, more thoroughly and more effectively about how you carry and when to employ your emergency lifesaving gear. If you're ever forced to ask yourself that horrible question — "Should I shoot?" — we want you to be as mentally and physically prepared as possible. We cannot give you specific answers to every situation. We can give you examples that will force you to think and to decide for yourself. The more information you have and the more often you consider the various possible outcomes of various possible scenarios, the more likely you are to make the choice that is correct for you given the totality of the circumstances at the time of the incident. There are no easy answers.

This is not a textbook. This is a thought-provoking collection of stories that will provide you great insight and a real chance for you to think about the question, "Should I shoot?"

Stay alert, stay focused and stay safe.

Ed Combs
Associate Editor
Concealed Carry Magazine

CHAPTER 1
SECTION 1: AM I READY?

WHAT IF?

By Sammy Reese

You just topped off your tank and now you need something cold to drink for the ride home. While you are in the back of the gas station pondering what will quench your thirst, you hear someone yell, "Give me the money!" At first, you think it might be on TV, but you quickly realize the store is being robbed.

You are carrying concealed and have to make a split-second decision to intervene on the clerk's behalf or be a good witness for the responding police. Your most basic instinctual response is to want to help. You could draw your weapon and order the suspect to drop his weapon (if seen) and to lay down on the floor with his hands on his head. We've seen this on TV and in movies, so it must work, right?

FOOD FOR THOUGHT

The store is being robbed, not you. They have insurance and hopefully a really good camera system to capture the suspect's image for law enforcement to make a case when he's caught.

For this argument, let's say the crook has demanded the cash from the register and has a small pistol in his hand. The clerk is following the company policy of opening the register and getting the cash out. Can you legally use deadly force to protect another from great bodily injury or death? The crook has a gun pointed at the clerk, whom he's ordering to hurry up and fill the sack with cash. This is happening in milliseconds … what to do?

You stay hidden, watching everything you see and hear. The crook exits the store, jumps into a car and drives away. No one is hurt. You, the clerk and the cameras have a great description of the suspect and the car.

WHAT IF?

Let's say you go with the option to draw your weapon and try to stop the crime in progress. Now the crook has a decision to make — comply or fight his way out.

"What if…?"

I use this while responding to radio calls and you should be using it when you plan for everyday life. What if the crook is part of a team? After all, crabs run in pairs and crooks run in bunches. What, you didn't notice the layoff guy in the back corner looking at the sunflower seeds? He's the guy whose job it is to shoot anyone in the back who tries to be a hero and stop the robbery.

What if there is an off-duty police officer in the store who's being a good witness when you pop out with your gun? Are you really friend or foe? What if you have your wife or child with you and the shooting starts because the crook is a two-striker and has no desire to go back to prison for life? After the shots start flying, who knows where all those bullets are going to go?

There are lots of "What if?" questions here. Hopefully, while hiding behind the candy display, this isn't the first time you've thought about what you're going to do if you're caught in the middle of a robbery.

Train hard and constantly think about the "What if?" questions and how you will respond. It might not work as you planned, but at least you have a plan, have thought about options and aren't making it up on the fly.

THE GOOD SAMARITAN

By Sammy Reese

The concept of a "Good Samaritan" pitching in usually conjures up an image like this one, but there can be a lot more to it.

just read in the news that a concealed carry permit holder attempted to intervene in a domestic violence circumstance and ended up being shot and killed. I don't have all the details and I'm quite certain the media will put a spin on the event to suit their needs, so getting all the facts might take some time.

A man shot at a woman in a parking lot outside of a store. One round went into the ground and another went into the woman's leg. The attacker attempted to flee the scene. A husband and father of three witnessed the shooting and went to his vehicle to retrieve his pistol. When he attempted to stop the attacker from leaving, the attacker shot the man in the head, killing him instantly.

DECISION-MAKING

I can't tell you what to do or when to do it, but I can give you some insight to help you expand your thought process, give your software (brain) as much of an upgrade as possible and push you to be proficient with your hardware (self-defense tools).

When I read about the above incident, my first thought was, "Why?" Why did this gentleman make the decision to do what he did? We all should have a line in the sand, so to speak, as to when we will get involved. I plan to make you think about all kinds of "What if?" situations and discuss plans and your individual line placement.

I recently wrote about all the "What ifs?" when caught in the middle of a convenience store robbery. The example I gave had no shots fired. In this case, based on reports, the attacker fired two shots at the woman and later one fatal shot at the Good Samaritan. Do the first two shots change things? To me, it shows the attacker had crossed the line from brandishing a weapon during an argument and was now somewhere between assault with a deadly weapon and attempted murder. In this case, the woman was hit in the ankle, so was he a bad shot?

WHY DO YOU CARRY CONCEALED?

Based on what I know of the situation, I have to go back to the reason I carry a concealed weapon: to protect my family and myself. I'm not a cop anymore. Even if I was, if I was off-duty during this event, I'd be in witness-and-report mode. If I was with my family, I'd get them behind the best cover I could find. It might be in the truck heading the other way. I'd call 911 and give the dispatcher a play-by-play so responding officers would know as much as possible before they got on scene: suspect description, type of weapon seen, how many shots fired, suspect's direction of travel, type of vehicle, number and type of injuries the first responders are going to have to deal with, etc. One thing I can guarantee is there will be cops coming with lights and sirens going. Depending on where you live population-wise, there might be a lot of them coming and they will have all kinds of tools at their disposal to take the attacker into custody.

A good man lost his life doing what he thought was the right thing based on his training and experience. I wasn't there, but what I can do is use this incident to create thinking and dialogue for those who carry concealed. I want the good guys to make good decisions. Is there a possibility that if the bad guy is not stopped, he will drive off and continue shooting people? Sure, that's possible, but for argument's sake, this isn't an active shooter. He did what he did and was leaving. What should you do? What would you have done if you witnessed the same scene? What if you decided to carry a two-shot derringer with you that day? What if you had your grandma with you? Lots of "What if?" questions. Keep adding to the list and keep working the plans so you are as prepared as possible.

THE LINE IN THE SAND

By Sammy Reese

If escape isn't an option, such as an attack when your vehicle is disabled, sometimes you have no choice but to employ deadly force.

Years ago, my FTO (field training officer) would quiz me throughout my shifts and ask me all kinds of questions. The one question I've never forgotten and ask myself quite often is, "Where is the line in the sand?" Will I disobey a direct order to disengage a pursuit of a vehicle in which a child has been abducted? Will I shoot the same person in the back as they flee from me with the child as I lay on the ground with a blown-out knee? Every day, we would play the "What if?" game and work on every possible angle we could come up with.

It's been a long time since I was in Mike's car, but I still play the "What if?" game to see where my line in the sand is on all types of "Oh $#@!"-type life events. I quiz my wife, kids and students every chance I get — "If you find yourself (fill in the blank), what is your plan? What is your secondary plan? Oh, I'm not done. What's your third plan?"

MY NIGHTMARE

One of the nightmare scenarios I think of a lot is what I would do if an attack were to occur while I'm with my family.

I've already made up my mind that if I'm carjacked at the gas station (weapon seen) — and if I'm alone and not going to be taken in the vehicle — the truck is his. It's just a truck and insurance will cover it. I'm not going to use deadly force to fight for a 2006 pickup.

If the bad guy says he's taking me, though, I've already drawn the line in the sand. I've seen the end result of a carjacking/kidnapping and it's a horror I won't ever forget. The same applies if my family is in the truck. He's not getting them, and I will fight at a level the crook never dreamed existed; I will not let him take my family.

What if the above happened and you weren't armed because you decided to take a day off from concealed carry? The bad guys don't take a day off and neither should you.

ACTIVE SHOOTER

Another nightmare is the active shooter/ rapid mass murderer killing everyone he sees in the mall while I'm there with my family. In my mind, I have to protect my family at all costs. My primary objective is to get them out of the immediate area. If we can get out of the structure, that would be my first choice.

If I couldn't evacuate my family, I would search for the best cover or concealment I could find. It might be a storeroom in the back of a store or a maintenance closet. I carry a small revolver as a backup to my primary concealed carry pistol. It's a habit I started back in my cop days, and I continue to do so today. In this type of scenario, I'd be giving it to my wife or one of my kids. Yes, they all can shoot. Two of us would make for a better defense than just one.

Would I go hunting for the bad guys after I got my family to safety? That's a question I ask myself a lot, and the more I ask it, the more I decide it depends on all kinds of factors. That's not a cop-out either. I would have to be very confident I had my family secured where no one would be able to get them. We all bring different levels of training and experience to the table. The decisions we make will all be different.

My line in the sand if I am solo is one I've considered a thousand times or so. I couldn't live with myself if I ran to safety and let others get slaughtered. Doing everything possible to stop the threat is probably not the best choice in that sce-

nario were I simply aiming to make it to rocking chair age, but that's my choice.

I don't plan on charging the machine guns like Audie Murphy though. I'd go into hunt mode and use sound tactics to put the shooter(s) under duress. By this, I mean using proper movement and accurate fire to let them know they have resistance and it's not the unopposed slaughter they'd hoped for. In most active shooter events, the bad guys beat feet or kill themselves when the good guys arrive.

The new breed of terrorist attack is very well-planned and usually has multiple shooters who are extremely well-armed. A recent one took place about an hour from where I live. Yes, ISIS is here despite what the politicians are telling us. I wish I had all the answers for every possible scenario, but no one has those answers and no one can tell you what to do. The decisions we make need to be based on our level of training and the info we can gather in a very short amount of time to formulate a plan.

What's your nightmare? And what have you done to prepare for it?

CHAPTER 4
SECTION 1: AM I READY?

ROAD RAGE

By Sammy Reese

One of my old patrol partners had a saying: "The fastest way to turn a human being into a complete idiot is to put him behind the wheel of a car." We've all seen people do things while driving that caused us to shake our heads and wonder if the driver did, in fact, have a fully functioning brain. (If you haven't, please tell me where you live; I want to move there.)

The phenomenon we call "road rage" has been around for longer than I've been alive. I can remember driving with my dad — not in a car seat, and probably not even with a seat belt — listening to him yelling obscenities (and giving what I would later learn was not a finger you should walk around showing) at some driver who must have broken one of his rules of the road. What can I say? Pop had a temper and wasn't afraid of expressing his displeasure with other drivers.

At some point, these car-to-car arguments cross the line and become physical confrontations where normally calm individuals beat the crap out of each other — or worse — for what one party considers improper use of a motor vehicle. All you have to do is watch the evening news and you'll come across a story where someone ends up dead as the result of road rage and the other guy gets to spend the rest of his life in prison.

Road rage comes in many different forms. The yelling and finger gestures are like football players fighting: They have all the gear on and nothing happens except a ref throws a flag if they don't calm down. What concerns me is when hand gestures turn into a physical attack. I've been the victim of road rage a few times, and the worst incident became something more.

When my daughter, Hannah, was about 4 years old, we were in my wife's SUV driving down a two-lane road. I was in the passenger seat. Hannah was in the back middle all secure in the best kid seat money can buy. The vehicle in front of us was going slowly; I assumed the driver was looking for a parking space in front of some nearby condos. He made about three or four stops and, on the last one, my wife pulled out to pass him. When she did, he started to move forward again, so she honked the horn to let him know we were passing. We continued for a few blocks and stopped at a red light.

I saw a vehicle in the side-view mirror approaching and it was closing fast. The

car swerved into the oncoming lane and came at our SUV from the driver's side, stopping inches from the driver's door. I had no time to exit the vehicle, so I drew my concealed weapon and dove across my wife's lap, presented my pistol out the window and yelled at the man as he exited his vehicle, "Stop or I will shoot!"

I'll never forget the look on his face when he looked down the barrel of my .45-caliber pistol. He froze in place and put his hands up. I told my wife to get going as I held the man at gunpoint. After some evasive driving through the neighborhood, we stopped and called the local sheriff to report what had just happened. Time from start to finish was measured in seconds, not minutes, for me to make an assessment and then act on it.

What would you have done? Have you done a "What if?" for this type of event in your head? I hope you do now and figure out some response to this and any other road-rage-type incident.

To this day, I have no idea what set that driver off. He was never found, and he certainly didn't dial 911 to report that someone had just pointed a gun at him. I can say I'm thankful I was carrying concealed that day and didn't take the day off.

I'm not sure why tempers flare so drastically over perceived indiscretions on the road. When we accidently bump into someone on the sidewalk, we say something like, "Sorry," or, "Pardon me," and we go about our business. This doesn't seem to be the case in traffic.

What I can say is de-escalation is the best option (or, more simply, the best fight is the one you aren't in). If you've angered another driver, a simple "Excuse me" wave might calm things down. If the wave doesn't work and he or she won't let it go, you can slow down and let the driver pull away. Exit and create space.

What if you can't get away? Call 911. Tell the operator what is happening. Remain calm and do the best you can to create space.

If you are followed and attacked, what's your plan? There's a lot to think about, so take some time now to consider what you will do when a simple trip to get groceries or pick up your kids from school turns into a rolling nightmare.

RESTAURANT ETIQUETTE

By Sammy Reese

Hopefully, if you are reading this, you already know how to behave in a restaurant. What I'm talking about in terms of etiquette is what your plan is when something goes bad while you are seated in a booth or at a table with your family. By going bad, I'm talking a takeover-type robbery, where the suspect or suspects want more than just the cash in the register; they want the patrons' watches, wallets and everything else. On the extreme end of bad, a nut off his meds decides to start shooting patrons or hacking on them with a machete. If you are thinking you only go to restaurants in nice neighborhoods and this won't happen to you, my mission here is to get you thinking about what would happen if it did and what your plans are if it does.

BASICS

Start with the basic decision of where you should sit. You might not have your choice of table, but you can make sure you sit where you can get the best view of the front door and as much of the establishment as possible. I know it sounds cliché, but sitting so you don't have your back to the door isn't just a movie line … it's common sense. If you can see the bad guys out the front window of the establishment gearing up, you might have time to evacuate your family before the bad guys make it inside. Trust your gut. If something looks wrong, get out and re-evaluate.

Do you know where the exits are? Sure, there are signs over the doors, but can you get out through the kitchen if need be? Where is your closest exit and a backup if the first option is blocked? Can you throw a chair through a window? If you need your concealed weapon, can you draw it from the position in which you're seated? This one can be practiced in the comfort of your own home and done live-fire on the range. Have you talked to your family about what to do if "X" happens? I trained my kids when they were very little to follow my in-structions without hesitation. If I told them to get down on the floor, they did it.

PLANS

If you find yourself in the middle of the takeover robbery, what's your plan of action or non-action? If all the robbers want is my money, my old beat-up G Shock and the engagement ring I gave my wife are theirs; insurance will cover the loss.

What's the plan if it goes sideways and they start shooting people? I've said it before: I can't tell you what to do. I can, however, ask whether you've practiced drawing and shooting from the seated position so you know what your capabilities and limitations are. Are you prepared to take the shot? Can you safely evacuate your family from the building? Or is the floor under the table the best option so you can focus on employing deadly force?

I highly recommend force-on-force training with Simunitions if you can find a facility at which to train. I've learned more from running scenarios based on "What if?" questions and getting stung by paint pellets than any other form of training.

Keep in mind that bad things can happen anywhere, at any time — not just in restaurants. Any place people congregate is just as much a target as a secluded parking garage or back alley. They all have their dangers, and we should prepare for every environment in which we might possibly find ourselves. If the motivation is robbery, the more victims in one place, the higher the yield. If the motivation is mass murder, we already know anywhere from schools to malls can be targets.

Having thought through as many scenarios as possible makes you that much more prepared. Remember the primary mission is to keep your family safe.

INSIDE THE HOME

By Sammy Reese

It's 3:30 a.m. and you're sound asleep until you hear the sound of glass breaking. You sit up in bed, trying to shake the sleep from your head while your ears strain to hear anything. You ask yourself, was it a dream or did I really just hear glass break? You decide to grab your pistol from the nightstand safe and go investigate in your nighttime "repel boarders" gear — skivvies, barefooted, with a pistol. Is there an intruder or is your mind playing tricks on you?

Off you go down the hall toward the kitchen when you hear the sound of a cabinet closing. You yell into the dark kitchen as you round the corner, "I have a gun!" and come face to face with your daughter. You have a loaded pistol pointed at your pride and joy. Your heart rate is at more than 350 beats per minute, and when you realize you almost shot your daughter, you feel faint and sick to your stomach. Your daughter couldn't sleep, so she went to the kitchen for a glass of juice. She dropped the glass pitcher and was trying to be quiet while she cleaned it up.

Luckily, the only damage is a broken pitcher. Things could have turned out tragically, and they do more often than they should. If you keep a gun in your house to protect your family, you have to put thought and training into how you will defend the occupants of your castle.

The first step is knowing the law. Does your state have what some call the "Castle Doctrine," or the law where you, as the homeowner, don't have to first attempt to flee before you employ deadly force? The second step is what I call fortification — making your home as impenetrable as possible without having to dig a moat around it. Having a whole-house alarm system is a good start. Crooks are looking for easy targets, and hopefully the alarm sign will get them to move on. If not, the alarm sounding has a tendency to get people's attention and cause them to get out of dodge. To support the alarm, have proper lighting around your home's perimeter. For some reason, bright lights can keep the bad guys at bay. I've added a big dog to my home-defense plan. When she barks, I don't tell her to be quiet — I find out why she's on alert.

I keep a gun handy for when the fortification doesn't work or the crooks don't care about bright lights, locked doors and an audible alarm. Luckily, we had an incident happen in our home many years ago where the alarm went off due to a bad sensor. We had a plan and I had the equipment: a handheld flashlight; a pistol with a weapon-mounted light; and a bandoleer to hold spare magazines, a light and first-aid gear. I learned a long time ago that no plan survives first contact, and our plan went to crap from the beginning. I didn't realize how loud the alarm was when continuously sounding. The dog hid under the bed and I wanted to also. The noise was disorientating to the point where I had a hard time thinking and communicating with my wife. The 911 operator couldn't hear my wife at all. Let's just say we learned a lot from the experience and have made some adjustments to our "repel boarders" plan.

If you encounter someone in your home, you have to be able to identify the threat before you employ deadly force. I keep several handheld flashlights for searching and I have weapon-mounted lights on handguns, shotguns and rifles that are set up for home-defense. Searching with only a light on a loaded weapon means everything you cover with the light is also covered by the muzzle of the weapon. I would much rather shine a light into my kids' eyes or on the drunk neighbor who walked into the wrong house than a loaded weapon.

I can't tell you when to shoot. That decision has to be based on the perceived threat, but, inside your home, the intensity level is much higher since you have to protect your family. Make sure you make plans and then practice them. Going deaf at oh-dark-thirty is not the time for either.

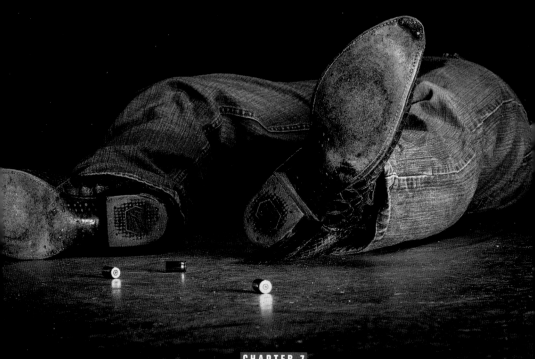

DISPARITY OF FORCE

By Sammy Reese

You and your family have just had a fun-filled day at the county fair: lots of rides and games, and you totally blew the "trying to eat only good food" diet on all kinds of funnel cakes, hot dogs and deep-fried everything. Walking to your truck, you comment to your wife that you don't remember having walked so far to get in to the fair. That's when you hear a voice from a few rows over yell, "What the hell are you looking at?"

You turn to look and, through the crowd, you see a group of five tatted-up shirtless guys who appear to be weight-lifters. One of them notices you looking over and he starts toward you, bellow-ing, "What the *&^% are you looking at?" You notice the other four are following him. As they close in, you realize these boys are all really big. The first two ap-pear to have cauliflower ears, and from the look in their eyes, they mean busi-ness. What do you do?

Use of force, especially deadly force, requires certain criteria be met before we can employ it. At its core, deadly force requires that we be in fear for our life or of great bodily injury (GBI) before we can use it to stop a threat (or, in the above scenario, multiple threats).

Today, we play the "What if?" game as it applies to a group of what at least ap-pears to be unarmed thugs but who are definitely of superior size and appear to be in great physical shape. I mentioned the cauliflower ears because, in my world of training Brazilian Jiu-Jitsu and coach-ing MMA fighters, I know those come from very hard training in either wrestling or other combat-style martial arts.

Disparity of force laws are different in some states, but let's apply the "reason-able person" test: What would any rea-sonable person in your position perceive from being in the middle of the storm in the fair parking lot? Disparity covers many standalone aspects — size, strength, age, number and skill of the assailants — and, when you combine them, especially in this case, it multiplies the threat. I know from time spent in the gym that very powerful and talented fighters can come in very small packages, so I've learned to never judge a book by its cover. The guys and girls I train with are all awesome people, but I know of some schools that are known to train thugs to be better thugs.

Back to that fair parking lot — what are you going to do? My family is my first concern. I'm going to tell them to run, get help and call 911. This gets them out of the danger zone and gets help coming, and it also shows I'm trying to find another option than fighting. I'd try to run, but with them only 20 feet away, I wouldn't get far on my bad ankle. I know trying to fight even one of these monsters could get me killed or crippled. Five of them would only make my demise quicker. I'm left with no choice but to defend myself with my con-cealed firearm.

What would you do? Have you thought about how disparity of force applies to your self-defense plans? If not, it's time to do some more research on the laws of your home state and the other states in which you carry a gun for personal defense.

CHAPTER 8
SECTION 1: AM I READY?

STAY VIGILANT AND KEEP YOUR SKILLS SHARP

By Sammy Reese

"Should I shoot?" is a moot question if you aren't carrying your gun or you don't have one within arm's reach while you are in your home. If you have a concealed weapons permit or are blessed to live in a constitutional carry state, the gun you have at home while you are out and about can do nothing for you. The same concept applies when you are home and all your guns are safely locked away when you need one to save your life. Please don't take it for granted or conduct your life in the mode of, "Bad things don't happen where I live or travel." Plan for the worst and the rest is gravy.

Unless you live under a rock or have zero contact with the outside world, it doesn't take much to grasp things have gotten really bad. Five Dallas Police officers lost their lives in the line of duty — murdered in cold blood. Several more officers in other states have also been ambushed. There are a few places I put the blame for lighting the fuse, so to speak. It starts at the top; then add in the media who won't let the facts get in the way of a good story. With tension already at an elevated level and then adding emotional kerosene to the fire, it makes for the perfect storm. It's going to get worse before it gets better, I'm afraid.

An argument on Facebook between two "friends" turned into a deadly confrontation for an off-duty police officer in Missouri. The suspect decided duking it out on the keyboard wasn't getting his point across, so he went to the officer's home and forced entry by throwing a planter box through a door. The officer's family was in the home and he used a firearm to defend himself and his loved ones. What if he didn't have a firearm nearby or on him? This story could have had a much different ending.

Yes, it has gotten this bad. What was once just a site to look up old friends and, for some, a place to share every aspect of their day has turned into a launching pad for violence, so please act and prepare accordingly. I'm not saying not to voice your opinion on "your page," but be mindful that some folks, for whatever reasons, are looking for a fight that goes beyond the keyboard.

Playing the "What if?" game here, ask yourself what you would have done if a similar event happened at your home. Are you prepared to defend your loved ones? If you have already thought about it and have a couple plans to deal with someone breaching a door and entering your house, then you are ahead of the curve. If you haven't envisioned this happening at your house, now is the time to get a plan (or three) worked out and make sure the entire family is on board.

Taking the planning a bit further out of the house, what if the suspect had decided to ambush you while you were walking to the car or mailbox? I'm not trying to scare you into putting bars on your windows and never leaving the house. I'm trying to get you mentally prepared — let's call it permanently locking you into Condition Yellow (relaxed but aware of everything going on around you).

Situational awareness and proper training with your firearm could be the difference between being a victim or being someone who prevails in a deadly force encounter.

CHAPTER 9
SECTION 1: AM I READY?

SEE THE LIGHT

By Sammy Reese

Prior to a recent range session with a good friend of mine, he showed me the new rig he was using for concealed carry, complete with a weapon-mounted light. A light on a concealed carry gun isn't anything new, but what surprised me was his statement. He said something like, "Since I have this weapon-mounted light, I don't need to carry a handheld flashlight anymore." This took us down the road of, "Guess you will be pointing a loaded flashlight at everything and everyone you need to identify as possible threat or friend." The look on his face was priceless.

"I didn't think of that," he mumbled under his breath.

Weapon-mounted lights are great tools and I have them on several handguns, shotguns and rifles, but I am a firm believer in getting competent with a handheld light. The technology found in modern flashlights is utterly amazing to me when I look back at where they started. Back in the day, 60 lumens was considered a really bright compact light. Today, you can find smaller packages utilizing hundreds of lumens.

As we've discussed at great length, our personal responses to "What if?" scenarios will depend on our individual circumstances and our own "line in the sand." Anything that can be done to help us prevail in a deadly force encounter is a good thing in my book.

Several years ago, my wife and I were sitting on a bench in our old neighborhood watching the sun go down over the ocean (it's a West Coast thing). There were probably 20 or so other people doing the same thing. When the fireball melted into the ocean and the crowd slowly dispersed, we stayed talking about life and where we wanted to go for dessert. The little park had lights, but there were many dark spots because of trees and bushes. I noticed a guy about 30 yards away who kept looking over his shoulder at us every few seconds. I wasn't overly concerned but was definitely in alert mode. I told my wife about the guy and said that if I stood up, it was time to leave if he came our way.

About five minutes later, I could still see him but not clearly and decided it was time to go. As we walked, he started at us at a trot, asking quite loudly if we had some money. I had my handheld flashlight in my left hand and immediately hit him in the eyes with the beam. His hand went up to shield his eyes. I told my wife to get moving toward the car. I told the guy in a clear voice, "I have no money for you. Leave us alone." He tried to walk toward us, but the combination of the light in his face and his hands up trying to shield his eyes made it really slow going for him. We were moving off line and creating space the entire time, which felt like minutes to me but was more likely 30 seconds from beginning to end.

To answer the question — yes, I was armed, but in this case, if I didn't have the light to literally light him up, the gun being introduced would have been more of a problem than a solution. The light gave us time to get out of Dodge. It stopped his advance, and when he brought his hands up to shield his eyes, I was able to see his hands were empty.

If all you have is a concealed handgun and no means to identify other force options at your disposal, maybe it's time to rethink your personal-defense plan.

CHAPTER 10
SECTION 1: AM I READY?

SOFTWARE UPGRADE

By Sammy Reese

Sometimes, defending the castle has more to do with software than hardware. What I'm saying is it doesn't matter what type of guns you have or how good your alarm system is; if everyone who lives in your house isn't on board with the security plan, bad things can happen.

A good buddy of mine lives in the nice part of town (if you were to drive through the neighborhood, you'd probably agree). It's all newer homes and, for the most part, everyone knows everyone and they all get along.

He was home on a Friday, upstairs in his office while the kids were playing downstairs. He didn't hear the knock at the door, but his 7-year-old son did. His son opened the door to see a 20-something white male who asked if his parents were home. Before the boy could answer, the bad guy pushed past the little boy, who was now screaming at the man. By the time dad figured out something was wrong, the family German Shepherd and the bad guy had a meeting in the entryway. The dog took a big chunk out of the bad guy, who was now running for his life down the street and leaving quite a blood trail. (Yes, the dog got a nice steak dinner for doing his job.)

Sometimes, luck — combined with some proper planning — is all on which we have to depend. In this case, the dog had been trained in basic protection work and took the protection of the pack very seriously. The dog was usually upstairs lying on his bed in the office. On that day, he chose the cool tile in the entryway. My buddy is a gun guy and has several in the house for defending the castle. He told me he came out of the office unarmed because he thought one of the kids had been hurt. He never heard the knock at the door. He keeps a handgun in the office but, in this case, never retrieved it.

After the incident, we talked at length about how to better prepare the family both in and out of the house. A camera system covering the perimeter and interior was added to the Christmas list. The kids already knew they shouldn't talk to strangers. Now, if someone comes to the door, the boys know not to open it; instead, they get Mom or Dad and the adults use the new wide-angle peephole to look outside. They talk to people through the door if they don't know who they are. Some might say it's rude, but for the security of the family, the neighbor or salesmen will get over it.

The kids and wife know he has guns to protect them, and now his wife is getting proficient at using them. She's a great student and has embraced her role as "mama bear" to protect her family with a firearm if need be. The kids shoot with dad, but now they are a part of the plan and are included in the "What if?" questions they drill on as a family.

It's never too late to get the whole family on board with a security plan. Is your crew ready?

DATE NIGHT

By Mark Kakkuri

It's been a while since you and your significant other have been out on an honest-to-goodness date. While the last couple of "dates" at least had some element of eating out, you ended up going to the big-box home supply store to pick up things you needed for the house (which means there was house stuff to do when you got home … which pretty much deflated them as date nights and turned them into something not very romantic). But tonight's different. No house projects are calling and you two are thinking about the menu at your favorite restaurant and then coffee and dessert at the local coffeehouse.

You've had your concealed carry permit for more than 10 years now, you carry regularly and your significant other is used to your about-to-leave-the-house routine: You chamber a round in your single-stack 9, carefully holster it and then carefully insert the holstered gun inside your waistband at 4 o'clock. Then, a spare magazine goes in a magazine holster attached to your gun belt on your weak side.

After a short drive into town, you're both sitting at a table in a small but popular restaurant, looking over the menu. Since you're big on situational awareness, you're not only looking over the menu, trying to decide what to order, you're also looking over the menu at the other patrons in the restaurant. You've gotten good at spotting other people who might be carrying concealed — every now and again a pistol stock prints behind a shirt — and generally keeping an eye on things. Your significant other has picked up on this too, and, at times, can spot a DLR ("doesn't look right") or even a concealed carry purse. You're not paranoid, but you also generally pick a seat and table that gives you a view of the exits and most of the people in the room.

Thankfully, dinner is quite enjoyable and there's no cause for any kind of alarm, let alone defensive action. So, it's on to the local coffeehouse — just a short walk up the street — which specializes in homemade cheesecake and hand-crafted coffees. The coffeehouse is jammed with patrons who are standing or sitting on a lot of "vintage" furniture and are blocking exits front and rear. You've been in this local coffeehouse many times and, while it's great dessert and coffee, from a tactical and defensive standpoint, it's a nightmare: narrow entries and exits, a single aisle down the middle with hardly any room and people everywhere. You and your significant other order at the counter and get a table. You get a seat with your back to the wall — a small but helpful point of relief for you.

This part of your date night is going well too, when you notice a couple walk in. Nothing really catches your attention about this couple except that the man has a somewhat nervous look on his face and you immediately notice he's constantly tugging at his white, straight-hemmed, untucked shirt, sort of pulling it down around his waist. Except it's not riding up in any way. You watch them walk through the coffeehouse. The man stands up straighter than most and continues tugging at his shirt, usually with the thumbs and index fingers of both hands, at 8 o'clock and 4 o'clock. They look like a nice enough couple and, thinking the best, you figure he has a concealed pistol license and is probably carrying a gun. A good guy. But you keep an eye on him nonetheless.

At some point, you forget about the other couple and finish your dessert and

■ What some call "simple purse-snatching" can become a deadly force incident the moment the predator decides he wants more than money.

coffee, enjoying the date night and promising yourself you'll do this again soon. You and your significant other leave the coffeehouse, strolling out on the sidewalk, where you immediately bump into some friends and strike up a conversation. After a few minutes of chatting, the couple you noticed earlier comes out of the coffeehouse. They turn away from you and your group, walking arm in arm. And that's when you see the clear outline of a full-sized pistol in the small of the man's back. Her arm around him has pressed his shirt against his back, causing the gun to print. He goes for another tug with the hand not around her, but to no avail: The gun still prints clearly. And he continues walking very erect, trying to give the shirt as much slack as possible. You smirk, grateful to know others are carrying but hoping the man can improve on his concealment methods.

As the couple walks away, arm in arm, their path runs headlong into four young men who, by their appearance, look like typical high school kids. The kids split into twos as the couple passes between them. Suddenly, one kid on

the man's side sucker punches the man in the back of the head while the other kid on the man's side swings a kick at the man's shins. Their strength and timing are well-calculated; the man doesn't have a chance. He goes sprawling forward, collapsing on the ground, holding his head with both hands. At the same time, the other two kids on the woman's side have also acted: One kid pushes the woman toward the man as he is falling while the other kid grabs her purse, ripping it from her arm. The woman trips over the man and crashes to the ground with him. Two of the kids take off running down the street. The other two (one with the stolen purse) take off running up the street, toward you.

Should I shoot?

SCENARIO 1

Your friends hear the commotion, but you hear it and see it. They turn and look at what you're looking at. For a moment, you're all stunned, watching what looks like a common purse-snatching in progress. Except it all seems to be going in slow motion. Two of the kids are running right toward your group. Angered by their actions, not sure what to do but wanting to help, you instinctively pull your friends away from the path of the two thieves and, at just the right moment, swing a kick at the leg of the kid with the purse. Your foot connects with his ankle, causing it to move behind his other leg while he's in full stride, effectively tripping him. He screams and falls in a sprawl to the ground about 5 feet from you, dropping the purse, which causes its contents to spill out. Scraped and bruised, he starts to pick himself up while he looks back at you with shock and anger in his eyes. On the ground in front of him are some of the contents of the stolen purse, including a wallet, some change, a smartphone and a holstered revolver. The other kid continues running.

SCENARIO 2

You hear a shout from behind you, "Stop right there!" The kid in front of you looks past you and a look of horror crosses his face. You freeze, thinking the voice behind you might be a police officer, but you're also watching the kid's hands and the holstered revolver on the ground. The kid doesn't seem to have noticed it … yet. You turn your head slightly and, out of your peripheral vision, you see that the man who was attacked is on his feet, limping toward you, gun in hand. You're pretty sure he's not coming for you, but who knows what the man is assuming at this point? Your friends are melting away from the path of the man … but you're directly in his path. At this point, the kid makes his move, lunging in the direction opposite the man to make a run for it, leaving the purse and all its contents behind. The man tries to chase the kid but the pain in his leg and head is too great. Instead, he looks down at the purse, sees the holstered revolver and then looks directly at you.

SCENARIO 3

The commotion has drawn a crowd and the man seems dazed. Your mind is racing, but you calmly say, "I'm here to help, buddy. Can you put your gun away?" The man seems to gather his wits quickly, realizing you're not a threat, and clumsily holsters his gun in the small of his back, pulling his shirt over it.

"This is your friend's purse," you say, gesturing toward it.

The man sees the holstered revolver on the ground and immediately stoops down to collect it and the rest of the belongings. You stoop down with him and again offer to help. He rubs his head, nods and then walks over to where the woman is to see if she's OK. She's now sitting on a bench and several people are with her, helping her treat nasty scrapes on her knee and elbow and a cut over her eye. You carefully place the holstered revolver and other items back in the purse and walk them over to the couple. Across the street, two police officers on bicycles notice the commotion and crowd and ride over to check out the situation. You start thinking through everything that's happened, reviewing details and wondering whether it was wise to intervene like you did. The police officers roll up.

"What's going on here? Is everybody OK?" they ask.

In what way would Scenario 1 or 2 have had to change in order for you to be justified in drawing your gun and shooting? What if, in Scenario 3, any of the four kids showed up at the scene while you and the police officers were all there?

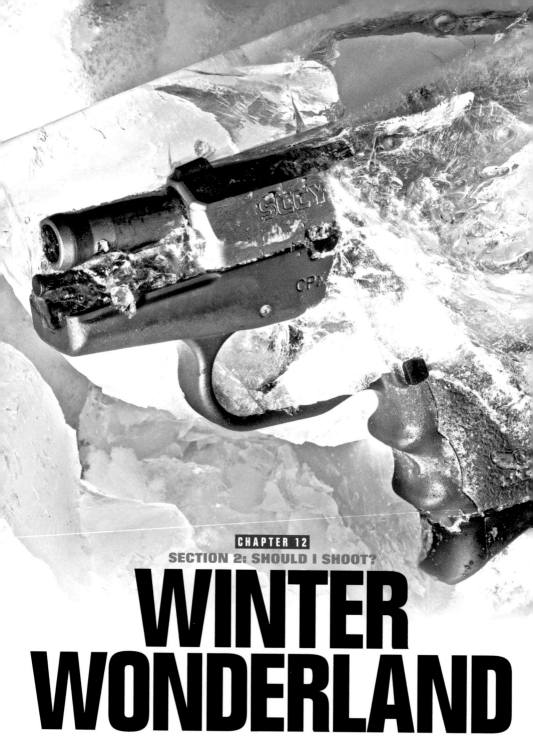

WINTER WONDERLAND

By Ed Combs

"Cold weather" means different things to different people. To some, "cold" is what happens when it's no longer sunny and 75 degrees every day. To others, it's not "cold" until your face gets numb within a minute of walking outdoors. Regardless of where you fall on that spectrum, cold weather changes how most carry concealed. I'm not just talking about gear and rigging; I'm talking about how to scan for potential threats when almost every man you see is walking around with his hands in his pockets.

Basic human threat assessment involves the following concepts in the following order: *whole person, hands, demeanor*. What this means is that when determining whether an individual likely presents a threat, you first look at the whole person, then you look to see what his or her hands are up to and then you look at his or her face, body language and general deportment. *Whole person* tells you basics, like whether he or she appears to be a full-grown adult male or a pre-adolescent female; *hands* tells you whether he or she is holding something and what it might be; and *demeanor* tells you what he or she might be up to. It's deceptively simple, and it can be anything but easy.

Say you're returning to your vehicle after an evening meeting. The church (or wherever) is in the Old Downtown area, so you had to park a block and a half away. It's dark, but the streetlights are on and some businesses are still open. As you cross the street, a 20-something man wearing a loose parka, dirty, baggy jeans and untied work boots comes around the corner of a building at the end of the block and, when he spots you, slows his pace. You move farther to the right of the sidewalk; he mirrors you. He rolls a ski mask down over his face, digs his hands into his pockets and continues ambling toward you.

In the spirit of this series, ask yourself: *Should I shoot?*

Well ... of course not. He's a man on a public street wearing a ski mask with his hands in his pockets. In all likelihood, that's because it's 22 degrees outside; for all you know, he just that moment walked outside and is heading home from work. Moreover, when you first saw him, he was a block away — all of 88 yards. That said, now he's 50 yards away and almost moving at half-speed; it at least seems like he wants to make sure your paths cross.

Should I shoot?

The answer is still absolutely not. He might be drunk, he might be injured ... you have no idea why he's acting like that. But you need to start considering that there might be something dangerously wrong with the situation. If you haven't already, this is the time to cross the street or, even better, walk into an open business if one is nearby.

So you cross the street and he follows. *Should I shoot?*

We're still not there yet, but this is definitely the time to get your hand on your sidearm and prepare to issue strong verbal commands. This is the time to have your flashlight in your non-gun hand (you do have a flashlight, right?) and to be ready to shine it in his eyes while warning him to stay away from you. You really hope this is just a terrible misunderstanding on your end, but if it isn't, you want to get out of the situation without being forced to shoot. Everything's already gotten very weird, but hopefully, at worst, it will conclude with nothing more than a call to 911 to tell the dispatcher that you had to draw your weapon on an attacker who then fled.

He's within 25 yards, and he's again positioned himself on a collision course with you.

You step over a concrete parking marker into the well-lit parking lot of a shuttered furniture store; so does he, and he's getting closer. You begin to move laterally, you shine him in the face with your flashlight and you yell that he needs to get away from you. He quickens his pace, begins to yell something you can't understand and begins to pull his hands out of his pockets. Without realizing it, you've already drawn and your front sight is squarely trained on his sternum.

Should I shoot?

Now he's 10 yards away, and as the adrenaline dumps into your system and auditory exclusion sets in, you can see his mouth moving behind the mask but you can't hear what he's saying. You're still moving and you're still yelling, and you can't see what it is he's holding. You realize that this is actually happening and that if he gets much closer you're going to open fire.

Should I shoot?

Here's the bad news: You still don't know.

If you shoot and he turns out to be a mentally handicapped man who thought you were his neighbor who gives him rides to the store, you're finished. You will likely lose your job and any money you've managed to save, and you'll have a higher chance of regaining those than you will of regaining your reputation. Depending on the dynamics of the shooting, you can expect professional protestors and rioters to pour in from out of state. Expect to have to pull your kids out of school. Worst of all, expect to be tortured by guilt for the remainder of your days. Expect the worst.

If you shoot him and he turns out to be a repeat-offending violent predator who was holding a stolen .45 with which he was going to pistolwhip or shoot you before taking your wallet and car keys, your situation will be slightly better but might not even seem like it. Depending on the dynamics of the shooting, it could be almost as bad.

The solution is to never let someone acting so strangely get that close to you without alerting him, in no uncertain terms, that you do not want him near you. Shine him with your flashlight. Do everything in your power to tell him that you are not an easy meal and that he needs to get away from you, immediately. Equally importantly, do everything in your power to alert the world to the fact that you are a reluctant participant in this violent encounter. You didn't go looking for it, you didn't want to take part in it and you tried to escape from it, but you were unfortunately forced to end it before your attacker could murder you.

Should I shoot?

The answer is almost never yes, but when it is, only accurate gunfire will suffice. Making that call will fundamentally alter your life, so the more thought you put into it now, the better.

> ## "THE SOLUTION IS TO NEVER LET SOMEONE ACTING SO STRANGELY GET THAT CLOSE TO YOU WITHOUT ALERTING HIM, IN NO UNCERTAIN TERMS, THAT YOU DO NOT WANT HIM NEAR YOU. SHINE HIM WITH YOUR FLASHLIGHT. DO EVERYTHING IN YOUR POWER TO TELL HIM THAT YOU ARE NOT AN EASY MEAL."

NIGHT SHIFT

By Ed Combs

Home invasions are some of the most violent and terrifying crimes against which we must be prepared.

"Should I shoot?" is a question you never want to have to ask when it's another human in your sights. That aside, those of us who carry concealed make it our business to be ready to defend our lives and the lives of our loved ones, and sometimes "Should I shoot?" is a question that needs to be answered immediately.

After the 2016 car-and-knife attack at Ohio State, there was an online meme going around of the scene from *Raiders of the Lost Ark* in which Indiana Jones shoots a scimitar-swinging bad guy. It's a pretty cut-and-dried example of what cops used to call a "good shoot" back before cages in squad cars and polymer frames: Bad Guy clearly presents himself and makes his intentions known, Bad Guy has a weapon and begins to close with Good Guy, Good Guy shoots and ends the threat Bad Guy presented.

I don't know about you, but scimitars aren't seen too often in my parts (at least not yet). The question of whether to employ deadly force is usually a lot less Hollywood.

Let's say you're asleep in the middle of tomorrow night and you wake to the sound of your locked front doorknob rattling. After you realize that, yes, that *is* your locked front doorknob rattling, you secure a firearm and a powerful flashlight before calling 911. As you confirm that everyone's accounted for, you tell the operator that someone is trying to get into your house and that, no, you are not expecting any visitors. Everyone who's supposed to be in the house is already there and, yes, you've personally confirmed that. No, you do not intend to go investigate and, yes, you will wait for law enforcement to arrive unless whoever it is comes to you.

Then you hear the doorjamb break, followed by erratic, heavy footsteps in the entryway. You're frightened but kind of relieved to realize that your hearing's become more acute than you can ever remember it to be; you can hear a piece of the broken doorjamb snap off as it's snagged on something. You can hear giggling and what sounds like both a male and a female voice. You can hear a shoe hit your floor as if it was dropped, and you can hear someone clumsily trying to shut your now-broken front door. Without realizing it, your training's kicked in: You've dropped your phone on the bed, you've moved away from the line of your bedroom door and you're now standing in an offensive posture with your light and weapon at low ready.

You hear additional footsteps coming toward your bedroom door and now your vision has caught up with your hearing: Even in the low light of your darkened bedroom, you can see the doorknob begin to turn.

Should I shoot?

Such a circumstance brings into tight focus what is popularly known as "Castle Doctrine" law. You are in your residence, you are minding your own business and someone breaks in. You, as the legal resident, are allowed the legal leeway to assume that this invader intends to harm you and defend yourself accordingly.

Should I shoot?

Now we're back to all of that difficult decision-making … that difficult decision-making that has to happen within the next quarter-second. Let's look at what we know:

Most burglars enter residences in the middle of the day, when they have the highest chance of finding the place deserted. Actual burglars don't want anything to do with anyone.

Most home invaders are usually either silent or dynamic in their entries. They usually either sneak in and have you overwhelmed before waking you or they smash in like a natural gas explosion and overcome the residents with violence of action.

What you heard was neither of those things.

Should I shoot?

Well, let's remember what we need in 99.99 percent of combat shooting: target identification, target verification and target isolation.

On the one hand, you have identified a verified, isolated target: someone who isn't supposed to be in your residence who kicked in your front door and is now turning the knob on your bedroom door. Plenty of you have already clicked this window closed; you've basically said, "The knob starts moving, so I shoot. What would you expect me to do? Whoever it is shouldn't have been in my house."

Well, maybe.

> ## "MOST BURGLARS ENTER RESIDENCES IN THE MIDDLE OF THE DAY, WHEN THEY HAVE THE HIGHEST CHANCE OF FINDING THE PLACE DESERTED."

On the other hand, angry as you might be about the brazen violation of your personal security, personal safety and the sanctity of your home, I come from what most folks would call a "big-time drinkin' state" (and, depending on the time of year, so do you).

You heard the locked doorknob rattle, you heard the door break and then you heard … laughter. You heard a shoe come off.

At least one person in my high school class broke into his parents' home in a rather spectacular fashion while extremely intoxicated. A few years ago, one acquaintance of mine was placed in the county detox facility after walking through the plate-glass front of a hotel in a manner described as "like the liquid metal guy in *Terminator 2.*" On more than one occasion, I've gone to the wrong hotel room and tried to get in, and that was just from extreme travel fatigue.

Do home invaders take their shoes off? Sometimes.

Should I shoot?

CHAPTER 14

SECTION 2: SHOULD I SHOOT?

THE DROP

By Ed Combs

Almost all defensive training of any kind — armed or unarmed — stresses that, "There's no room for a fair fight when your life is on the line." That's very true, and I don't want you to ever forget it. Where this can get dicey is in trying to decide when, exactly, your life is no longer on the proverbial line.

Real life is rarely as clean-cut as the movies. Come to think of it, it's rarely even as clean-cut as training scenarios, even those run in high-quality schools. Real life has a tendency to be messy and unpredictable.

How messy and unpredictable? Allow me to insert you into an actual armed robbery that went down a while back.

Picture yourself in a small, narrow convenience store, waiting in line to pay for your beverage. The man at the head of the line pulls a pistol and, in no uncertain terms, initiates a robbery. He orders all five of the rest of you to back up against the wall opposite the register and away from the door. You're at the back of the line and too far away to immediately disarm him, so you and everyone else comply. As all of this happens, another young man moves out of the line and locks the only visible door of the store, which is up by the register; at this point, it's worth assuming they're working together.

You walk backward with the group and keep your hands in the traditional "surrender position" taught by countless instructors: palms out, elbows bent, biceps on your sides. The man with the gun returns his attention to the cashier and you make your way back with the crowd, all of you coming to rest about 30 feet from the counter.

You've calmed your breathing and you're running the math: At this range, you're confident that you can be out, up and accurately placing bullets within a second and a half. You silently take in all of the information that you can.

The one who's at the register is holding a full-sized pistol in his right hand and a drawstring backpack in his left. The one who locked the door is watching the guy with the gun, but he's also glancing over at you — yes, *you* — every few seconds. The one holding the gun is wearing skinny jeans and a dark T-shirt; the other one's hands are empty and he's wearing long khaki shorts and an untucked flannel shirt.

For now, T-Shirt is concentrating on the cashier, who is shaking and crying as he clumsily empties the bills and change from the till into the bag. He's begging for his life, and it's making T-Shirt mad. Flannel over by the door is nervously slapping his left fist into his right palm, and he still keeps pausing whenever he scans past you. (Who knows why? Maybe he thinks you look like someone who might be carrying a gun.) All told, T-Shirt seems to be all business, while Flannel looks like he wants to leave as soon as possible.

The money from the till is now in the backpack. As T-Shirt realizes cinching the drawstring will require both hands, he readjusts his grip on the gun and, as if in slow motion, drops it. His eyes bulge, his left hand shoots out to grab it and, though he tries to bring it in for a fair catch, he actually knocks it away from himself. It goes skittering across the floor, coming to rest 15 feet from him and 20 feet from all of you. For what seems like 30 seconds but what is probably only a half a beat, everyone just stands there, motionless. T-Shirt starts to lunge — you can't tell if it's for the gun or the exit — and Flannel is frantically trying to unlock the door.

Should I shoot?

Let's see.

T-Shirt is obviously dangerous. He was just threatening to murder all of you if you didn't do what he said, but he's dropped his gun, which might mean any number of things. It might mean that he'll realize the

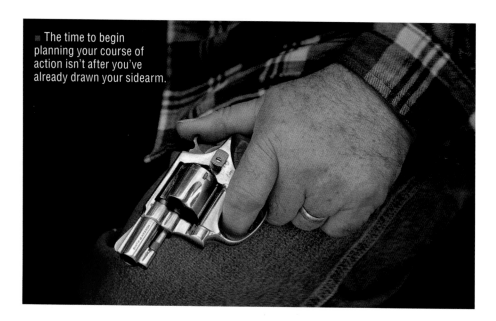

The time to begin planning your course of action isn't after you've already drawn your sidearm.

whole situation's now officially out of his control and, as such, he'll just try to get away with the money. It might mean that he wants to get hold of that gun and use it to cover his and Flannel's exit, only shooting if he deems it necessary, whatever that might mean. To a guy like that, "necessary" might mean that he'll only shoot if any of you move, but being the kind of guy who would threaten to murder strangers for money, it might also mean that he's a violent psycho who sees dropping that gun as embarrassing enough to right his mind by popping a few of you for laughing at him.

Moving on, everything you know about human body language has told you that Flannel wants out and that he thinks you are a potential threat to him and T-Shirt. If he's been through the system before, he knows that if someone gets shot and killed right now, he'll go down for what my home state calls "Felony Murder" — basically a life sentence because he knew exactly what the plan was when he walked in with T-Shirt and locked the door. Flannel doesn't appear to be armed at the moment, but that doesn't mean he isn't dangerous and

it doesn't mean he doesn't have something concealed under that big billowy shirt.

Both of them are currently concentrating on only one thing — getting away with this armed robbery — but unfortunately, you have no idea if that includes re-acquiring that pistol.

Should I shoot?

Well, how quickly can YOU be out, up and accurately placing gunfire? How much do you want to bet that Flannel can get the door unlocked before T-Shirt gets hold of that pistol? How close are they to the poor guy working the counter? Has he moved?

Do you make the bet that T-Shirt is going for that gun and, therefore, is about to present an imminent, unavoidable deadly threat to you or others?

Or do you look out for No. 1, ride it out and count on the poor marksmanship of this nation's criminal class?

IDENTITY CRISIS

By Ed Combs

The "if he's in my house, he's dead" crowd might not like to hear it, but if you can avoid having to shoot somebody, for God's sake, don't shoot. For a healthy private citizen, there's nothing even remotely pleasant about having to shoot someone other than the knowledge that you — prepared and trained to accomplish such an unpleasant task — were there when you were needed to preserve innocent life.

Making that decision can be hard though. Dead's dead, and bullets can't be called back. Killing's hard on the average person and, even though no one has much sympathy for the criminal, putting him down hard will be the worst chapter of a bad book for his family. If you don't really have to shoot, I beg you not to.

Complicating matters further, deciding whether to shoot is almost never a red light, green light affair. Don't complain; you knew that when you got your permit, and if you didn't, let's you and me go get some lunch at the park.

It's a slow day — almost no one around — and let's say that, on our way to the charity hot dog stand, I end up waiting outside a public bathroom for you to come out so we can continue our leisurely stroll. I'm concerned that I look like some kind of skulking pervert because I'm hanging around outside a men's room in a public park, and, thus distracted, before I realize what's happening, a young man has what looks like a K-frame revolver with a 4-inch barrel stuck in my face. From where I'm standing, the bore on it looks about as big as an oil drum as he says, "Gimme all you got."

Slightly flexing his clenched fist back to threaten me with a pistol-whipping if I don't comply, I'm pretty sure I see daylight for a fraction of a second; more accurately, I'm pretty sure I don't see any cartridge rims between the cylinder and the frame. I slowly raise both of my hands into a tra-

ditional "surrender" position and agree to give him my property. He appears to slightly relax, and I slowly reach my left hand into the pocket that actually contains my backup gun.

Should I shoot?

I'll say short answer "probably" and long answer "no, but..."

On the one hand, though I do pretty well for a fella who's never worked as a firearms historian, I would never claim to have seen every last revolver on the planet. Additionally, in a situation like the one described here, I'm under terrible duress. This guy's waving a gun in my face and demanding my property, which means that what he's really saying is, "I'm ready to murder you. Give me your money."

Did I see that right? Were there really no rims there, or did I misidentify nickel-plated cases against the bright white sky? Can I get a look at the chambers in the cylinder? Do I see anything that looks like bullet noses in there?

Or do I quit wasting my time, pretend to comply and then initiate stopping him before he finally decides to murder me?

But dammit ... just by how big the gun seems in his hand and how the T-shirt is hanging off of him, this is a very young man, maybe even a kid in his mid-teens. If I shoot at him from here, I'm going to hit every time, and enough of these 88-grain jacketed hollow-points to stop the threat he presents will likely also kill him. He should have thought about that before sticking a gun in a stranger's' face, but killing a kid is still killing a kid, and killing a kid is to be avoided whenever possible.

Hang on ... is that a pellet gun? For use as training aides, plenty of pellet guns are manufactured to look and feel exactly like their legit counterparts. Atop that, the cylinders seem kind of small. Son of a ... I think this kid is pointing a pellet gun at my

Whatever you decide to do, you need to understand that trained, smooth movement — not untrained hurrying — wins the day.

face. Or is it one of the old .22-cal I-frame Smith & Wesson "Kit Guns" that he stole from somewhere? Even if it isn't, a pellet through the eye or nose at this range could easily kill me. Didn't I recently see an article or an ad or something about how some guy just took a 600-pound wild boar with a pellet gun?

Wait a second … I'm standing around outside a bathroom because I'm waiting for someone. When you come out, the kid pointing a revolver in my face will likely get spooked, and there's a good chance he's going to either shoot you or me or hold both of us at gunpoint.

It's been a second. Time's running out. I have to move. I have to give him my wallet or begin the process of stopping the threat that he poses. Giving him my wallet in no way guarantees my safety, as he isn't wearing a mask as almost all robbers do when they're looking to get away clean.

Such a situation is a lot more common than you might think and, if you haven't thought about a situation like this, you need to. You might live in an area where this kind of violent crime is rare or you might live in an area where it's common. Either way, all Walmarts sell pellet guns and all criminals can get ahold of firearms.

Some kids do stupid, dangerous things.

Some pellet guns wind up in the hands of stupid, dangerous people.

Some stupid, dangerous kids wind up with firearms.

Some pellet guns will kill you as thoroughly as a firearm chambered in .22 LR.

Some days are worse than others.

Should I shoot? Should I fight?

I'd love to hear your answer.

CHAPTER 16
SECTION 2: SHOULD I SHOOT?

KNIFE!

By Ed Combs

Here at *Should I Shoot?*, we're more concerned with, as Lt. Col. Dave Grossman would say, the "software" side of the concealed carry equation than the "hardware" side. I love to talk guns and holsters and knives and flashlights as much as anyone, but this is about generating discussion and critical thought. We're here to run as many scenarios as possible and, in doing so, encourage all responsibly armed Americans to practice weighing options and making measured decisions. Nothing about any of that is simple, nor is any of it easy.

Say you're standing in a hotel room packing to leave. Since you're clothed and you're not in a place that bars you from carrying, your EDC sidearm is right where it's supposed to be — charged and secured on your person. You hear several shouts outside and what is very clearly the word "knife."

You walk over to the sliding screen door and see a heavyset man in his mid-50s slicing at the air with what appears to be a regular old kitchen knife. You also see a group of men and women scattering away from him. Just as you see this, he weaves out of your line of sight and the shouting intensifies. You slide the screen door back and step out onto the balcony with your phone to your non-gun ear, and the 911 dispatcher tells you that they've been alerted to the situation and that units are on the way.

So, there you are: one story up on a hotel balcony, wearing a sidearm that's charged and ready to go, looking down on a parking lot where … well, let's go over what, exactly, you know at this point.

You've personally seen a knife-swinging man who, at least once, lunged in an aggressive fashion toward about 10 other people. Those 10 people were concerned enough about his behavior to shout and run away from him and, now that he's weaved his way back in front of the balcony, you see that a few of the crowd are approaching him in an attempt to talk him down.

Should I shoot?

Before shooting even crosses your mind, you need to rapidly assess your options. Minor permutations notwithstanding, here's where we are:

Option 1: Do nothing else. You called 911, they know what's up and they have squads pointed in your direction. Stay away from the window and mind your own business. You've already done more than most folks would do.

Option 2: Do nothing else but stand there on the balcony and observe, prepared to duck back behind the security of that cinder block exterior hotel wall. Be, as they say, "a good witness." Concentrate; get the details right. Take notes if possible.

Option 3: Yell to the man that he needs to immediately drop the knife. Punctuate your point by drawing your sidearm and pointing it at his chest.

Option 4: The man presents a direct-and-imminent threat to innocent life. Keep your weapon holstered but start your autogenic breathing, get down there and see if your help is needed.

Which option is the wisest? Well, let's walk through them.

Option 1: Local law enforcement being what it is, there's a halfway decent chance that the multiple professionals who are currently on their way will know this guy by sight. They handle exactly this kind of behavior in exactly this area and, depending on where we're talking about, they might do so on a weekly basis. They're also in possession of less-lethal force options like TASERs, 12-gauge bean bag rounds and pepper spray. Most importantly, from where you're standing, if they have to shoot him, they'll be backed up by a police department, sheriff's office or state police agency. It might be harder to swallow than a tennis ball, but this might be one of those times that you step back and let the pros do their thing.

Option 2: Atop everything covered with Option 1, if you're out on that balcony, you might be able to provide valuable information to law enforcement for what could range anywhere from a routine police report to a full-on mass murder investigation.

NOTE: Options 1 and 2 also mean that you might have to live with the knowledge that you — armed and at your level of training and experience — stood by as a person or persons got murdered by a madman. That would be tough to handle, but let's keep moving.

Option 3: Drawing your sidearm and issuing commands might sound good on paper, but what, exactly, do you think you're going to do from up there? Are you not just a competent but also a good shot at however far away he is? Do you know how your pistol shoots from elevation? How much experience do you have with moving targets? If this guy's just having a particularly bad day and acting out, what's to say that hearing your orders and seeing your firearm won't escalate the situation, maybe even prompting him to grab someone just so he can murder them in front of you? (We won't even get into target isolation or him running under your balcony. In case you were wondering, I consider this the worst option of the four.)

Option 4: You'll insert yourself into a hot scene that will soon contain cops responding to a "crazy man with a knife" call, and you're not in uniform. Moreover, you're about to intervene on what might be a random attack, a child custody argument, a psychotic break or a weird drug episode (and maybe some combination thereof). You have no idea what relationships exist between the man with the knife and the individuals around him. You don't know whether he was attacked or whether he's on a murderous rampage. You don't even know what was happening before the knife came out, but there you'll be, right down in it, trying to work out exactly where you fit into the whole picture.

I don't like any of those options.

Personally, I get down there as quickly and discreetly as possible, but then again, I'm former law enforcement. I have training and experience in mitigating violence and dealing with emotionally disturbed persons — training in de-escalation, discreet NON-escalation and unobtrusive observation. (Those last two are harder than they sound.) I need to be there with a sidearm ready to save lives, but the best-case scenario is everyone stays away from him until the cops arrive and no one even suspects I realize what's going on.

What do you do and, equally importantly, why do you do it?

CHAPTER 17
SECTION 2: SHOULD I SHOOT?

LUNCH DATE

So, over the last few chapters, we've studied several scenarios that explored whether deadly force would be the best course of action in a given situation. All of them were designed specifically for that reason: to get you, our readers, to discuss different thought processes and outlooks on defensive violence and to make everyone think a little more than they otherwise might have about the gun they carry every day. This installment will be no different, but it will involve a physical position that is all too often neglected in many training circles.

Say you're sitting at a two-chair table next to the window in a fast-casual restaurant, waiting for your order to be brought out to you. Your chair is of the swivel variety and it is permanently affixed to the floor. You're reading a book or the paper or your phone — or whatever you'd be doing in such a situation — when a woman in the booth immediately across the restaurant from you begins yelling at the man across the table from her. It's loud enough that it makes everyone uncomfortable, and as you scan your eyes past them, you notice the man smoothly but very quickly bring a pistol up from under the table and conceal it under a burgundy cloth napkin next to his right hand. The woman is crying, but it appears that he's warned her to remain as silent as possible as she very suddenly places both of her elbows on the table, clamps both hands over her mouth and tries to muffle as much of her crying as she can.

The man is in his mid-30s and extremely large; he appears to be about 6 feet 5 inches tall and probably weighs more than 300 pounds. The woman is in her mid-40s and is of average build; she is probably 5 feet 5 inches tall and 140 pounds. They are facing each other in a restaurant booth immediately to your right, and there is a pair of square four-chair tables between you and them, neither of which are occupied. The woman is now obviously trying to regain her composure and the man continues to whisper to her in a hissed, low tone. You have no idea what's going on, but you can tell that it's not on the up-and-up and you can see that the man's already drawn a weapon. From your right shoulder to his left earlobe is about 20 feet.

Should I shoot?

What I just described are the circumstances that led up to a shooting that occurred some number of years ago when an off-duty police officer grabbing a sandwich spotted a violent predator meeting with the mother of a girl he was threatening over a drug debt. It was an extremely, almost excruciatingly difficult situation, and it was happening in a restaurant filled with innocent people.

But enough about the off-duty cop for now. Let's get back to you.

So, there you are, not able to just pretend you didn't see that gun come up from under the table. You can surmise that the man is implicitly threatening the woman's life with a pistol, and you can surmise that if she had her way, she would be far away from where she is right now. You know that this is exactly what human trafficking, kidnapping, rape and all kinds of other nightmares look like, and you know that you really ought to do something in order to help that woman and stop that man.

From where I sit, you have a few options.

You could get up, walk out of the restaurant as if you have no idea what's going on, get in your vehicle and then dial 911. This would probably be the safest course of action and the one that would afford you the highest chances of escaping the incident unharmed. After you're out of the restaurant, the decision of whether to flee would be up to you, but no one ever said that hanging around the scene of an armed kidnapping was a SAFE course of action.

You could get up, walk out, call 911 and then try something Hollywood, like pulling a fire alarm. The goal there would be to get everyone else out of the restaurant and bring the authorities into the picture without the man seeing you holding a phone. The upside is that everybody would leave the restaurant; the downside is that "everybody" includes the man and woman, and who knows what they'd do next.

You could get up, walk to the restroom, call 911 and then return to your table. After there, it would be up to you to figure out how and when to draw without losing the element of surprise. Remember, it certainly doesn't look like the man knows that you know that he's got a pistol under that napkin. You're pretty sure that you could get a clear shot from where you are, and big as he is, he's still completely below the line of the cinder block wall that forms the main partition in the restaurant. The man has put his left arm up on the top of the bench seat, exposing his left armpit directly to you, and you're almost positive that a round from your sidearm wouldn't make it through his entire chest cavity *and* the wall behind him.

Should I shoot?

With his arm up like that, he's presenting you quite a shot. A string of rounds through the armpit will certainly deliver devastating results, and it's basically what deer hunters are after when they "shoot right behind the shoulder." But would those shots be immediately incapacitating? At that range, a bullet below the ear right at the TMJ certainly would be, so it's not that you're out of options. It does, however, raise three additional questions:

1. Have you trained to make shots that are that precise at that kind of distance?

Heading to so-and-so's shooting school for another defensive pistol class is all well and good, but none of the perfect scores I've ever shot required that I hit something the size of a (potentially moving) cherry tomato at 20 feet within a second of drawing my gun and absolutely, positively hit it on the first shot or somebody dies.

2. Have you trained to access your firearm from a seated position?

We all start out assessing a holster the same way: We install it in the intended position, clear our sidearm of any and all ammunition and begin to practice our draws. As fast as you might be with your current setup while standing, have you trained with it in a seated position? Do you know exactly how you will mount that gun in order to deliver your shot? And what is your plan for getting off the X after you've taken your shot?

3. Speaking of which, are you certain that you can land that threat-stopping "light-switch" shot so after the bullet hits him and does its thing, he won't be able to get his hand on that pistol and start firing?

You're basically in a hostage crisis but haven't yet revealed yourself to be the sniper. If you do elect to shoot, you have to completely neutralize the man who looks all the world like a guy who's either already kidnapped or is in the process of kidnapping the woman across the table from him, and you probably have to do it in one shot.

4. Come to think of it, are you prepared to articulate exactly why you elected to employ deadly force against a stranger who was seated across a table from a crying woman?

A prosecutor or district attorney might make the argument that, yes, the man you shot had a gun on the table under a napkin, but you had a gun in your pants; to the average juror whom neither attorney got removed during the selection process, which sounds weirder? Who's to say he had any less of a right to his gun than you had to your gun? (Never mind that the man in question might be a convicted violent felon. That kind of detail has a way of finding its way out of scripted in-court statements.)

Should I shoot?

If I should, at what am I shooting? What am I doing after I take my shot? And how am I going to articulate to my attorney exactly why I did what I did?

'YOU MAD, BRO?'

By Ed Combs

These scenarios are all about the more unexpected angles of going about armed, the kind of stuff that some concealed carriers never even consider. They're always difficult scenarios, and that is entirely by design. That said, I pull the specifics directly from past personal experience, experiences of other current and former law enforcement officers, and raw footage of violent crimes. The scenarios that I present here are real, and the way I present them is designed to make you and all other concealed weapon permit holders think more deeply and broadly about the defensive use of force than you otherwise might.

Say you're walking through the parking lot of a grocery store and you say something under your breath. Maybe you mumbled to the person next to you that it's cold or hot or rainy. Maybe you're alone and mumbled one of those statements that we seem to mumble more often as we grow older. It was a non-statement; it was just one of those things that happens sometimes.

You continue to walk toward the door of the store, but when you're about 20 yards away from it, you feel a hand on your shoulder as it spins you around. You almost lose your balance, and as you get your hands up and orient yourself, you see who's connected to that hand: He's about 5 inches shorter than you but is about as muscular an individual as you've ever seen. His face, neck and arms are covered with tattoos, he's wearing black jeans, black Converse All-Stars and a tight black T-shirt, and he's demanding that you repeat what "you couldn't have possibly been stupid enough to just say" to him.

Well, what do you know ... it appears that he's certain he heard you.

NOTE: Yes, I know that some of you guys are Ronins who live in caves, drinking gasoline while putting cigars out between your toes. Yes, I know that a lot of you will swear up and down that this could never even remotely possibly hap-

pen to you. Yes, I know that you're just SO situationally aware ALL the time, and that anyone who could ever, under any circumstances, be snuck up on shouldn't even be allowed to live in the United States of America. If this is the case, then I would ask that you either humor me or pass this scenario along to a mere mortal who could use the help.

Let me reiterate that you didn't really say anything at all, let alone to him. No one reading this would be foolish enough to walk around insulting strangers, even under his or her breath, because this is exactly the kind of disaster that such behavior can generate out of thin air. You really were just mumbling a song lyric or an old saying about walking in the cold, and this entire exchange is a terrible misunderstanding.

You tell him so as you raise your hands and back up, but the little bugger is extremely fast and it's hard for you to keep track of where he is for more than about a second. His language is intensifying; he's now bragging about how many men he's killed with his bare hands and how he isn't afraid to "go back inside" for killing a such-and-such like you.

There's now a crowd forming, and some of the people have pulled out phones and are very clearly recording what's happening. You keep moving away from him, but the crowd makes it hard to maneuver; he's still all over you, and now he's demanding that you strike him. You again tell him that you have no intention of fighting with him, but this only seems to make him madder.

Then he says it: "******, I'm gonna kill you. You gonna die today. You hear me?"

The crowd immediately backs away, and some of them actually flee the area altogether.

Should I shoot?

In this specific scenario, we're getting into a pair of crucial legal areas referred to as "victim-perpetrator factors" and "disparity of force."

How old are you? Are you, like our bad boy here, also a starkly muscular prize-fighter who could probably kill the average person with a single right to the back of the jaw? Are you over the age of 40? How about 50? Are you older than 60? Do you walk with a cane? Would you describe yourself as downright elderly? Would you describe yourself as disabled, and would others agree? What is your experience with single combat, unarmed or otherwise? How's your eyesight? Arthritis? What are your knees up to these days?

Just to reassure some of the folks who think I go too hard on the private citizen and bring up too many concerns for the predator, what does the crowd appear to be doing? Do they appear to know this man? Do they appear to be siding with him? Have any of them begun to verbally assault you? Are any of them yelling things like "Worldstar!" or "Take him!"? Are you incapable of elbowing anyone out of the way, let alone what appears to be an entire high school's worth of gawking under-achievers?

You'd never seen this man before this interaction, but from what you know about him, he's extremely dangerous even if all he has in his pockets is Chapstick. He's told you about how many people he's killed and how he's been to prison, and now he's actually said aloud that he intends to kill you. Under such a circumstance, you have no choice but to believe him.

Should I shoot?

As in any use of force, you need to be ready to articulate exactly why you did exactly what you did. In most law enforcement agencies, any time an officer lays a hand on a citizen outside of a handshake, that officer has to explain in writing exactly what led up to and the justification for that use of force. Such a document is called a "Use-of-Force Report," and it will be used internally and, if necessary, in court.

If you're forced to shoot someone to save your own life or the life of another, you will have to do the same.

Should I shoot?

Just as you don't have to wait to be shot or stabbed or clubbed to shoot an attacker, you don't necessarily have to be punched or kicked before shooting either.

Should I shoot?

If your life or the life of a loved one is immediately and unavoidably in danger, the answer is basically always "yes." If not, the answer is always "no."

I'm still a comparative youngster who's roughly the dimensions of a decent-sized black bear. I also have a few years of calming down meatheads like this guy under my belt, so I might not (even though he's just told the assembled crowd that he intends to kill me). If I can't calm him down or get out of the crowd, that might not make much of a difference.

I also understand (as should all of you) how dangerous that assembled crowd could be regardless of my relative youth and experience. I understand that if I am forced to shoot this man, the chances of the crowd scattering are better than the chances of them all attacking me at the same time, but not so much better that the latter isn't crossing my mind. If they all rush me at once like they mean it, they'll basically neutralize my skillsets apart from rapid target acquisition and engagement until either I run out of ammunition or they get tired of getting shot.

I think I might still have a chance of talking him down, and I'd really rather get out of this without having to shoot a local hothead in front of 30 of his closest admirers. I've done so under similar conditions in the past, so at this point, it's still worth a try. He's running out of time, though … and so am I.

How about you?

LONG SHOT

By Ed Combs

Greater and greater numbers of Americans are carrying concealed, not only for self-defense and the defense of loved ones but also so they can be prepared to stop rapid mass murder if necessary. Whether it's against a terrorist with an international political agenda or simply a madman, this nation is one of the only on Earth where private citizens are allowed to fight back with effective means.

Complicating this is the fact that even though gun sales have remained strong for several years now, a lot of those guns aren't exactly what you might consider "duty guns" or handguns designed for counter-offensive use. A lot of them are what you might call "get-off-me" guns: micro-framed pistols chambered in .380 ACP and five-shot revolvers chambered in .38 Special. I'm not going to stand here and say that no one can hit much past 15 yards with guns like that, but I will stand here and say that most folks who own one don't train to. Why would they? It's a "belly gun," and most people end up using their guns to defend against close-in, face-to-face attacks.

It's not just private citizens either. Most law enforcement officers who have to fire are firing at assailants well within 25 yards, often no farther away than the average private citizen is from his attacker.

"Most," however, isn't "all."

A few months ago, a deputy with whom I briefly served was on duty with a different agency and, at a full run, stopped a school shooter with his service sidearm, a .40-caliber Glock 22. He was patrolling past a high school prom, and as soon as he was able to visually confirm that what he saw was, in fact, a young man with a firearm who'd already shot innocent persons, he immediately closed with and stopped an active deadly threat to the individuals inside and outside of the school building.

I'm ashamed to admit that I hardly remember this officer — I'd maybe worked a shift or two with him before leaving law enforcement to work full-time at *Concealed Carry Magazine* — so I do not recall what he was like as a shooter during training or qualification. "Shooting qual" hardly enters into such a situation though; anyone who's in the least bit experienced with firearms will recognize what he did as truly outstanding shooting. Engaging a moving target with a sidearm under the extreme duress that only a rapid mass murder in progress can bring on and scoring incapacitating hits while you yourself are running is not only extremely admirable, it's something that all who go about armed should occasionally (if not regularly) train for.

Even if you suffer limited mobility or other limiting factors, shooting on the move at something that is also not stationary isn't a weird range drill ... it's the kind of shooting that you as a concealed carrier are the most likely to have to employ. Even in the "most common" circumstance listed above, your target will most likely be moving at least a little bit, and you need to be moving in order to present to your attacker no better a target than necessary.

That's close-in though. What about when you can't smell the threat's breath?

Say you're pulling into the parking lot of a large store and, when you track some movement out of the corner of your eye, you see a young man behind the wheel of a parked pickup truck speaking animatedly into a cell phone that's held in a bracket on the dashboard. He's wearing all black clothing, but you can see large pockets and, as such, you can't tell whether he's wearing a vest of some kind over a black t-shirt or whether he's wearing a cut-off black BDU blouse. You can't quite tell; you're driving and your attention is split between him and the other vehicles moving about in the area. You glance back and see what you swear is the front sight aperture of either an AR- or AK-type rifle bobbing around his face, and he's started moving and twisting in the cab of the truck. You're about 35 yards away now, and his door pops open.

Yup, that certainly appears to be an AK-pattern rifle, and that certainly appears to be a vest covered with magazine pouches.

Should I shoot?

Rather than run down a list of the options as I see them, I want to focus on one very specific decision: Do you, at that moment, reach for your cell phone or your firearm?

If your answer is cell phone, exactly who are you going to call and exactly what are you going to say to them?

If your answer is firearm, what are we talking about here? Are you reaching for an LCP or similar pocket .380? Are you snapping the "truck gun" out of the roof rack and feeling especially grateful for the 30-round magazine of 7.62 NATO you have on hand? Maybe something in-between? Do you drop it into gear and commence to ramming speed? Or do you sit there like a lot of folks will, reinforcing the reality that not making a decision is, in and of itself, making a decision?

Should I shoot?

To a law enforcement officer, the most important point of order at that moment would be to ensure that the man getting out of the vehicle with a rifle does not get into the large store and start shooting. If you're a sworn officer of the law, you immediately verbally engage him to clarify what exactly is happening and, if necessary, you do everything in your power to keep him from getting inside and starting to shoot, period.

But private citizens aren't law enforcement officers.

The cop or trooper who just drives away from this scene isn't just letting down his department and wildly shirking his duty,

he's breaking the oath that he swore and fundamentally breaking the trust he is supposed to hold between himself and the community he serves. If it can be proven that he knowingly and intentionally fled the scene of a rapid mass murder, there will definitely be professional repercussions for him, and he would also be open to civil suits brought by the families of the murder victims.

A private citizen? Your average Joe Range-Bag who carries a concealed sidearm just to be safe rather than sorry?

The private citizen always has the option of just driving away.

Should I shoot?

The circumstance in the parking lot described above is a heck of a challenge to take on, but it's one that everyone who carries should at least think over before (God forbid) they'd have to decide to investigate, accept or decline it. All of this is compounded by the fact that you don't yet even have an articulable, concrete reason to shoot at this man. For all you know, he's one of those open carry activists and this is his way of showing everyone in town what a big boy he is now. Maybe he was live-streaming a Facebook rant about how unfairly targeted open-carry activists are and how he's about to peacefully walk into this big-box store with a GoPro strapped onto his chest to prove it.

Maybe.

But I wouldn't bet lives on it.

What say you?

HOME ★ SWEET ★ HOME

CHAPTER 20
SECTION 2: SHOULD I SHOOT?

KNOCK, KNOCK'

By Ed Combs

A few chapters ago, I offered a scenario in which you were awakened in the middle of the night by the sound of your front door being kicked in, and it raised some interesting questions about the implementation of deadly force inside the home.

A lot of people likely saw it as a very cut-and-dried situation, but some probably did not. That's fine; what we're after here is discussion and critical thought. The body can't go where the mind hasn't been, and I want all concealed carriers and possessors of home-defense firearms thinking a heck of a lot about the possible circumstances surrounding the potential use of deadly force.

Say you're standing in your kitchen one morning at about 7. Pick a reason why you're there — finishing the dishes from breakfast, helping your kids prepare for the day, finally getting around to eating breakfast yourself, whatever. As this scenario unfolds, I want you to be concentrating as hard as you can on the following questions:

- Where is your closest firearm when it's 7 in the morning and you're standing in the kitchen?
- At what point would you access a firearm in this scenario?
- What are the steps it would take? And how long would it take for you to complete them?

So, there you are and you hear screaming outside. If you live in a house, it's out by the road. If you live in an apartment or a condo, it's out in the parking area. (If you live in the middle of nowhere, see if you can think back to the last time you lived near people.)

The screaming is a woman's voice telling a man named Frank to "just go away." The man is also yelling, but you're unable to tell what it is that he's saying. You hear glass break, and then you hear glass break again.

Looking out the window, you see a man with a 3-foot piece of rebar hitting a car, smashing its windows and denting every surface he can touch. A woman is yelling at "Frank" to "just get out of here," but when he turns toward her, she runs to a door, enters the residence and closes it behind her.

Frank follows, tries the door, finds it to be locked, kicks it once and walks away. He approaches the next door, tries it and finds it to be unlocked. He enters, holding his piece of rebar, and you hear shouting. You hear glass break. You've dialed 911 by this time and the operator tells you that there are units on the way and that you should remain in your residence.

So you do.

By this time, Frank's been run out of the residence he entered and, as he's walking back toward the cars, you see a trickle of blood running down his forehead from the middle of his hairline. He's back to hitting cars again, but he hasn't gotten to yours yet. You're watching out your window and, for a second as he turns around, your eyes meet and Frank stops swinging his piece of rebar.

And he starts walking toward your door.

Your door is locked, and at his current pace, it looks like Frank's going to be at the threshold in about five seconds.

Should I shoot?

No.

If you're going to employ deadly force against an assailant, three conditions must be present: Jeopardy, Ability and Means. (The acronym JAM is a popular way to remember them.) "Jeopardy" means you are in unavoidable jeopardy of death or great bodily harm. "Ability"

means that your assailant has the physical ability to deliver that death or great bodily harm to you or another from where he is. And "Means" means your attacker has the tool or physical superiority he will use to deliver it.

As it stands now — at least for the next few seconds — Frank is still on the other side of a locked door. If you're not holding a weapon and if you haven't taken up a defensive posture by now, you're crazy, but again, Frank does not yet have the ability to deliver death or great bodily harm to you. He's still outside, and the last locked door he tried he kicked once and then walked away from.

Now those five seconds have passed, and you hear the knob rattle. It's locked.

Then you hear the first kick. The door holds.

Then you hear the second kick. And the third. And the fourth. Now the doorjamb is starting to give way.

Should I shoot?

What you've seen so far is an extremely agitated man who is destroying property and who has violently entered a residence. He is holding a deadly weapon — a piece of steel rebar — and appears to have already been in one physical con-

frontation. He is now literally smashing open the locked door to your home, and as you do not have a legal duty to retreat from your own residence, you are:

• Clearly in jeopardy
• Facing a man who has the ability to inflict death or great bodily harm
• Facing a man who is holding a deadly weapon in his hands

As silly as this whole circumstance might sound, it is a combination of two different very real incidents: one I experienced as a law enforcement officer and another that is one of the more unbelievable videos you'll probably ever see. If you Google "machete-wielding intruder shot on camera," you will see the cell phone video of a man in Pocatello, Idaho, named Twain Thomas literally smashing through an apartment door like Jason Voorhees before the resident shoots him three times. In the ensuing wait for emergency services, Thomas admits that he was, in fact, looking to kill the resident.

Thomas absorbed three rounds. Those three rounds put him on the ground, but he survived the incident to receive a good long hitch in prison. He was holding a machete, so as soon as he went down and wasn't moving, the resident stopped

■ Secure your firearms however you wish when you're not carrying them, but carry them whenever and wherever you can.

shooting. (I've said a few times that defensive shootings are rarely cut-and-dried affairs; sometimes they are.)

So back to what I asked you at the top.

Where is your closest firearm when it's 7 in the morning and you're standing in the kitchen?

Do you actually carry a firearm whenever you're not in bed or bathing? Do you keep other firearms in your residence specifically for on-site security, or is your daily EDC sidearm also your home-defense gun? If it isn't immediately on your person, how long does it take you to get from your kitchen to wherever it is?

At what point would you access a firearm in this scenario?

If you're not already wearing that gun, at what point do you realize that you really need to be holding a gun? Is it the screaming? Is it the glass breaking? If we're talking about a long gun, do you have a way to sling or otherwise secure it so you're not just walking around with a rifle or shotgun at port arms? If you're already wearing an EDC gun, do you pull it or do you access a different weapon? Are you a believer in the old adage that your sidearm is "only for fighting your way to a rifle?"

What are the steps it would take and how long would it take you to complete them?

Are you literally just a proper draw away from your emergency lifesaving gear, or do you have to access a firearm from storage? Are all of your firearms squirreled away in a gorgeous $7,000 vault, or do you have other arrangements? Do you have a biometric lock box, a regular old keyed unit or do you have firearms otherwise secreted around your home? Are you more than the proverbial "three seconds away" from a firearm?

Should I shoot?

Assuming you've been issuing strong verbal commands that he cease all hostile activity from the moment the kicking started, what happens next? Is running out a different exit even an option? Does your residence only *have* one entry/exit point?

"Castle Doctrine" laws aside, I'd love to hear your answers.

CHAPTER 21
SECTION 2: SHOULD I SHOOT?

WHEN DO YOU CALL 911?

Well, we've all had a pretty harrowing few months here at *Should I Shoot?*, what with all of the random attacks and razor-thin margins for error and borderline exchanges of gunfire. Let's take this week off and just have a seat, pour a cup of coffee or a tall tea, put our feet up and scan the local news.

Let's say that you're doing just that and come across a story about a semi-rural man in your area who shot an intruder in his home.

The resident heard a scratching noise in his dilapidated garage at about 10 one night. Thinking it was likely the raccoon that had recently been raiding his trash cans that the county demanded be stored "indoors or otherwise secured," he grabbed and charged a 20-gauge pump shotgun that he'd left by the door in hopes of getting a shot at the furry little bandit as it ran out into the wooded area behind his garage.

When he got to the unlocked door that connected his kitchen to his garage, he still heard the noise, so he opened the door very quickly and jumped through it, slamming it behind him. (The last thing he wanted to do was have the raccoon get into his house.) Turning on the light and grabbing the doorknob of the door that led to the backyard, he saw ... a middle-aged man pulling a knife from the sheath on his belt while stumbling toward him, eyes bugged out, obviously very startled and angry.

The resident instinctively pointed and fired a load of No. 6 birdshot into the upper chest cavity of the burglar-turned-attacker, who promptly died before the resident could even dial 911.

Well, dang. Neither was expecting THAT.

This happened about 20 years ago to a mild-mannered semi-rural individual who owned a pump shotgun for a few rounds of clays every summer and the occasional trip to a pheasant farm with some bud-dies from work. There wasn't a violent or even particularly aggressive bone in his body; in fact, his blubbering on the phone made the 911 dispatcher initially think that *he* was the one who'd been shot, and then when his wife came downstairs and learned what had happened, she grabbed the phone and made it sound as if *another* man had been shot since the resident first called. Like they so often are, this deadly force encounter quickly went from a completely normal evening to a complete disaster in the span of seconds.

So, you're reading this story on your phone or in your local paper and it gets you thinking:

What if he'd gone out there with a broom to shoo the animal out the door? What if his wife had gone out there with a broom to shoo the animal out the door? What if, rather than his survival instinct fortunately kicking in and saving his mild-mannered hide with the shotgun he was fortunate enough to be holding, he'd been holding a broom that would have turned the circumstance from a rather clear-cut defensive gun use into the world's most exciting karate tournament?

All of this gets you thinking about the line we read in so many of these use-of-force stories: "The homeowner took up a firearm and went to investigate."

So, in a break from form, I guess I have to ask:

Should I call?

If you hear "a noise" that seems out of place — night or day — do you call the police before you do anything else? Maybe the non-emergency number, just to let them know that you heard something weird and you're going to investigate?

Well ... no. Were you to call your local police non-emergency number every time you heard a strange noise, you would quickly become that department's least-favorite citizen. (Believe it or not, some people actually *do* call the non-emergency number every time they hear a noise; any dispatcher could tell you stories you wouldn't believe.) Moreover, were you to call 911 every time you heard a weird noise and didn't stop after several stern talking-tos from shift sergeants, you would likely be literally jailed.

What makes this a serious problem is that quite often, after someone has no choice but to employ deadly force in self-defense, a common question from the anti-gunners is, "Well, why didn't he call the cops?" (Spoiler alert: Had he thought that the situation merited a call to the cops or had he the time to do so, guess what? *He would have called the cops.*)

I mean, think about it.

If I know that I have a load of laundry in the dryer and if I know that there are rivets on some of those jeans, I'll understand that there will likely be some noises emanating from that dryer. Every now and then though, I'll hear something odd enough coming from my laundry room that I'm going to walk over and make sure that the washer isn't unbalanced and making a run for the guest bedroom.

And when I do so, I'll be — at least in the eyes of the law — "taking up a firearm to go investigate."

As someone who is basically always carrying a handgun or handguns whenever he's not sleeping or bathing, I am by definition "taking up a firearm to go investigate" anytime I go anywhere to investigate anything.

Should I call?

"AS SOMEONE WHO IS BASICALLY ALWAYS CARRYING A HANDGUN OR HANDGUNS WHENEVER HE'S NOT SLEEPING OR BATHING, I AM BY DEFINITION 'TAKING UP A FIREARM TO GO INVESTIGATE' ANYTIME I GO ANYWHERE TO INVESTIGATE ANYTHING."

If I'm going anywhere on my property and I'm carrying a gun, if I end up having to use it to defend myself, all of a sudden, now I'm a guy who "took up a firearm to go investigate" and didn't call emergency services before doing so — which, to be honest, doesn't always play the best in a police report or in a prosecutor's opening statement.

My rule of thumb is that if I'm not specifically thinking that what's about to happen will possibly be dangerous, I never call *anything* in. If I do think that something might be dangerous and I am specifically headed over with a firearm, I'm calling 911 and explaining exactly what's going on (situation permitting, of course).

Problem is, the latter is only about 0.00001 percent of anyone's daily activities.

So, let's say you hear something at 2:30 tomorrow morning, and it's weird enough that you're hopping out of bed. It could be the furnace, could be the water heater, could be the dog ... you have no idea. Since the world can be a not-so-nice place when it's dark, you grab a flashlight and a sidearm.

Should I call?

I'd be interested to know what you think.

CHAPTER 22
SECTION 2:
SHOULD I SHOOT?

THE TRENCHCOAT AND THE CROWDED CHURCH

By Mark Kakkuri

On a Sunday morning somewhere in Michigan, dozens of people, including you, are entering one of many suburban churches. This particular church sits on the edge of four communities, three of which are described as typical, middle-class suburbia — you know, Starbucks, indoor trampoline park, nice community college. The fourth community is a poorer, economically distressed community — roads not well kept, a few burned-out houses, lots of stray animals.

In recent months, the church, an icon in its community for more than 60 years, has endured several thefts and has seen an increase in people showing up on the premises looking for handouts. As a result, while trying to meet legitimate needs in the surrounding communities, the church has just started a scratch security program to help deal with any problems or even threats that might arise before, during or after Sunday morning worship services. The small security team isn't pre-disposed to assuming trouble will most likely come from the economically distressed community, but they weren't expecting it to show up in a suit, tie and trenchcoat.

A little background: Michigan law requires anyone with a concealed pistol license to have permission from the church's presiding officers before carrying concealed on premises. And, because you're a law-abiding citizen and a faithful attendee, you obtained that very permission several months ago. You don't always carry your single-stack 9 (with one spare mag in your weak-side pocket) in the church, but on this particular Sunday, you do. Moreover, you've talked to the church's security leader about possibly joining the team and taking a shift every now and then. It seems like a good way to participate in the life of the church and you want to help. As such, you're 10 times more vigilant than the average churchgoer, grateful to worship freely in America but also aware of recent violent incidents at other churches around the country. In short, you're realistic about the threats.

It's 10:39 a.m. and the service starts at 10:45 a.m. You've taken your seat on an aisle about 10 rows back from the front row. You have a clear view of the stage and the pulpit is just to your right. You watch other people file in and take their seats. The pianist is playing a welcome tune. People are greeting one another, getting kids situated and sipping their coffees. Then you spot a man you don't recognize wearing a long trenchcoat. He's looking for a seat about 30 chairs to your right but in the front row. He's also looking at the stage, looking behind him, etc. It's a little strange, but "not every trenchcoat means a gun is hiding underneath," you chide yourself, trying to think the best…

Then the man takes off his trenchcoat, moving in such a way that you see he is not only wearing a suit and tie but, under the suit coat, also a shoulder holster with a large, semi-automatic pistol. The man folds his trenchcoat and places it on the seat next to him and then adjusts his suit coat, trying to wrap it around him more but not actually buttoning the coat. He picks up the bulletin and looks through it, waiting for the service to start.

You immediately but nonchalantly get up, find the security team leader and discreetly let him know what you saw. He finds another security team member, reports what's happening and then takes a seat directly behind the man with the shoulder-holstered pistol.

Then the church service officially starts. You participate in the service as you can but are quite distracted by the man who is carrying the large pistol. Thoughts of all types cross your mind: What if this man is a law enforcement officer? If so, he's exempt from having to get permission from the church's presiding officials. What if he's a private citizen with a concealed pistol permit? Maybe he too has gained permis-

You might be surprised just how irresponsible and unreasonable some people can be with their firearms, both at home and out in public.

sion and you just don't know about it. He's clearly not a part of the church's security team and his holster and apparel have not done very well concealing his pistol. What if he does something during the service, such as getting up and approaching the stage during the minister's message?

But the service goes without incident and the man carrying the concealed pistol behaves, for all intents and purposes, like a typical churchgoer — standing when you're supposed to stand, sitting when you're supposed to sit, singing when you're supposed to sing, etc.

Right at the conclusion of the service, one of the security team members approaches the man, greeting him with a friendly smile and an offer of a handshake. You discreetly make your way over to try to listen in on the conversation and possibly be of help, just in case something goes awry. The security team member who sat behind the man comes around to his front and starts an interchange:

"Hi, how are you today?" the security team member says. "My name is Bill. Are you new here?"

"No, I used to come here several years ago," the man replies. "Just visiting today."

"I see. Well, we are glad to have you," Bill says. "Say, I happened to notice you're carrying a concealed pistol. Can you tell me why you're carrying in this church?"

Bill has a pleasant but firm look on this face. The man's eyes widen as he hears Bill's question.

"Oh! Well, I, uh, I have a concealed carry license and carry everywhere," he says.

He starts pulling his jacket closed, trying to better hide the gun from view.

"I see. Well, according to the laws of the State of Michigan, you're not to carry on church premises without permission from the church," Bill says.

"Right, yeah, but I've had all the training, so it's, you know, totally safe," the man says.

As he stammers through his answers, you see him getting a bit red in the neck and face, fidgeting more, unhappy to be confronted in this way. He stands up. Bill stays cool and collected.

"Sir, here's what I'd like for you to do," Bill says. "First, you should know I am an off-duty police officer and a member of the church's security team. While we appreciate the 2nd Amendment and your desire to exercise that right, state law as it stands today prohibits you from carrying on premises without the church's explicit permission. I'd like to ask you to leave the premises immediately."

Bill gestures as if to show the man a path to the exit.

"If you come back — and you are welcome any time — you are to leave your gun in your vehicle," he says.

You're still in the church sanctuary, watching this conversation unfold from about 10 feet away, to the back of the man but in the clear line of sight of the security team member. Dozens of people are all around, chatting with one another, oblivious to the conversation-turned-confrontation. At this point, any number of scenarios could play out.

Should I shoot?

SCENARIO 1

The man puts on his trenchcoat and quickly and deliberately heads for an exit. He's clearly steamed on being called out for carrying on church premises. Not knowing him or his intentions, you and Bill follow him out of the building and to the parking lot — sort of an escort out to help make the point. He turns and looks back at Bill with a scowl, shaking his head. You guess the man won't be back. Hopefully, this situation is over, only to be brought up as a matter of training for the next security team meeting.

SCENARIO 2

But as he gets in his car, you see him fumbling with his coat. He puts his car in gear and the tires squeak a bit as he makes a quick backward movement out of the parking spot. He somewhat erratically drives toward the main entrance where you and the security team member are standing. He spins the steering wheel with one hand and brakes hard, putting the car about 50 feet in front you, driver-side door toward you. He glares out his window at you both. Neither hand is visible and he

just sits there for several seconds. His driving has caught the attention of others in the church parking lot and they've stopped to give attention to this bizarre standoff. Questions race through your mind: What is this guy doing? Where are his hands?

SCENARIO 3

All of the sudden, his door flings open and he steps out but stays behind his door. One of his hands is on the top of his car door; the other appears to be reaching inside his suit coat, as if going for a draw. You think back to the sanctuary: Was the gun under his right arm or his left? "His left, definitely," you think. So, he's likely right-handed. Which hand is reaching inside his suit coat now? His right. While you watch his hands, you — and everyone else nearby — hear his exclamation: "I know my rights! I've got the training! I'm not here to hurt anybody!" Then both of his arms go up in the air in the shape of a "Y" — a sign of exasperation or frustration — and he sits down back in his car, slams the door and tears out of the parking lot. Bill is already on the phone with the local police, relaying the events as well as the man's license plate number and vehicle description.

Should I shoot?

While some of the man's behaviors were bizarre and unwise, he never presented a threat with his gun or any other weapon. At one point, his driving might have been construed as hostile, but this was in a crowded parking lot with enough room between him and you to allow you to seek cover or escape.

How would any of these three situations have had to change in order for you to be justified in drawing your gun and shooting?

CHAPTER 23
SECTION 2: SHOULD I SHOOT?

THE ACCIDENT

By Mark Kakkuri

It's 7:05 a.m., as typical a Tuesday morning as ever. You're in your SUV, driving to the office. You live in a half-suburban, half-rural area, but it seems there's always a healthy dose of rush-hour traffic. The commute, only 11 miles, often takes 20 to 30 minutes when the weather is good. Any amount of precipitation might double your driving time.

It's winter and there's a light snow falling. Traffic on the southbound two-lane road has backed up, more than you expected. As you brake and take your spot in line, you look at the other drivers around you. Most are showing signs of frustration, some are looking at their phones and some are glancing at their watches. You look in your rearview mirror and watch the driver behind you throw his hand, which had been on the top of the steering wheel, up in the air as if to say, disgustedly, "Well, this is just great."

As you and other drivers inch forward around a curve and over a slight hill, the reason for the backup becomes apparent. It's not the weather, at least not directly. It's what looks like a fender-bender: Two southbound vehicles are partially pulled over on the right shoulder but are still on the road enough that traffic has to carefully go around them. The vehicle in front is a new black sports car, and the vehicle behind it is a very large, older pickup truck. Probably an accident, you think, but there are no police officers on the scene. At least not yet.

As you inch up on this scene, you see the rear bumper of the sports car has been significantly damaged. The front of the pickup truck, equipped with an old, rusty grill guard, has no visible signs of damage. But you quickly lose interest in the vehicle damage when you see a man, presumably the driver of the sports car, out of his car, standing between the two vehicles, gesturing at the truck driver. The truck driver is still inside his truck. The sports car driver wants him to get out.

You've heard of road rage but haven't seen what looks like it's going to turn into

an active fight or heightened confrontation. Your attention to the situation hits its apex when you see that the driver of the sports car is carrying a handgun in his right hand. Looks like a Glock. Right out in the open.

To make the situation worse, a couple passing drivers lay on their horns, gesturing their displeasure at the delay caused by the two vehicles on the side of the road. You wonder: Do they not see the gun? As you take all this in, you hear the distant wail of a siren; sounds like the county is on the way. The sports car driver is still gesturing to the truck driver, pointing at him and then pointing to the shoulder of the road and beckoning him to get out. The driver of the truck does not seem to be responding.

At this point, your SUV is in the right lane and you're looking at the scene through your windshield and your passenger side window. And suddenly you realize you're about to be uncomfortably close to a man with a gun who's just been rear-ended.

You've had a concealed pistol license for more than 10 years but have never had to use your gun, let alone put your hand on it in a scenario where you felt even a bit threatened. But, today, with this situation brewing, you find your right hand has moved toward the passenger seat, toward the side-zip pocket of your shoulder bag, where your handgun resides in a holster attached to a stiff panel — an off-body concealed carry solution you got for Christmas.

Should I shoot?

SCENARIO 1

As you inch forward, passing the sports car, your eyes remain on its driver. You turn your head back and forth, watching the vehicle in front of you, then watching him directly and then, as you pass him, watching him by using your side and rearview mirrors. He seems engrossed with the pickup driver and something on the other side of the vehicles. All of the sudden, the sports car driver moves from between the two vehicles and starts walking southbound, next to his car. In fact, he is walking toward you, approaching your vehicle's rear passenger side. Your eyes dart from the road in front of you — blocked by traffic — to the gun in the man's hand. He seems to be looking right into your rearview mirror. And now he's gesturing at you to … what, pull over and stop? Seriously?

SCENARIO 2

Your heart pounds as you watch this unfold, seemingly in slow motion. Does nobody else around you notice? Or care? The vehicle in front of you has stopped and so you have to stop. The sports car driver is now directly outside your passenger-side window. Your window is up. Your doors are locked. Your right hand is now moving to unzip the side-zip concealed carry pocket, which is going to be difficult with one hand. Escape seems impossible; you're blocked in by traffic, but you don't want to leave the relative safety of your vehicle. You're watching the sports car driver immediately outside your vehicle. You can't see his gun any longer and he's now turning toward your vehicle, about to engage you in some way. Your mind races as you contemplate what you'll do if he bangs on the window or yanks on the door in an attempt to open it.

SCENARIO 3

The sports car driver peers into your vehicle and you lock eyes with him. His right hand comes up and he presses a sheriff's badge to the window while signaling with his left hand for you to roll down the window. You glance at your rearview mirror at the sports car and notice its headlights flashing in an alternating pattern and red and blue flashing lights in what looks like a damaged grill. It's an undercover sheriff's vehicle. Relief pours over you as you slowly move your hand from the zipper pocket of your shoulder bag and rest it on your car's shifter. The sports car driver, a county sheriff's officer,

raps his knuckles on the window with a friendly smile. You roll it down all the way.

"Hey buddy, I'm Lt. Christiansen, Grove County Sheriff," he says. "Can you pull over for a quick minute and help me out? I just hit a deer with my car, which in turn resulted in the poor guy in the truck hitting me. My car won't budge and I want to move it further off the road and onto the shoulder. Not sure what the truck driver's doing; he's probably in a bit of shock. Anyway, I have a tow strap and I figure your SUV would have no trouble with this while I wait for a wrecker…"

"Sure, glad to help," you respond. "But for your safety and mine, I want you to know I have a license to carry a concealed pistol and I do have my gun in the car with me — in this shoulder bag, in fact."

"OK, buddy. Thanks for letting me know," he says. "You keep your gun in your bag and we'll be good, OK?"

"Yes, sir."

"Thank you."

"Um, Lieutenant, didn't you have your gun out a second ago?" you ask. "What was going on with that?"

"Yep, unfortunately, I had to put the deer out of its misery," he says. "It's laying just off the road on the other side of my car."

As you carefully pull off the road and position your SUV to help the police officer, you reflect on the presumptions that abounded in the scenario and how things turned out to not be what they seemed. A vehicle hitting a deer, an unmarked police car, a plainclothes officer, a scared pickup truck driver, the possibility of slippery roads, rush hour traffic, a law enforcement officer who had to put a hurt deer down and blocked traffic patterns. Plenty of opportunity for an accident to go from bad to worse.

In what way would Scenario 1 or 2 have had to change in order for you to be justified in drawing your gun and shooting?

THE ASSAILANT AND THE ATTENDANT

It's Friday, 4:56 p.m. You and your co-worker have labored through another week of corporate dysfunction and are looking forward to dinner and a hockey game. You both have had your concealed carry permits for a few years and carry just about everywhere you go. *Just about* everywhere. The only places you don't carry concealed are the ones denoted by your state's laws: places of worship, bars, educational institutions, hospitals, courthouses and entertainment venues seating more than 3,000 people. You'll be in two of these places tonight. You don't carry in your office, as company policy forbids weapons. As such, your gun spends business hours in your vehicle's glove box.

It's a 30-minute drive from your office to downtown where the restaurant and hockey arena are located. You've made this trip dozens of times, and you always carry your gun, because downtown is still downtown (and one of the cities near the top of the FBI's list of most violent).

Upon arrival at the restaurant, you and your buddy dutifully place your handguns in the glove box. The restaurant, is, after all, a bar, and you're planning on celebrating the start of the weekend with a drink or two. The restaurant is crowded, but you and your buddy are able to get a seat at the bar where you enjoy the house special — pulled pork with mac and cheese — and your buddy downs a large cheeseburger. Comfort food at its finest.

You both roll out of the restaurant, stuffed but satisfied, looking forward to the game. It's just a 10-minute drive to the arena, but parking in this city is usually a disaster. As you negotiate the traffic, you and your buddy scout for people managing small, private lots offering close parking spots. For just a few bucks more than a typical garage parking fee, you can get a really good spot. Easy in, easy out.

Just beyond the next intersection, only about 75 yards from the arena, you both spot a guy holding a sign that reads, "$25" — red characters spray-painted on a white board. It's $10 more than you'll pay at the parking garage, but the parking garage is three blocks away. You and your buddy look at each and shrug as if to say, "Why not?" As you approach the parking area, your eyes meet those of the guy holding the sign. You point to his lot as if to ask if he has spaces available. He nods vigorously and waves you over, his hand full of cash from those he's already parked. Your buddy pulls a 20 and a 5 from the cash in his pocket as you start making the turn into the lot. You stop the car at the lot entrance and roll down your window to pay the attendant.

Just then, out of nowhere, a guy in sweatpants, running shoes and a hoodie comes up behind the attendant and swings what looks like a nightstick right at his head. Your eyes must have bugged out a bit as you saw this, because the attendant was looking right at you and then turned to look over his shoulder to see his assailant coming. Deftly ducking out of the way, the nightstick misses its mark. But the assailant is quick to reverse the momentum of his swing and try again. This time, he brings the nightstick down on the attendant's left arm, between the shoulder and elbow. He lands the blow with a thud, causing the attendant to scream in pain, buckle at the knees and drop the sign and all his cash.

Should I shoot?

SCENARIO 1

Immediately, the assailant swings the nightstick at you, striking your car door and yelling, "Stay in your car, man!" while frantically trying to grab the $10 and $20 bills all over the ground and all over the attendant, who is on also on the ground, holding his left arm with his right hand and writhing in pain.

At this point, your buddy has opened the glove box and retrieved one of the two guns inside and is attempting to open his door. You put the car in park and instinctively thrust your door open, which hits the assailant right on the top of his head, causing him to stumble backwards.

"I told you to stay put, man!" he screams, reaching under his hoodie, into his waist, and drawing a trench knife — brass knuckles with a built-in 6-inch blade. You pull your door shut, lock it and then see your buddy rounding the front of the car, gun in hand. You retrieve your gun from the glove box and look out your car's window.

SCENARIO 2

As soon as your buddy reaches your side of the car, the assailant sees him — and his gun — and drops most of the cash and scrambles to his feet to run away. Your buddy pockets his gun and kneels down to help the parking lot attendant. You holster your gun, open your door and get out to help. The commotion has drawn a few onlookers, but no police. You get out your phone and dial 911. The dispatcher converses with you casually. She tells you a police officer will be along soon. Meanwhile, you and your buddy help the parking lot attendant pull himself together. His left arm has a nasty bruise but is not broken. And, frankly, he seems more concerned that you have called the police than the fact that he was just assaulted and almost robbed. He wants to get back to his job of collecting his money for this lot. Just then, the assailant returns, walking around the corner, facing the three of you. He is standing about 30 feet away. The nightstick and the trench knife are not in view. Then again, neither are his hands. Instead, they're bunched up under the front of his hoodie.

SCENARIO 3

It's clear the assailant and attendant know each other. They both unleash a stream of verbal threats, each taunting the other to come over and settle this once

and for all. You and your buddy stand by the attendant, watching the assailant. Your buddy has his hand in his pocket, on his gun. Every now and then, the assailant's left hand comes out from under his hoodie to aid his verbal assault with an obscene gesture or pointing. His right hand stays hidden. This goes on for a several seconds. How you got tangled up with these two is beyond your comprehension, and you dismiss most of their shouting and threats ... until the assailant takes two steps forward and shouts, "You gonna try to shoot me again?"

That's when both you and your buddy realize he's talking to the attendant. At this point, you glance at the attendant and notice he too has his right hand under the front of his shirt. He's stopped yelling, but his eyes are fixated on the assailant and he's breathing heavily. You're getting a bad feeling about this standoff, but it's at that point you see the red and blue lights of an unmarked police car light up about two blocks away. Immediately, the assailant changes his demeanor to "uninterested citizen taking a walk" and starts walking away from the scene. The attendant shuffles over to the parking lot hut and goes inside. You and your buddy are left standing there when the police car rolls up.

Two officers get out and ask for your IDs. You go through the normal steps of informing them about your concealed pistol licenses, which they appreciate but take virtually no interest in. They ask you and your buddy a few questions, indicating they are more than familiar with the feud you just witnessed. Both police officers go to talk to the attendant and then get in the car and enter a brief report on their car's laptop.

Should I shoot?

How would any of these three situations have had to change in order for you to be justified in drawing your gun and shooting?

SEEN AND HEARD

By Mark Kakkuri

The sound of breaking glass is unmistakable, especially at 1:50 a.m. as you are lying in bed and the rest of the house is dark. Quiet. Asleep. That sound...

It didn't make a crash like someone dropping a beer bottle in your tile foyer. No, it was lighter and more scattered. More like a window being tapped out by a tool. Maybe a small hammer. It was distant but distinct.

Break-ins aren't common in your neighborhood, and you're a normal, everyday private citizen in a modest suburban subdivision where all the homes look alike. But you know criminals aren't too picky when they're desperate. And, apparently, they're clumsy too. Just the same, you reach over and put your hand on your biometric handgun safe. It reads your fingerprint and, in half a second, the door pops open and a small light comes on inside. You wait for your eyes to adjust. Yep, there it is. Your 4-inch-barreled .357 Magnum revolver — stainless steel, loaded with .38 Special +P defensive ammo, equipped with a laser-aiming system — is inside, ready for service.

The rush of adrenaline now has you wider awake than ever as you simultaneously sit up, listen and ready your gun. As you bring the revolver out of the safe, you accidentally bang the cylinder against the side of the safe with a clunk. Freezing mid-motion, you listen. Nothing.

You set the gun on the bed and move your feet around, trying to locate your shoes while carefully moving your hand over your nightstand, looking for your tactical light. Ah, there are the shoes. And there's the light. And there's your mobile phone on a charger on your nightstand. All of your motions seem out of order as you try to carefully dress while straining to hear.

This isn't the first time you've thought about what to do if there is an intruder in your home, but it's the first time you've ever been awakened like this. Your bedroom is on the second story of a typical colonial-style house. All the bedrooms are upstairs, but there's no one in the house but you. If you can get to the top of the stairs — right outside your closed bedroom door — you can hold an excellent tactical position. Anyone coming up those stairs can be warned, and, if they are a true threat, easily targeted. And looking down those stairs affords you a view of the front door and living room, and, to a degree — because the houses in your subdivision are so close — your neighbor's house.

It only takes a few seconds to get your bearings, get dressed, put your phone in your pocket and stand up, gun in one hand, tactical light in the other. But it seems like several minutes. Every few seconds, you stop cold, listening. Listening hard. Hoping to hear nothing, but if there's something to be heard, you're hoping to hear it and simply gain more information about whatever is going on. All you can hear — or feel — is your heart pounding.

You move stealthily to your bedroom door and, gun at the ready, open it quickly, stepping back and briefly shining your light into the hall. Nothing. Peering around the doorframe, you look down the stairs, which are just to your right. The exterior lights on your house are on, so there's some light coming into the living room. You can see your furniture. Everything looks normal. You stay there for a minute, just watching, allowing your eyes to grow more accustomed to the dark. And listening.

Your living room is bordered on three sides by large windows with transoms. During the day, an enormous amount of sunlight can pour in, making the room exceptionally bright and cheery. At night, you sometimes close off the views by twisting the stick control on the mini blinds. Last night, you left them open. All of these windows, as best as you can tell, are intact. You can also see out the windows into the side yard. Your neighbor's kitchen window is 30 feet away. And that's when you see it: the silhouette of a human figure, in your side yard, moving near your neighbor's window, looking into it.

Are your eyes playing tricks on you? You carefully move down a few stairs to get a better view while staying in the shadow and not using your light.

Sure enough, it's a person. Looks like a male, probably 5 foot, 10 inches and 250 pounds. Dark baseball cap, gray hoodie, blue jeans, maybe tan work boots. Beer bottle in hand. You know it's not your neighbor because your neighbor is not a he but a she — a nurse who is, in fact, working her late shift tonight. She's not one for late-night visitors and this guy's middle-of-the-night visit simply doesn't look right. At this point, you've forgotten about the noise of the glass breaking. It's time to call the police on a very suspicious character.

So, you pocket your tactical light and dial 911. It is answered almost immediately. "County Dispatch, what is your emergency?"

Just then, someone bangs heavily on your front door and a woman's voice yells a name you don't recognize. With your focus on the man in the side yard and on trying to call 911, the banging and yelling startle you so much you drop your phone, which bounces down seven steps, coming to rest face-up.

The pounding on the front door continues and the yelling of a name continues. You watch the man in the side yard turn around and look in the direction of your front door, which is uncomfortably in the same direction as you are. He yells something toward the other person, then hisses, "Be quiet!" while gesturing with both hands, palms down, in an up and down motion as if to say, "Keep it down!" Then he walks out of sight, presumably toward your front door.

The person at the front door grasps the door handle and tries to open it. It's locked, of course, but the person twists and rattles and shakes the door. Your mobile phone display is still lit up, "911" showing on the screen along with a timer counting up the seconds and minutes while the call is connected. You stay stock still on the stairs, heart pounding, hands shaking, holding your revolver in sort of a low-ready position. The man in the side yard returns into your view and this time looks not into your neighbor's window but directly into yours. Right into your living room. Right at your phone. Right up the stairs. Does he see you?

Should I shoot?

SCENARIO 1

The man quickly pulls back from the window and goes toward the front of the house. The banging and yelling continue. The door rattles and shakes. You seize the moment, quickly descend a few steps, grab your phone and lunge back up the stairs.

Did the man see you? You put the phone to your ear and catch the dispatcher mid-sentence: "...no response on the line, 4210 and 4240 are en route, sir."

Relieved the dispatcher is still on, you stammer out a situation report: "I, I, I've got someone banging on my front door, yelling, and some weird dude in my yard. No idea who they are."

The dispatcher is calm and reassuring: "You say they're outside your house. OK, what is your location?"

"I'm inside my house," you reply. "They keep banging on the door, trying to get in. I have no idea who they are."

"Stay on the line with me," the dispatcher says. "We have officers en route to your location."

SCENARIO 2

The man who was in the side yard must have convinced the other person near your front door to cease the banging and

yelling because it all suddenly stops. Well, the banging stops. Now two people are in a heated argument right outside your front door. One of them has a gruff voice — this one you presume to be the man from the side yard. The other voice indeed is female. You can't understand what they're saying because they're yelling over each other.

You stay put on the stairs, gun in hand, trying to relay what you can to the dispatcher, including the fact that you are armed. At that point, blue and red flashing strobe lights fill your living room as two squad cars pull up into your driveway with a screech and the sound of doors opening.

A commanding voice resonates over a PA system: "You two on the front porch: Hands up and face the house!"

Suddenly, there's a huge crashing noise and your front door violently swings open. The man from the side yard bursts through the doorway but trips over the threshold and falls hard into your foyer.

SCENARIO 3

He ends up lying on his side, howling in pain, grasping his left shin with both hands. You drop your phone, level your gun at him, retrieve your tactical light and shine it on him. Police officers are approaching the porch, guns drawn. The man's hands are still on his shin as he groans in pain.

From the PA system you hear: "Homeowner! Put down your gun and keep your hands in view! We are entering your house!"

You comply, putting down not only your gun but also your tactical light. A police officer appears at your door, shining his light at the man and then at you.

"Stay right there, it's over," he says, but you're not sure who's he's talking to.

You stand still, arms out, showing your hands as a second police officer steps in to handcuff the man.

Should I shoot?

How would any of these three situations have had to change in order for you to be justified in shooting?

EPILOGUE

In a situation like this, you might not ever find out the whole story, but here it is: The police successfully arrested the two people outside your home on multiple charges. Both were found in possession of controlled substances and both were intoxicated. The woman, in fact, was diagnosed later at the hospital with acute alcohol poisoning. The man was armed with a neck knife and a modern .40-caliber pistol with all the serial numbers scratched out. Both were known drug dealers.

Eventually, police would learn that the couple, in their stupor, were looking to visit another dealer in a subdivision across town but couldn't figure out how to get there and somehow ended up in your yard and at your front door. The sound of breaking glass you initially heard that night was the result of the man tossing a rock at your neighbor's upstairs window in an attempt to signal the dealer he thought would be in there — a pre-arranged code between the two parties. He picked too large a rock and threw it way too hard. And thus began a rough night that thankfully ended well.

CHAPTER 26
SECTION 2: SHOULD I SHOOT?

ELEVATED AWARENESS ON THE TRAIN

By Mark Kakkuri

It's 10 a.m. on a crisp, winter morning and you, your significant other and three other couples are driving in a minivan from your suburban homes into the city to hang out. The day's downtown plans include checking out the farmer's market, shopping in some stores in various pockets of the city, having lunch at one of the popular burger joints, taking a tour of the city's art institute and, if everyone is up for it, enjoying dinner at the newly opened BBQ restaurant. You arrive downtown, park in a public parking area, lock the car and begin walking.

Downtown is a mixed bag. There's a lot of good going on in the city, which happens to be one of the largest in the nation and, unfortunately, high on the FBI's list of most violent. But, despite decades of urban decay, the past three years have seen the formation and growth of most of the stores and restaurants you'll be visiting today. So, there are nice, cleaned-up areas that are well-populated. Most consider these areas fairly safe despite literally being across the street from more run-down areas. But the nice areas are few and far between. As positive as things seem, the city's rough condition does not improve in three years or even 10 years. So, there are still parts of the city — known for gangs, arson, violence, drug abuse, you name it — everyone knows to avoid.

You and your friends have lived in the suburbs for years. As such, all the city's vices are well known to you and are fairly easy to avoid. Plus, the improvements in the city — the shops, the restaurants — are very good and you want to do your part to see them succeed. Just the same, you and one of your friends have concealed pistol licenses and both of you are carrying today. You are carrying a Glock 19 (with a round chambered, of course) inside the waistband at 4 o'clock, with a spare magazine in your front left pocket. Your friend has a Smith & Wesson .38 Special in his front right pocket with a full Bianchi Speed Strip in his front left pocket. As a matter of awareness, you and your friend discuss all these facts with each other. You also go over Col. Jeff Cooper's Color Codes and agree that both of you will be, at a minimum, in Condition Yellow (relaxed but aware) all day. You're not paranoid but prepared. You're not a tactical vigilante but a trained shooter who will find every way to avoid a problem. You're not afraid to defend yourself or your friends if something should happen. Like every time you holster your pistol, you hope to never have to use it.

The outing downtown starts off well and turns out to be a lot of fun. The markets and shops you visit are brimming with people, lunch is fantastic and everyone is pleased to see the city — at least some parts of it — seemingly alive with activity. Everything your group has enjoyed so far has been within easy walking distance, but for the visit to the art institute, you decide to ride the city's elevated train. It's an unmanned, unattended, automatic transportation system — sort of like a string of buses that glide along an elevated rail — traveling in a loop around the city, stopping at various locations. The fare is 75 cents, whether you ride it for one minute from one stop to the next or whether you ride it all day — which some people do, either because they are homeless or bored. To board the elevated train, which you can do at several locations around the city, you enter a sort of terminal and place coins or a dollar into a wall-mounted, automated fare system. The machine pumps out a token and you then drop the token into a coin slot at a turnstile. Push through the turnstile and then it's up a couple flights of stairs to the boarding area.

■ Suspicious behavior is suspicious behavior, regardless of location.

Your group is walking toward the terminal. Your buddy's in the lead and you are bringing up the rear. Everyone's having a good time and looking forward to the train ride because it'll take about 10 minutes for the train to get you to the side of the city with the art institute, which means you'll get to enjoy a brief tour of some of the city while you look from your seats in the train. You all enter the terminal, where your group immediately starts digging in purses and wallets for dollar bills to pay the fare. That's when you, about to walk into the terminal door, decide to take a look over your shoulder. And that's when you spot him: a man in hi-tops, baggy jeans and a light blue hoodie about 25 yards down the sidewalk, staring at your group. He starts walking toward you with a determined gait.

You get your buddy's attention and nod over your shoulder.

"Light blue hoodie," you say. "Let's get moving."

Your buddy gets it and immediately starts encouraging your group to engage in a bit faster movement and less conversation. Both of you have moved from Con-dition Yellow to Condition Orange (specific threat). Some of the others in the group quickly acknowledge the wisdom in hustling to the train. Eight loud out-of-towners with handfuls of cash deep in the city … no one panics, but the group moves with a little more gusto up the stairs to the boarding area.

Your buddy is still in the lead and you're still bringing up the rear. At the top of the stairs, you look back and see the man in the light blue hoodie has jumped the turnstile and is beginning to ascend the same stairs you are on. He takes them two at a time.

The train is waiting, doors open, and there's hardly anyone around or on board. You and your friends board the train and you have a moment for a quick conference with your buddy on what to do. For all you know, light blue hoodie is on his way to work and wants nothing to do with you. But the purposefulness in his movements just doesn't seem right. You and your buddy agree to have your friends sit at the end of one of the train cars, with you both standing nearby, creating a sort of human gate between your friends and everything else. You all get in position and the train doors are about to close when, at the last second, light blue hoodie sneaks through the closing doors on to the same train car as you and your friends. He turns and looks right at your group.

SCENARIO 1

The train car you and your friends are on contains your group and the guy in the light blue hoodie. You size him up: about 5-feet, 9-inches tall, 160 pounds, stocky. You remember his deft leap over the turnstile and the two-stairs-per-step climb. Nimble. Agile. Your right hand looks like it is resting on your waist at 4 o'clock, but your thumb is actually between your waist and the grip of your pistol. If you need to, you can get your gun out in half a second. Your buddy has his hand in his front pocket, but only you and he know his hand is on his gun. Both of you are standing, holding a support bar with your weak hands as the train pulls away from the station, completely on autopilot. Both of you take occasional looks at light blue hoodie. You don't want to stare, but you want him to know that you are completely aware of his awkward presence. The man holds one support bar in each hand while he continues to look at your group. He's about 15 feet away.

SCENARIO 2

You and your buddy look at each other and you both know you need to get off the train at the next stop. The situation is just too weird and you both prefer to avoid confrontation, not aggravate it. The train plods toward the next stop, which is probably a minute or so away. You and your buddy continue to stand guard, hands on or near guns, your friends giving their full attention to the situation. The other guys in the group have moved closer to you and your buddy, just in case.

Just then, the guy in the light blue hoodie moves toward your group, slowly walking about three paces. His right hand goes into his hoodie pocket while his left hand grasps the next available support bar. His face has a smug look on it. Not quite combative or angry but not friendly. He continues to look at you and your buddy and even looks at your hands every now and again. With the man's advance, you and your buddy now opt for a full-on stare to let him know, as best as a look can communicate it, not to mess. This is Condition Red for both of you, the identification not just of a potential threat but a potential target.

SCENARIO 3

The train rolls to a stop at the next terminal and the doors automatically open. You and your buddy each take a step forward to allow your group to disembark the train behind you. You keep your hands on or near your guns and your focus completely on the man in the light blue hoodie.

Your friends file out and your buddy follows, always facing the man in the hoodie, and the two of you more or less walk backwards out of the train. The man in the hoodie is smirking at you but is not moving, which is a great relief. Your group walks on while you and your friend continue moving away from the train, slowly starting to turn away from the train but keeping your eyes on the man in the hoodie. The train doors automatically close and the trains pulls away, taking light blue hoodie to wherever he is going.

How would any of the scenarios have had to change in order for you or your friend to be justified in drawing and firing your guns? How would you have handled any of the logistical decisions, such as whether to board the train, where to stand or whether to engage the man in conversation?

A CONCEALED CARRY FIT

By Mark Kakkuri

You and your friends carry concealed just about everywhere you legally can. But you're not a bunch of vigilantes out looking for trouble. You're not a bunch of tough guys out to prove a point. You're a group of friends who shares a common bond in that you do what you can to preserve life, to protect others and to be prepared. As such, you and your friends often share advice and tips on concealed carry — everything from the latest guns and gear to the best tactics for safety and protection of life. And, when you're out together, you make it a point to be aware while you responsibly enjoy yourselves, because you never know when trouble might spring up.

Thankfully, all that has sprung up lately is you and your friends noticing when other people are carrying concealed. You've picked up on some of the cues — a person constantly fidgeting with covering garments, sometimes directly adjusting a gun/holster rig, and more. While it's somewhat comforting to know the popularity of concealed carry is growing exponentially, at times, you wish more people would read the myriad resources available to them to help them carry concealed really well. After all, concealed is supposed to be concealed.

Your state not only allows concealed carry but also open carry. While you're grateful for these rights and glad they can be exercised, you prefer concealed carry to open carry. You want the element of surprise if you have to deal with an attacker, and you don't want anyone seeing you with a gun and possibly targeting you for the theft of it. It would be foolish for someone to try it, yes, but you're all about minimizing opportunities for trouble. For the most part, people who are open carrying don't cause any trouble and they don't create much concern for you either. Every now and then, however, you find someone carrying a gun who seems to be caught somewhere in the middle. To put it another way, that person thinks he is carrying concealed, but something has happened to his covering garment; his gun is not concealed but is on display for all to see.

So, as you and your friends are enjoying conversation over coffee at the local coffeehouse, you notice one other customer — a stocky guy in jeans and a red sweatshirt — engaged in the concealed carry fidget. Clearly this person has a duty-sized pistol on his hip and he is doing his best to keep his shirt from riding up too high and revealing anything. He pulls at his sweatshirt when he's standing and he pulls at his sweatshirt when he's sitting. You discreetly nod in his direction and your group nods to one another in understanding — you all know what's going on. He doesn't seem to be a threat, but he's certainly worth watching.

Then, into the coffeehouse walks a gentleman wearing khaki pants, a golf shirt, a light tan jacket zipped halfway up and a baseball cap. As he walks through the door, the wind blows in just a bit, creating a draft behind him that almost blows his hat off. The man reaches up, catching his hat just in time, but in doing so, the draft billows his jacket, causing it to rise and then settle behind the stocks of the black pistol it was hiding just one second ago.

It's a typical black polymer-framed pistol and he's carrying it in an outside-the-waistband paddle holster — also black plastic. With the jacket caught behind the pistol's stocks, the rig is on display as the man walks through the coffeehouse, oblivious that he has gone from concealed carry to open carry in a very unique turn of events.

You and your buddies watch this unfold but act nonchalant. While the man might be no threat, you don't know this for sure. For all you know, he's here to rob the place. So you watch in a heightened state of alertness. Hardly any of the other customers even notice the man, let alone the gun, but it's just a matter of time before they do.

The man in the light tan jacket heads to the counter. As he does, you and your friends notice the man in the red sweat-shirt has risen from his seat with his eyes locked on the man in the light tan jacket. Red Sweatshirt makes his way through the coffeehouse toward Light Tan Jacket.

Should I shoot?

SCENARIO 1

The man in the red sweatshirt comes up behind the man in the light tan jacket and taps him on the shoulder. The man in the light tan jacket turns around, a puzzled look on his face. You watch these two have a brief conversation and see the man in the light tan jacket look down at his gun and then quickly pull his jacket over it to conceal it. By the expression on his face and his general demeanor, you can see the man is clearly embarrassed. He looks around the coffeehouse to see if anyone else noticed. A few have, but they don't seem to be doing anything about it. The man in the red sweatshirt walks toward the front of the coffeehouse, scowling and shaking his head.

SCENARIO 2

The man in the light tan jacket places an order at the counter and waits for it to be served up. He looks around nervously, obviously wondering who else spotted his gun and how they might react. He looks at his watch. He looks toward the front of the restaurant, hoping to catch a glimpse of the man in the red sweatshirt, but he's nowhere in sight. Finally, his order is delivered to him at the counter and he gathers it all up quickly. While he does, his jacket rides up again, revealing the muzzle of the gun on his right hip.

SCENARIO 3

The man in the light tan jacket turns around to head for the exit but stops and stares. You see why: Two uniformed police officers have entered the coffeehouse, followed by the man in the red sweatshirt, who is pointing at the man in the light tan jacket. One officer walks toward the man in the light tan jacket while the other stays with the man in the red sweatshirt. The man in the light tan jacket calmly explains what happened to the officer, the same signs of embarrassment showing on his face, while the officer runs the man's ID.

Meanwhile, the man in the red sweat-shirt has grown agitated as the other officer questions him and asks for his ID. All the customers are now enraptured in these two confrontations, but more so the one involving the man in the red sweatshirt. At one point, the officer dealing with him tells him to walk outside and gestures accordingly with his arms. The man in the red sweatshirt doesn't take too kindly to the officer's request, but starts moving toward the door. But not without using his arm to push away the officer's arm in an act of defiance. And that's when the officer, in a deft move, grabs the man's arm, twisting it and pushing the man face down to the ground.

Red Sweatshirt unleashes a stream of profanity, but the takedown affords the officer the opportunity to spot the man's concealed gun. Keeping the man's arm in a vice-like grip with one hand and keeping him pinned to the floor with his knee, the officer pulls the man's gun, drops the magazine and racks the slide on his boot, ejecting a live round from the chamber. At this point, the other officer comes over to help and the situation is soon over. The man in the red sweatshirt is arrested, the man in the light tan jacket is warned and you and your friends have a lot to discuss.

At what point in Scenario 1, 2 or 3 would you have been justified in drawing and firing your pistol? Would you have interacted with the man in the light tan jacket? What about with the man in the red sweatshirt? Would you have offered any information to the police as they were handling the situation?

THE WITHDRAWAL

By Mark Kakkuri

Saturday, 9:30 a.m. It's a typical day for you as you plan to drive from home into town to run a few errands. All your stops are listed out in order on a piece of paper so you can drive the shortest distance and make the fewest turns. On the list: returning a defective tool to the big-box home goods store, picking up some dry cleaning, picking up a prescription for your mother and then heading to the bank to get some cash for the week. In addition to your list, you grab your keys, your wallet, your folding knife, your mobile phone and your gun — a single-stack 9 you carry inside the waistband, in front, near your appendix.

Getting situated in your car, you place your mobile phone in a carrier attached to a vent on the dashboard. This setup allows you to talk hands-free and also see the screen when you drive — not that you allow it to distract you, of course. You head out, windows down, enjoying the moderate temps during this Midwestern spring day.

The return, dry cleaning and prescription pick-up take only several minutes apiece. As you turn into the bank parking lot, you pull up to the one drive-through ATM lane. A couple people are ahead of you, so this shouldn't take too long. With the bank building on your left, your car faces the bank's main parking lot, where there are several cars and a few people going in and out. You glance at a placard on the wall: Saturday lobby hours are 9 a.m. to 1 p.m. With all the online and drive-through capabilities available, you can't remember the last time you physically entered your bank. But, apparently, people still prefer to handle these kinds of transactions with a teller, face-to-face.

The person in the car at the ATM finishes and pulls away, turning to the right. The next vehicle — the one in front of you — is a big pickup truck with flames painted on the side, large mudder tires and an enormous rusty hitch. The truck moves up to the spot next to the ATM and stops. The driver rolls his window down. You move your car up right behind it. The car behind you moves up as well.

Just then, the truck lurches forward about 5 feet and the driver jumps out. He has a bandana half-covering his face, his right hand is in his right jacket pocket and he's pointing it (whatever it is) directly at you. He signals you to stop or stay put by holding up his left hand with his palm toward you. Totally caught off guard but trying to figure out what to do — because everything you're seeing is so surreal — you put your hand on your gun and prepare to draw.

You've had a concealed pistol license for years, and you've carried a concealed gun for just as long. Even though there have been a few instances where you were in a heightened state of alert, you've never had to draw on anyone. The thought races across your mind, unbelievingly: Would today be the day?

Should I shoot?

SCENARIO 1

Convinced you'll do as you've been told, the man removes his right hand, empty, from his jacket pocket as he moves to the rear of his truck. Reaching over the truck bed, he pulls out a massive chain and begins fastening it around the ATM. He fastens the chain to the truck hitch, looks directly at you, points at you and gives you the same stop or stay hand signal. Then he jumps back in his truck. Is this really happening? In broad daylight?

Gathering your wits, you reach with your right hand to your phone, hold down the home button, which brings the phone's personal assistant feature to life.

"Call 911," you say.

"Calling 911," the phone assistant answers obediently and starts the call.

SCENARIO 2

The driver of the truck puts his vehicle in drive and inches forward, taking up the slack in the chain. When it becomes taut, the driver guns it. Both rear tires howl as they spin, straining for grip on the pavement. Smoke starts billowing from each tire well as the truck jerks to the left, the chain tight as can be. You roll up your windows as your phone connects to a 911 operator.

"911, what is your emergency?"

You do your best to relay what is happening 10 feet in front of your car, that you're stuck in the position you're in and that the driver probably has a weapon of some kind. The operator asks you to hang on while the police are dispatched. In these few seconds, the driver's actions have caught the attention of several people in the bank parking lot. A few immediately get on their phones, presumably to call the police.

Just then, the truck engine idles and the chain slackens. The man jumps out of his truck, looks at you, looks at the ATM and then jumps back in the truck. He guns the engine, the chain tightens and the tug-of-war continues. You're still stuck, unable to go forward or backward, but relatively safe as long as the man thinks you're going to continue to obey him by staying put in your car. At this point, you've withdrawn your gun from its holster and are holding it in your strong hand. You're relaying as much as you can to the 911 operator.

SCENARIO 3

The commotion caused by the truck draws the attention of a bank security guard, who appears from the main entrance of the bank. As the guard rounds the corner to view the ATM lane, he instantly recognizes what is going on and draws his gun on the truck driver, shouting for him to stop. The guard is facing you just as much as he is facing the truck driver.

Just then, a portion of the ATM machine gives way, causing the truck to lurch forward a few feet before being halted again. The security guard treats this as an act of aggression by the truck driver and fires two rounds at the driver — or, at least, through the windshield. You're unable to see whether these shots have any effect, but the truck engine returns to idle and the chain goes slack again.

Just then, it's all lights and sirens as the police roll into the bank parking lot. The squad cars screech to a stop to the front right of the truck. The officers get out and draw their guns from behind their open squad car doors.

The 911 operator is telling you the police should be on the scene and asks if you're OK. You start to open your mouth to answer when the driver of the truck opens the truck door and jumps out. He points a gun in the general direction of the security guard and squeezes off a couple shots while moving toward the rear of his truck — toward you. The security guard returns fire, missing the man but hitting your windshield, which shatters into a spiderweb but stays in place. Through it, you can see the truck driver approaching you, his gun pointing directly at you.

At what point during Scenario 1 or 2 would you have been justified in drawing your gun and shooting? How would you handle Scenario 3?

THE GUN STORE

By Mark Kakkuri

It's Saturday morning and you're driving to the gun store. You own several guns already and you've had a concealed pistol license for about five years. You always carry — even to the gun store!

Today you're carrying a snub-nosed revolver, a gun you intend to replace with a slim 9 you hope to purchase on this visit. The revolver you carry has served you well, but it only carries five rounds and, while that's probably enough for any situation you'd face, you'd just be more comfortable carrying a few more rounds on board while having the ability to quickly reload with a magazine if need be.

You arrive at the gun store, park in the back and walk around to go in the front door. As you open the door, a beeping noise announces your entry. You have nothing in your hands, but your snubbie rides in an inside-the-waistband holster at 2 o'clock — the same way you intend to carry the slim 9.

As you greet the staff, they ask you if this is the day you'll be picking up your new gun. The big smile on your face tells the story and you give a thumbs-up as you look over the selection of holsters.

The owner has the gun you're buying ready for you at the counter. It comes with a second magazine, a magazine loading assist tool and a cleaning tool. He also has the paperwork prepared in advance. All you need to do is to pick out a holster.

As you're checking out some Kydex inside-the-waistband holsters, a beeping sound announces another customer is walking through the first of the two doors to the gun store. Instinctively, you look up from the holsters toward the door — as do several of the staffers — to see who else is there to shop, browse or buy. It's a man and a woman. They're clearly not from the area. As they walk in, they look around nervously as if unsure where to go. One of the staffers greets them and asks how he can help them.

"We're just looking for some .22 for squirrel hunting," the man answers.

The staffer directs them to the end cap of the ammo aisle where .22 ammo is on sale. The man picks up one box of 50 rounds, pays for it in cash at the counter and then leaves with the woman and a small bag with his purchase in hand. All the staffers and you give a quizzical look at each other, shrug it off and go back to business. You find a holster and head to the counter to finish your transaction. While you're there, you ask the owner to add a couple boxes of self-defense ammo to your purchase.

You pay and the owner rewards you with a bag containing your goods. Saying goodbye to the staffers, they wish you well with your purchase as you head out the double front doors.

After you get to your car, you get inside and decide to take a minute to look everything over. Before you do, you carefully remove your snub-nosed revolver and holster and put it in your glove box. Removing the new pistol from its case, you open a box of ammo and load up the two magazines. You slide a magazine into the gun and it seats with a confident snap. As a general rule, you don't carry a gun until you've test-fired it with a couple hundred rounds or so, but you're so happy with how this new gun feels, you want to holster it and see how it rides on your belt. You look in the bag for the holster, but it's not there. The receipt shows you purchased the holster, but after a quick search of your car, it still doesn't show up. Maybe the owner forgot to bag it or maybe you left it back in the gun store. Leaving your revolver behind, you put your new gun in your jacket pocket and get out of your car for what should be a one-minute trip back into the gun store.

As you close your car door, you peer across the parking lot. About 15 cars away is the couple who entered the gun store while you were in there. They're standing next to a car with its door open and you can see a person sitting in the driver's seat. The couple is talking with the man in the car, but they're looking around nervously, just like they were in the store. Your path back to the front entrance of the gun store won't cross their location, but it will bring you closer to them for a moment.

The exchange between the man and the woman and the driver doesn't look right and you're immediately conflicted on what to do. On the one hand, it could be nothing. Or it could be a simple matter, such as someone accidently bumping into another person's car and now they're trying to work it all out. Or you could be witnessing a hold-up in broad daylight right behind a gun store. Or it could be something else.

SCENARIO 1

You decide to assume the best and start walking toward the corner of the building that will lead you to the front entrance. Your hands are in your pockets and your strong hand is on your new unfired pistol. Mentally, you kick yourself. The revolver would have been a better choice. You know that gun. Worse, you didn't chamber a round.

As you walk, the threesome comes into better view. You turn your head just slightly and strain your eyes to see what you can. The man and woman are standing very close to the driver, between him and his open car door, making for an intimidating conversation at the least. The driver of the car is a young man who seems to be trying to explain something to the man and woman. The woman has a purse pulled in next to her and the man has his hands in his pockets. All three are speaking a different language. The couple is clearly aggravated and occasionally raise their voices at the young man. You keep walking.

SCENARIO 2

As you round the corner of the building, out of sight of the threesome, you stop and listen to see if you can determine not only what's going on but also what, if anything,

you should do. You hear the argument between the three escalate.

Carefully peering back around the corner of the building, you see the woman with her hand out toward the young man. He hands her some cash. The man is standing there with his hands in his pockets. The woman puts the cash in her purse. Then the man and woman step back and urge the young man out of the car. The arguing and the exasperated gestures continue as the young man exits the vehicle. They all nervously look around the parking lot but don't see you watching. Then the man and woman get into the young man's car, start the engine and begin to drive away.

SCENARIO 3

The young man, showing obvious signs of frustration, walks in a determined manner away from your post. The man and the woman in the car circle the gun store parking lot and then turn onto the street adjacent to the sidewalk you are on. They are heading right toward you, slowly.

The woman is in the passenger seat — the side of the car you are on as you begin walking toward the front of the gun store. They pull up right next to you and she rolls her window down, looking right at you. You're nervous and you can't see her hands, but she has her purse on her lap.

Just then, the owner of the gun store comes around the corner with your forgotten holster in his hand, his openly carried 1911 in plain sight. The woman and man in the car see the gun store owner, exchange some brief words of warning or command and speed off.

Should I shoot?

How would Scenario 1, 2 or 3 have had to change in order for you to be justified in drawing and shooting your pistol? What are the assumptions you made as the scenarios unfolded?

CHAPTER 30

SECTION 2: SHOULD I SHOOT?

THE FILL UP

By Mark Kakkuri

Driving home from work one weekday, you pull into a gas station to fill up and get something to drink. Pulling up next to the pump, you put your car in park and turn off the ignition, clipping your keys to your belt. You also retrieve your subcompact pistol from the backpack on the seat next to you and tuck the holstered gun into your belt — appendix carry. Your jacket will cover it nicely while you make this quick stop. Putting your gun on, even for quick errands like this, has become second nature to you. And you've seen enough gas station security video footage to know how quickly an incident can go down.

Normally you'd pay at the pump with your debit card, but because you're getting a drink from the gas station, you decide to go in, get your drink and pay for the drink and gas all at once. In the gas station store, you quickly glance over the myriad of refrigerated soda pop available to you and instead decide a large cup of coffee is the way to go. The commercial coffee machine is just completing a brew cycle, so you're assured it'll be a fresh cup. Small pleasures.

Holding a large empty coffee cup in hand, you're just about to pull the coffee machine handle and fill your cup when you hear an electronic chime behind you. It's the sound of the gas station door, which is about 30 feet away, being opened. You instinctively look over your left shoulder and over the aisles to see who came in. The customer is an enormous man wearing gray sweatpants, a sweatshirt and work boots. He's also wearing a baseball cap and large, dark sunglasses and — of most interest to you — he has a messenger bag worn across his body, hanging off his right side. His right hand is tucked inside the bag.

The man walks up to the counter and hands the clerk a note. The clerk nervously takes the note, reads it and then looks up at the man. The man motions with his left hand toward the cash register and then uses his right hand to put the messenger bag on the counter. His hand is still in the bag, but you can see the clerk has a clear view of what's inside. The clerk then punches a few buttons on the cash register, the cash drawer opens and the clerk steps back a few feet. At this point, the big man turns and looks around the store behind him and sees you standing at the coffee machine.

Should I shoot?

SCENARIO 1

As the man looks at you, his right hand comes out of the messenger bag enough so that you see he is holding something black. Given the clerk's reaction and the man's behavior so far, you're virtually certain it's a gun. You stand completely still as your heart pounds and your mind races. Then the man speaks to you.

"Stay right there. Don't try nothin'," he says. "No one has to get hurt."

You nod but say nothing. Your strong hand holds a large coffee cup and, regardless of what happens, you desperately want to free your hand in case you have to go for your gun. Then the man turns his attention to the register; reaching across the counter with his left hand, he methodically starts grabbing bills from the open cash drawer, putting the money in the messenger bag, even as his right hand stays inside it, wrapped around … whatever he's holding.

SCENARIO 2

The clerk has said nothing but has stood virtually frozen in place, just a yard from the cash drawer, eyes on the large man and the messenger bag. The clerk's hands have been at his side, but you notice his right hand moving toward his back. You look at the clerk with a determined stare, as if to say, "Stay cool, man. Don't try to be a hero."

The large man finishes cleaning out the cash drawer and then speaks to the clerk.

"Get me some smokes," he says.

Then the large man looks directly at you. "Don't try nothin'. Stay there," he orders.

The clerk turns around and reaches for the packs of cigarettes lining the area behind him. He grabs two packs and holds them out to the man, who takes them with his left hand and puts them in his messenger bag. At this point, the man brings his right hand out of the messenger bag. He's holding a large semi-automatic pistol, which he points at the clerk and then at you, in quick sweeping motions, as he begins walking backward toward the door.

SCENARIO 3

You've seen replica BB guns before and you've seen more than enough news reports where thieves have used BB guns in robberies or hold-ups. The guns are shiny black plastic. Often the would-be robber removes or colors the orange safety marker on the end of the barrel black in an obvious attempt to disguise the fact that the gun isn't real. But replicas they are, and most of them are very good ones, matching the exact dimensions of the real guns they are intended to replicate. The gun in the large man's hands looks real but not quite real, and you simply can't be sure as he continues swinging it back and forth, pointing it at you and then the clerk as he walks backward out the gas station door.

After he exits the gas station, he gets into the passenger side of a waiting late-model coupe, which speeds off before you or anyone else can see the license plate. You make a mental note of the make and model of the car and its general direction when it left the gas station parking lot while the store clerk dials 911.

In what way would any of the three situations have had to change in order for you to be justified in drawing your gun and shooting?

THE CREEPER

By Mark Kakkuri

Everybody knows him. He's the ultimate DLR, but to say he "doesn't look right" is an understatement. Whenever you see him, you go to Condition Orange without hesitation. And Condition Red probably isn't too far off. He's a weirdo, a creeper and, virtually 100 percent of the time, he's a he. Sure, there are females who fit this category, but not many. Males seem to own the DLR category.

And, while you're enjoying a quick lunch at a table in the food court of your local mall, you're looking at one. He's about 30 feet away. Average height, build and appearance. Nothing remarkable. A few tables and several chairs sit between you — more of a maze than a straight path — and about half are occupied with others who are eating lunch. He too is sitting at a small table, an empty lunch tray in front of him. His hands are in his jacket pockets and he's just sitting back, watching the myriad of people around him. No, not watching. Staring.

It's not his clothing or general appearance that doesn't look right; it's his demeanor. You've been at your table for about 25 minutes, during which you've consumed your entire lunch and sent a handful of text messages. He's been sitting in that same position, just staring, during that same time frame. It's his right to do so and, frankly, none of your business. It's just a bit weird.

Your table and seating position has you directly looking at him. He is directly in your line of sight. But his table and seating position face away from you so that you have a clear view of the right side of his face and body. As such, it is easy for you to keep an eye on him while you finish off your soda.

You look at your mobile phone. It's about 12:30 p.m. on a Thursday. The mall crowd is typical for a spring day: People employed in the area often drop into the food court for lunch. Several young families are in the mall, shopping or browsing. The seniors in the area have already completed their laps of the mall and are mostly enjoying conversation over cups of coffee. Every now and then a mall security guard walks by. All the guards are unarmed, but they carry two-way radios and handcuffs.

You've made it a habit to carry your gun concealed whenever you can, and today's no exception. Strapped to the area just above your left ankle is a five-shot, snub-nosed revolver with .38 Special +P rounds on board. Your dress pants cover it easily.

The Creeper hasn't really moved other than to stare at some people as they breeze by or move around in the dining area. As you watch him, you notice he tends to lock his eyes on younger children, which bugs you. The children are with their mothers, but their mothers are mostly consumed with navigating the lunch area and all the other kids, strollers and full shopping bags. You know the two largest cities in your area are hotspots for human trafficking and you can't help but wonder if this guy's looking for potential targets. But you talk yourself out of that line of thinking for now. After all, it's mere speculation. Maybe the guy just likes to eat lunch at the mall and hang out.

A young mother with two young children arrives at a table about 10 feet in front of this guy. She gets the stroller situated, somehow holding a tray with their food and drinks on it, and helps one child into a seat. Her purse hangs from her right shoulder. As she places the tray on the table, her purse slips off her shoulder, hits the floor and overturns. A small, black pistol in a tan leather holster slides out.

Should I shoot?

SCENARIO 1

You stand up and walk over to the woman with the intent to help her out.

But the weird guy has gotten up and seems intent to, well, do something also. He walks toward the woman and her children, or, rather, to the location where her gun is lying on the ground. The woman, seeing the gun fall out of the purse, attempts to reach for it with her right hand but inadvertently knocks over one of two sodas on her tray, soaking not only their food but also one of her children who is seated at the table. The man gets to the gun before the woman, reaches down and picks it up.

SCENARIO 2

The man stands there, holding the woman's gun and stares. He seems mesmerized or at least not sure what to do with the situation. The woman tries to simultaneously help calm and clean up her child while addressing the man.

"Thank you ... sir, that's my gun," she stammers. "I have a permit. I'll take it back now."

With her left hand, she is trying to dab her child with a napkin. Her right hand is extended toward the man. Her attention turns to her child, then to the man and then back to her child again. At this point, you have arrived to within 5 feet of the man and are at his right side, just behind him. The woman looks at you in desperation. You look at her and gesture to her with your right hand, open palm toward her as if to say, "Be calm." It's a tense situation all around, but you are compelled to try to help. So you address the man.

"Sir, everything's OK," you say. "Please give that back to the woman. It's hers."

SCENARIO 3

The man turns to face you. The woman's gun is in his right hand, still holstered. He stares at you and then slowly starts to extend the gun toward you. It's a small pistol, so he's holding its stocks with a thumb and index finger.

At this point, people in the immediate vicinity have started to panic and are clearing out of the area. A mall security guard strides up, speaking into his radio. The weird man's head darts back and forth as he takes in his surroundings, which are quickly turning to chaos. One of the woman's children has begun to cry, chairs are scraping against floors as people get up to leave quickly and the security guard yells, "Put it down! Put it down!"

The man's eyes grow wild and a look of panic crosses his face. As he looks over at the woman, you seize the moment and slap the gun out of his hand. It hits the floor and separates from the holster. The security guard lunges, pushing the man backward and they tumble to the ground. Two more security guards arrive. One immediately piles on the man and first security guard. The other reaches down and retrieves the gun and holster. He inserts the gun into the holster and tries to take command of the situation.

Should I shoot?

In what way would Scenario 1, 2 or 3 have had to change in order for you to be justified in drawing and shooting your gun?